PARSON WOODFORDE

Parson James Woodforde, 1740 - 1803
Painted by his nephew, Samuel Woodforde, R.A.

PARSON WOODFORDE

THE LIFE & TIMES OF A COUNTRY DIARIST

ROY WINSTANLEY

WITH ILLUSTRATIONS

MORROW & CO
BUNGAY, SUFFOLK
1996

First published Morrow & Co, Bungay, 1996

ISBN 0 948903 38 4

Designed and typeset by Morrow & Co, Bungay, Suffolk
Printed and bound by St Edmundsbury Press

CONTENTS

ILLUSTRATIONS

PREFACE

The main authority for the life of any diarist must be a diary. Between 1980 and 1989 the Parson Woodforde Society issued nine extensively annotated volumes of the complete diary text from its beginnings in 1759 to the last day of 1781, approximately half the total length of the diary. For the later period, 1782-1802, I have used the original manuscript in the Bodleian Library, Oxford.

The Parson Woodforde Society publishes a Quarterly Journal, which serves as a platform for discussion of the diarist's life and aspects of the diary. It has over the years built up a very comprehensive archive. New College and the Bodleian Library Oxford, both have important collections of primary source material. Other indispensable documents are in the hands of the Woodforde family, the most useful of these documents being the unpublished *Family Book* compiled by Dr. R. E. H. Woodforde.

It is both a duty and a pleasure to record the very great degree of help I have been given, not only during the composition of the book but throughout the long time I have been concerned with Woodforde. Much of the early research was done in Duke Humfrey's Library, that most beautiful and gracious part of the Bodleian. To work there must be counted a rare privilege. I am grateful to the Librarian and staff, Main Library, University of Birmingham; also to the Reference Department, City of Birmingham Central Library, and some of my former students who were working there.

I would like to thank the following who gave permission for the the use of illustrations for the book; George H. Bunting for the frontis, and illustrations nos. 1, 2, 3, 4, 5, 14 & 18; Dr W. J. Jordan of Bungay for illustrations nos. 6, 7, 8, 9 & 12; The Warden and Scholars of New College, Oxford, for illustrations nos. 10, 11, (both New College Archive, no. 9457) and 13; Norfolk Museums Service, cover (archive ref. 68.929), and illustrations nos. 15 (375.965) & 16 (1.953). My thanks are also due to Mrs Caroline Dalton, Archivist, New College, Oxford, Ms Norma Watt of Norwich Castle Museum, Ms Joanna Richards and Mr Sean Leahy for their advice and assistance in selecting and preparing the illustrations.

Most of all, I am indebted to the friends I have made through the Parson Woodforde Society, for illuminating argument, elimination of otherwise pervasive errors, and all the happy benefits of good fellowship. It is to them, as is fitting, that I have partly dedicated this book.

Halesowen   Roy Winstanley
February 1996

*To George Bunting
and the
Parson Woodforde Society*

INTRODUCTION

Although he was living in what some of his contemporaries termed "The Age of Reason", James Woodforde no doubt believed implicitly in many things which we no longer find credible; and some of his more endearingly irrational superstitions provoke merriment among sophisticated readers today. But he would certainly have rejected as quite unworthy of belief a prophecy that he would be remembered, even famous over two centuries after his death; or that this fame would come about through the diary which he thought enough of to keep for the greater part of his life, but at the same time referred to only once or twice, calling it a "trifling" book.

Its first introduction to the public took place in a typically modest and unassuming manner. In the last years of the 19th century the little market town in and around which so much of the diarist's early life was spent, possessed its own small periodical, *The Castle Cary Visitor*. The then owner of the diary, the Rev. Alexander Woodforde, allowed the editor to print a few passages from it, dealing with various aspects of local history. It was of course these, not the diary itself or the diarist, that would have interested the readers of a paper, the circulation of which did not extend very far beyond Cary and its environs.

In the early 1920's Dr. R.E.H. Woodforde, son of the clergyman who had made possible the printing of the first diary extracts, and great-grandson of "Nephew Bill" who features in many parts of the diary, was a G.P., living at Ashwell End, Hertfordshire. Among his patients was a career civil servant, John Baldwyn Beresford, son of a country vicar. The village surgery had no waiting room, but some of the patients were allowed to wait in the doctor's private sitting room. It was in this casual, quite accidental way that Beresford, recuperating from an illness and still under Dr. Woodforde's care, first saw the array of small books and booklets containing the diary. He was not only fascinated by what he read but also became convinced that selections from this diary would have a wide appeal if they could be published. He subsequently persuaded Oxford University Press to take sufficient interest in the diary to embark on the publication of a volume of extracts in 1923, entitled *The Diary of a Country Parson*. The diarist's name was relegated to a sub-title, since no one knew who Woodforde was; but it was from this title that we derive the practice of referring to the diarist as "Parson Woodforde".

To the surprise of everyone, *The Diary* was a best seller. There were two main reasons for this unexpected success. The first was that the publication of Woodforde's diary represented a wholly new kind of enterprise. There had been diaries before which, in variously abridged and mostly bowdlerized forms, had been published. However, their authors had been without exception people already well known. For example, Pepys' reputation as a diarist was built initially upon the name that he had made for himself as an administrator of the Stuart Navy. On the other hand, *The Diary of a County Parson* was the product of an obscure figure whose later fame rested solely upon the diary itself. And it was a different kind of diary from those to which early twentieth century readers were accustomed. The study of local and domestic history was in its infancy, and indeed, the success of the O.U.P. edition greatly stimulated interest in these previously unexplored aspects of the past. It prompted the hasty publication of diaries by other hitherto unknown people, some of whom were far from possessing the qualities that had been revealed in Woodforde.

The other factor that made for the book's favourable reception by the public was the time at which it appeared. The horror of world war was less than five years away, and was still fresh in the memory of practically everyone. Aided by the way that Beresford's selection had favoured the light-hearted, generally jocular approach, it was possible for a reader to go back to what seemed a simpler, kinder and more innocent world than that of the 1920's. Woodforde, who in reality has much to say about the seamier side of 18th century life, was quite perversely made into one of the great classics of escapist literature. The chilling fact that nothing would ever again be the same as it was before 1914 was slowly permeating the public consciousness; but people did not want to see the image of the future which had been revealed to them in the events of the previous decade. It was not only that Woodforde provided an imagined past as a refuge from the importunate present. He also seemed to give his readers the illusion of continuity, the idea of an unbroken historical chain stretching from past to present and the comforting assurance that in spite of all the evidence to the contrary, nothing had really changed.

In reality, the book is deeply flawed, and nothing less than the immense prestige of O.U.P. can have kept it going so long. Beresford was a cultured dilettante, not a scholar. His knowledge of the 18th century was slight, and he did not always understand its idioms, some of which he explains incorrectly. He appears to have shared the illusions of his readers about the supposedly peaceful qualities of the diary. How else could he possibly have written that

4

reading Woodforde is "like embarking on a long voyage down a very tranquil stream"?

The first volume was so much of a speculative venture that Beresford was obliged to say in his preface: "if public appreciation and support are forthcoming", it would have a successor. But neither he nor O.U.P. could have been at all sure that it would find favour, so the volume was prepared as though it was to be the only one. With his own clerical background, Beresford was really interested only in the second half of Woodforde's career as a beneficed clergyman in Norfolk. Consequently he galloped at top speed through the Somerset and Oxford years, covering the entire period from 1759 to 1776 in some 450 entries, hardly any of which are complete, a large number being rendered down to a mere line or two. Many others are chopped up to appear as snippets in the editor's commentary, which manages to be both intrusive and inadequate. In short, Beresford's treatment of the early parts of the diary exemplified Lord Ponsonby's dictum that "An editor can never be trusted not to spoil a diary".

The second half of the book, 160 pages out of 340, deals exclusively with the diarist's first six years as rector of Weston Longville, 1776-81. With so much more space at his disposal, the editor could afford to quote much more generously. This was still more evident in the four succeeding volumes, the publication of which between 1926 and 1931 was made possible by the great and unexpected success of the initial volume of extracts. From the second volume on, Beresford eschewed the commentary and took to writing footnotes, mostly on public affairs mentioned in passing by the diarist. These betray how inadequately he was equipped for the task. His sources are limited to the old D.N.B., aided by a handful of books which appear to have been utilized for no better reason than that he had them on the shelves of his own library, and many of which were out-of-date even in the 1920's.

The original five-volume Beresford edition, published when O.U.P. was at the height of its fame as a maker of fine books, is beautiful to look at and to handle. But for all this it is a sham, produced with an intention of making it like an authentic 18th century book, but in reality doing nothing to reproduce the conventions of Woodforde's manuscript. Whoever made the transcription did it carelessly, for the text is full of errors. Since O.U.P. have never submitted the text to critical examination, still less replaced it with a new one, these mistakes are perpetuated in modern reprints.

The O.U.P. edition got off to a good start, and for nearly 40 years there was no other way to read Woodforde except through their publications. An abridged version (1935) in a single hulking volume - this was the recension of a recension, since no attempt was made to go back to the manuscript - was not successful, but the same material when put into the *World's Classics* series was a veritable money-spinner, as is the paperback volume which has now replaced it.

An editor who reproduces not an integral text but a series of selections from it must, by the act of selection, impose his own criteria upon it, which reflect his own sense of the relative importance of different parts of the material. As a consequence, it is very difficult to avoid a certain amount of distortion. This certainly happened in the case of Woodforde's diary.

By omitting many of the entries which throw the clearest light on the diarist's character, Beresford produced a rather emasculated and featureless man, the motives of whose behaviour are often hard to decipher, because too much has been left out that might have elucidated them. The worst effects of his editorship concern the matter of food and eating. Here he succeeded in creating the "Parson Woodforde" of legend, the stereotyped clerical glutton whose main, indeed almost his sole, preoccupation lay in the direction of the dinner table and his meals. Although Beresford (unlike many later commentators) never brings a charge of gluttony and gormandizing against Woodforde, his determination to produce a volume which would appeal to the general reader led him to seize upon food as a subject that could be relied upon to hold his readers' attention. The result of this bias is that Beresford's selections produce a very unbalanced account of Woodforde's interests. It is ironic that if Beresford had edited the Somerset portion of the diary properly, and allotted an approximately equal amount of space to it as to the record of the Norfolk years, this imbalance could not have occurred, since it would not have been possible to find the examples of the kind of entry he wished to highlight. Woodforde, in fact, says very little indeed about food in the early years of the diary. Later, like so many other people, he paid more attention to what was on his plate and, as a householder and host, was concerned with providing himself and his guests with varied and well-cooked meals. But it is worth noting that he did not begin to list dinner, the one hot meal of the day, as part of his daily entry, until 1791, by which time he had been writing the diary for 32 years. As for breakfast and supper, scratch meals composed of leftovers from previous dinners, he does not at any time have much to say about them.

The mistaken image of Woodforde as another "Parson Trulliber" is compounded by modern misunderstanding of the way meals were served up in the 18th century and by the ill-founded assumption that because Woodforde listed all the dishes on offer at a particularly splendid banquet, he must have eaten his way through them all. Yet such ludicrous fantasies have always been part of the Woodforde legend. When in 1968 O.U.P. re-issued the five-volume edition, and again in 1978 when the paperback version came on to the market, the reviews of both were of the kind that might just as well have been written in the 1920's. The tenacity of the legend reflects a lack of knowledge of the diaries themselves and of the conventions which form the unspoken context of Woodforde's entries.

In 1969 a completely new Woodforde book was published, the first that had no sort of association with Beresford or the O.U.P. Comprising all the entries made during Woodforde's two periods of residence at the University, it appeared under the title of *Woodforde at Oxford 1759-1776* as one of the publications of the Oxford Historical Society (New Series, No. XXI), edited by Dr. W.N. Hargreaves-Mawdsley. In this book Woodforde and scholarship met for the first time. The text was more accurately transcribed than it had been in the O.U.P. edition, and within its chronological boundaries it is complete in itself. At the same time, it is far from an attractive book, having a rather cramped appearance which arose from the necessity for all the entries of the relevant period of the diarist's life to be crammed into one not very large volume. Hargreaves-Mawdsley knew a great deal about 18th century Oxford life, and many of his footnotes are valuable. But there is a curious bleakness about the work, perhaps attributable to the lack of pleasure the editor seems to have derived from the labour of transcribing and preparing the text for the press. Although Hargreaves-Mawdsley took on the task in fulfilment of a promise made to a late member of the Woodforde family who had been chaplain of New College and then Dean of Wells, he seem's determined not to allow his work to be tainted with any trace of partiality. He has little good to say about Woodforde, "that rather colourless man, whose stature one imagines to have been smallish"; "by any standard James Woodforde was a dull man"; and the underlying theme of his rather niggling introduction is that the diarist had no imagination, not the least trace of originality, and merely recorded what was there before his eyes, like a camera. One recognises a glimmer of truth in this, but it does not take us very far if we wish to recover aspects of Woodforde's character which are revealed by his diary. Woodforde may "by reason of his very mediocrity" be "representative of his class and age" but the appended list of his habits and preferences which supports this value-judgement must strike us as far too trivial to be worth anything as proof of the assertion. Woodforde waited a long time before he paid his debts to tradesmen, but disliked being "dunned", as he called it. His taste in furniture and liking for the engravings of Bartolozzi (this, by the way, based on a single diary reference) "mirrored the taste of many an academic". He gambled and he drank, and once attended a public execution as a spectator. It seems to have escaped this editor that many people whom he would have considered neither mediocre nor dull did all of these things. On balance, his carping manner is far less agreeable than the sentimental enthusiasm of Beresford. *Woodforde at Oxford*, issued in a subscription edition, never reached the general public at all.

At about the time it came out, the most important event in the history of Woodforde's diary, next in importance to the composition of the diary itself, took place. The Parson Woodforde Society was founded in 1968, and with it the epoch of serious enquiry into the diarist's life, career and surroundings began. It has made possible the publication of the present work, the first full-scale biography of the diarist ever to be written.

Over the years, James Woodforde has become an important historical personage. No book now written at any level on the social and in particular domestic history of England is complete without quotations from the diary. The trouble is they are always the same quotations, and most of them are trivial enough, leading the casual reader to the mistaken impression that the diary contains nothing else. My purpose in writing this book is to try and convince readers that I am justified in my belief that Woodforde's world is one that is full of interest. It must already be well enough known that the diary contains primary source material of the greatest importance, although so far only restricted use has been made of it by researchers and specialists. May I be permitted to hope that the publication of his biography will lead to the diarist becoming even better known, and given his rightful place as an authority on his own time and place in society?

As for the plan of this biography, approximately the first half is written in a fairly strict chronological sequence. After Woodforde took up residence in Norfolk, his life-style underwent no significant change in the 26 years that made up the rest of his existence. At that point, therefore, I abandon the chronological order, and the rest of the book is concerned with the various topics which a study of the diary and the diarist's life has suggested.

CHAPTER 1

ANCESTRY

Woodford(e) is a common enough name. As a place-name it occurs in several parts of the country. There was at one time an important family bearing this name, the Woodfords of Ashby Folville in Leicestershire. These died out about the middle of the 17th century, near the time when our Woodfordes were emerging into the professional world. Upon which, they coolly appropriated the armorial bearings of the extinct family, and its coat-of-arms may be seen on a memorial in the parish church of Ansford, Somerset, where James Woodforde, the "Parson Woodforde" of the famous diary, was born, and again on his own wall-tablet at Weston Longville, Norfolk, where he is buried. Some of the Woodfordes seem honestly to have thought there was a family connection between the two. James Woodforde's great-great-grandfather, who compiled a pedigree under the name of *Stemma Woodfordeiana*, believed that he was descended "from a younger slip of that house". But he was quite wrong, and his kin did not come "from Leicester or thereabouts". [1]

In fact they came from Northamptonshire, and the little village of Woodford, on the A604 road from Kettering to Huntingdon, some 6 miles from Kettering and not much more than that from the places where the early Woodfordes are known to have lived, was in all probability the ancestral home of the family. [2] They are found from the early 16th century living in two villages, Scaldwell and Old, about 6 miles from Brixworth and 9 miles from Northampton. Their way of life can to some small extent be recovered from a series of Wills now in the Northamptonshire Record Office.

The first of these, dated April 1513, is that of John Woodford of Scaldwell, and shows him to have been a man of some substance. His bequests are mainly in the form of sheep and other livestock. To read the document, in a heavily contracted form of Latin, reminds us that the world of the Middle Ages had not yet passed away, for it is full of pious offerings, "to the light of the Great Crucifix", "to the light of St Edmund King and Martyr". Eleven sheep and half an acre of corn are given to "my mother church of Lincoln". Only after these gifts had been enumerated did the testator come to his own family. Then another list is headed - "I give to my son Robert Woodford one cow and eight sheep". The Will informs us that he had another son, Eusebius, and that his wife's name was Agnes.[3]

The Robert Woodford mentioned in his father's Will moved from Scaldwell to nearby Old. He was certainly dead by 1576, at which date his widow gave directions that she was to be laid beside him, and probably by 1559, when one of his sons made a Will in which he is not mentioned. The Will of "Elizabeth Woodforde of Old Wyddowe" is in English. Medieval pieties have no place in it. She leaves 2d to "the mother church of Peterburghe", the new diocese set up at the Reformation. Otherwise her Will is mainly concerned with household utensils and clothing, of which there is a long, meticulous list.[4]

Robert and Elizabeth had several children. The second son, Thomas, is described as "husbandman". He was the testator of the 1559 Will, dying the following year. In it he mentions his mother, two brothers Edward and Richard, and a sister Alys. Edward was the eldest. Born in 1518, he married Marjery Ragdale; they had seven children. He lived to see the end of the Tudor dynasty, and died in 1604. His eldest son, another Robert, was born in 1562 and baptised at Old in 1564. His marriage in 1604 took place in some other parish, but was recorded in the parish register of Old. His wife, Jane Dexter, was about 22 at the time of her marriage. He died on 3 June 1636 and she survived him until 12 February 1648/9, when she died aged 66.[5]

An inventory of his goods taken a month after his death describes him as "yeoman" and shows that his entire effects, including household articles as well as livestock, standing crops and farm implements, amounted to only £36.12.6.[6]

So far, all these early Woodfordes had been working as basic food providers. Some, more thrifty, more industrious or luckier than others, would have been rewarded by greater prosperity, but all were in comparatively humble circumstances, carrying out year by year the unchanging routines of the land. One has to imagine them, not as "farmers" in the modern sense of the term i.e., as tenants or owners of enclosed farms, but as strip-cultivators, for they lived in the heart of the great Midlands belt of open-field or "champaign" country, where in the dark grey limestone "street" villages the older houses still turn their backs on the thoroughfare to face what were once the great unenclosed spaces of the open field. The movement from the farming communities upwards to the professional classes, sometimes to full gentry status, forms a pattern familiar to all those who have studied English social life in pre-industrial times; and so it came about with the Woodfordes.

The third Robert Woodforde was an only child, or at least the single surviving child of his parents. He was born at Old in 1606. We have a few details about his life, most of them coming from the autobiographical account written by his distinguished son, Samuel Woodforde D.D., F.R.S. He "had but ordinary education as born that I may say but to a meane Fortune". Leaving the villages where his ancestors had lived and laboured for so long, he went to Northampton where he became the servant of an attorney, Mr. John Reding or Readinge. Lawyer's clerks at that date, and for long after, were recruited by a process indistinguishable from that of apprenticeship to a trade. They worked in the office, employed in such routine jobs as copying out legal documents. If a clerk were attentive, and reasonably bright, he might expect to pick up enough knowledge of forensic business to enable him to take over the concern when his master retired or died; or to set up in practice himself somewhere else. It is to be presumed that Robert Woodforde did this, although we have no specific knowledge of when this came about. We know only that in 1636 Robert was appointed Steward of Northampton on the recommendation of Reding. At a meeting of the Court of Aldermen in that year Reding, the holder of the office, explained that his "much employment elsewhere" had caused "the defects and slackness" in carrying out his duties, of which there had evidently been complaints, and he "therefor made suit for the office on behalf of Robert his late servant. Whereupon the Mayor and Alderman did give the Voyces for an election and by the greater part of the Voyces then taken, the said Robert Woodforde was elected and chosen Steward whollie to succeed his master in the said office".[7]

Three years before, at the age of 27, he had married the 16 year old Hannah Haunch. Robert was, beyond all doubt, the architect of the Woodforde family fortunes, and if his personal rise to the status of a professional man was the first essential step, his ultimately advantageous marriage was the second and equally requisite factor.

The Haunch, or Hanch, family was of Northants extraction, but Hannah's father was a London citizen, living in the parish of All-Hallows-in-the-Wall, "next door to Carpenter's Hall". The young couple were married in the local church, which was a little over 30 years later to disappear in the Great Fire. Hannah's mother was born Susan Heighes, of Binsted, Hampshire. She came from a quite wealthy landed family, and was the heiress by whom Samuel

11

Woodforde, her grandson, inherited the property. It was in this way that the name "Heighes", borne by many of the later Woodfordes, came into the family.

But that was still in the future. Robert Woodforde was by no means a rich man. Although he had risen in status, he may well have been poorer than some of his relations who had stayed on the land. Robert and Hannah had 14 children. The family was ravaged by tuberculosis, and only three, or perhaps four, lived to adulthood. Robert himself died of the disease on 15 November 1654. After his death Samuel wrote of him with becoming piety: "No monys or lands my good Father did or could leave me God saw it not fit that he should leave them yet say he left me and all his children and widow an invaluable inheritance of blessings and prayers on which we to this day live plentifully". Robert was apparently the first of his family to keep a diary, an example of which was to be followed by many in coming generations. Part of it was published in the Ninth Report of the Historical Manuscript Commission in 1884. This reveals him, though a layman, as a far more deeply religious man than his descendant, Parson James. He was also a Puritan, everlastingly searching his soul and, in the time leading up to the Civil War, very much pro-Parliament and anti-Royalist.

Samuel was the eldest of his children. He probably owed his survival to having been brought up by his grandparents in London, far away from the Northampton home with its infection, disease and death. His grandfather's political sympathies were at the opposite end of the spectrum from those of his father. Samuel never forgot coming home from school and finding "the good old man all in tears" over the beheading that day of Charles I. Grief at the "Murder of our late Gracious Sovereign" and the death of his own son shortened his life. He died in the July following (1649); "tho' had he not been thus broken his Constitution promised many more years". Eleven years later Samuel composed a loyal poem on the return of Charles II.

Samuel was the first Woodforde who was at a great public school, St. Paul's, where he was admitted in 1647, aged 11, about three years younger than his schoolfellow Samuel Pepys. He was, likewise, the pioneer at Oxford, being entered at Wadham in March 1653/4.[8] He graduated B.A., but when his grandmother died in 1657, he decided not to return to the University, but to follow his late father's profession of the law. He was thereupon admitted as a student to the Inner Temple. The death of his grandmother had left him the immediate heir to the Binsted estate, the owner of which was her brother, Samuel's grand-uncle, Mr. Heighes. About 1659 he met

Alice Beale and although he had "expectations", neither he nor Alice had but much of their own. It was not until 1661 that Samuel dared tell his relations that he wanted to marry her, and when he did so it precipitated a great family explosion. But things were soon straightened out, and Mr. Heighes came round: "the 15th of April following being my birthday the good old gentleman of his own goodness was pleased to relent and took me into favour again and continued increasing till his dyeing day". There was thus no further obstacle to Samuel's marriage, which took place later in the same year. In 1662 the couple had a daughter, whom they named Alice.

Then tragedy struck. On 9 January 1663/4 Heighes, Parson Woodforde's grandfather, was born. A few days later Alice died of what modern medicine would call "post delivery sepsis" and contemporaries termed "childbed fever".Samuel was heartbroken and his anguished outpourings in his autobiography still have the power to move a reader.[9] But he recovered in time, and married Mary Norton, a delightful woman whose own diary deserves recognition. At the same time it reveals the parlous state of female education at the time, for it is the work of an intelligent and sensitive woman who can just about write and no more.

Samuel was a distinguished man, who had taken the family far from its bucolic origins. In his lifetime he was noted as the author of the *Paraphrase of the Psalms of David*, published in 1667, and John Aubrey calls him "Mr. Woodford the poet (who paraphrased the Psalmes)".[10] He wrote a good deal of other poetry, among which are two works addressed to his friend Izaak Walton, and an *Ode to the Memory of John Wilmot Earl of Rochester*. In 1669, when he was 33, he took Holy Orders, becoming the first of the clerical Woodfordes and founding the association of the family with the Anglican church. He became rector of Hartley Mauduit, near Binsted, and having influential friends in the church did not lack for other preferment, which included two prebends, one being the valuable one of Winchester. He died on 11 January 1700/1.[11]

All four of his sons became clergymen. Heighes Woodforde, Samuel's only son by his first wife, went to Wadham, his father's college. Samuel gave up the prebend of Ertham to him, and he became rector of Elvetham, Hants., a living which he later exchanged for that of Epsom. He married Mary Lamport, of a Sussex family, whose dowry was an estate at Pagham, near Bognor Regis. This remained a Woodforde possession until the early 19th century, and is often mentioned in James Woodforde's diary. Heighes had eight children, most of whom were born at Elvetham.

Late in his life, he made the long journey into Somerset to marry his eldest son Samuel to Jane Collins, as is noted in the Ansford register. He died 5 months later, on 4 January 1724/5. The couple he married became the parents of James Woodforde.

Revd. Samuel Woodforde, 1695 - 1771
Parson Woodforde's father

Jane Woodforde, née Collins, 1706 - 1766
Parson Woodforde's mother

CHAPTER 2

NEAR RELATIONS AND DIARY PEOPLE

For James Woodforde, the keeping of a diary was not the belated occupation of a lonely old man; nor did he, like Pepys and Kilvert, keep it for almost a decade and then drop it abruptly. On the contrary, his diary was begun at the age of 19, very soon settled down into a pattern of an entry each day, and was written for 43 years out of the 62 that were his life-span. And as he was born into a system of large familial groups, living close to one another in what was a largely static rural existence, we find that the early diary is full of his relations, many of whom now enjoy through him a sort of vicarious fame. Without some knowledge of his "nearest and dearest", it is scarcely possible to understand the diary.

His father, Samuel Woodforde, was born at Elvetham, on 22 July 1695. The family association with Winchester, which was to be the making of his son James' career, had already begun. Samuel's father Heighes, (adm. 1675), and his four uncles: Samuel (1681), John (1684), Robert (1687) and William (1693) had all been there. In his turn he was admitted in 1709, matriculated 1714 from New College and was a Fellow 1716-20.[1] He was for what could have been only a short time domestic chaplain to the Earl of Tankerville, information which appears on the monument which James put up to the memory of his parents in Ansford Church.[2] In 1719 Samuel was instituted as Rector of Ansford. Two years later he became vicar of Castle Cary, the neighbouring market town. These preferments came to him through the influence of his uncle Robert, rector of Yeovilton, Somerset, Treasurer of Wells Cathedral and Canon Residentiary.[3]

In his turn, Samuel looked after his own siblings. In the 1760's when James was writing his early diary, we find a number of his aunts and uncles living in Ansford, some of whom were in accommodation provided by Samuel. Elizabeth (b. 1699) always called by James "Aunt Parr", lived in a house by Ansford Churchyard. Apparently she had been widowed so long that no remembrance of her late husband survived into James' time. She was poor and died intestate because she had nothing to leave except a pile of old clothes which James inherited and some of which, years later, he handed down to his own niece, Nancy. On the other hand Anne (b. 1691), had probably been the paid companion of the

17

Countess of Derby, from whom she was receiving a life-annuity of £10 a year. She left a very useful nest-egg of £600 "in South-Sea Stock" when she died in 1773. Thomas (b. 1706), the only one of three brothers who did not go to Winchester, also lived at Ansford, for at least some time in a house provided by his brother Samuel. He seems to have been quite well off. He was a schemer, and his finally successful attempts to wreck the chances of James to succeed his father in the Ansford living in order to secure that living for his son, once drove the frustrated diarist to call him "my greatest Enemy". We shall meet him again.

Samuel also had a brother and sister who did not reside at Ansford. John was at Winchester, but his career there came to a sudden end when he was expelled, along with another boy named Robert Pescod, for "assaulting and beating" the "Hostiarius", or undermaster, in 1723. [4] This did his career no harm, for he ended up with the very well-endowed living of North Curry, Somerset. He died in 1760, and his sole mention in the diary, after his death, states in what part of Ansford churchyard he was buried. Jane, "Aunt Jenny", Samuel's youngest sister, was unmarried, and kept a boarding house in Bath.

James Woodforde always regarded himself as a Somerset man, and this was a justified claim through his mother. Five years after he had become rector of Ansford, on 12 July 1724, Samuel Woodforde married Jane Collins, aged 18. She was a minor local heiress and after the death of her father owned farmland and other real property in Ansford, including the "Lower House", which figures so prominently in the early diary. It was a small Tudor or Elizabethan manor house, occupied through nearly two centuries by one or other member of the Woodforde family, and finally burned down in 1892. The site has never since been built on.

Samuel and Jane had a family of four sons and three daughters, James being the sixth child and third son. They lost only one in childhood. This was Samuel, born 1731 and died 1733. All the others have become noted, even celebrated, diary "characters" : Brother Heighes, Brother John, Sister Clarke, Sister White, Sister Pounsett. The reader of Woodforde feels he or she knows these people, just as well as if they had been personages in a long family novel. The mysterious alchemy of wholly unconscious art has brought them to life and given them a place in history. Even after he had gone to live in Norfolk, whenever he returned to the West Country - and the only reason he undertook the long journeys was to see them again - they are there and we greet them like old friends.

James' eldest sister was Clementina Sobieski, born at Epsom in 1725. Her names come from the grand-daughter of John III Sobieski, King of Poland, who turned back the Turkish forces from the gates of Vienna in 1685; wife of the Pretender and mother of Prince Charles Edward of the '45. The choice of these names must infer some degree of Jacobite sympathies in Samuel Woodforde in his young days. But he had already received both his Somerset benefices before the child was born, and no doubt, like the vicar of Bray, he found no difficulty in reconciling his private feelings with service in the Anglican Church which had so completely accepted and supported the Hanoverian succession. Not surprisingly, she herself evidently disliked both her names, and took to calling herself "Sophy". On her marriage certificate at Ansford she is down as "Sophy or Sobieski Woodforde". Richard Clarke, a native of Epsom who settled in Ansford, was no doubt befriended by Samuel Woodforde, whose favour must have been necessary for the marriage between his wife's half-sister, Martha Collins, and Richard. Martha became the mother of James and Richard Clarke, the cousins who figure so prominently in the early diary. She died young and in 1754 Clarke and Sobieski were married. There is some mystery about her later life. Her husband built up a considerable reputation as a doctor, specializing in the inoculation treatment of smallpox and, out of several alternative and rival methods, following the type developed by the famous Baron Dimsdale. When he died in 1774 she was left well-provided for; yet in 1793 and again in 1795 she is found, seemingly in poverty, living in the London suburb of Hackney, with her son Samuel, always eccentric and now quite insane. Somehow Sobieski must have found her way back to her old haunts, for she was buried at Ansford in 1821, aged 96. She was the longest-lived of all the Woodfordes, who produced some striking examples of longevity.

Woodforde's brothers both made a mess of their lives. Heighes, born in 1726, was trained in the law, partially in London, but seems never to have done any law business except for the odd jobs tossed to him from time to time by members of his own family. In 1754 he eloped with Anne Dorville of Alhampton in the parish of Ditcheat, like his mother a small heiress. They were married at the Queen's Chapel of the Savoy, in London, at a time when such marriages had already been made illegal through the passing of Lord Hardwicke's Marriage Act the year before, by a man who not long afterwards was sentenced to be transported for this kind of offence. Doubts as to the validity of the marriage led to a second wedding, this time in Anne's parish church of Ditcheat, only three months before her eldest child was born. Heighes and Anne led a cat and dog life in her ancestral home until she threw him out of it. Unlike many surreptitious brides, whose property at marriage belonged by law to their husbands, Anne's possessions had been legally secured to her. This explains why she was able to live in comfort while Heighes endured miserable poverty, scratching round for odd loans until he died of "stranguary" in 1789. Of Anne's seven children, three were expressly repudiated as not being his. Three of the remaining four have become famous. Anna Maria, or "Nancy" is, next to Woodforde himself, the best known figure in the diary. Professor Wallace Notestein, in his book *English Folk*, says that her uncle has made her a minor immortal.[5] Nephew Bill, so "unsteady" in his youth, and with seemingly little capacity for earning his own living, also stage-managed an elopement, when he was 30 and his bride 17, fortunately with more success than his parents. Nephew Sam, whom Woodforde called "an uncommonly clever Youth", when he was aged 14, found influential patrons in the Hoare family, the bankers and creators of Stourhead and its famous gardens, who sent him to Italy to be trained. He became a successful painter and R.A. (1807). Only Juliana, the second daughter, is less well-remembered. She lived with her father and shared his threadbare existence until she died of pulmonary tuberculosis, aged 28.

Mary, the diarist's second sister, married Robert White, a farmer. Their home was on Ansford Hill, a hundred yards or so from the Parsonage where she had grown up. All the Whites' children died tragically young except one, the younger Robert, one of the most amiable and pleasant persons we meet in the diary. Elopements certainly ran in the family, for he went off with his cousin, Sophia Clarke, after meeting opposition from the Clarke family, who thought him "too much the Clown". Earlier than this, his father had refused to make him executor of his Will, bringing in the second son, James White, instead. This would have been regarded at the time as a slight and an insult. There was a fatal weakness in the White stock, a lack of resistance which had already appeared. In the next generation again all but one died, some as children, some as young adults, and none leaving any issue.

Jane, or "Jenny", was James Woodforde's favourite sister, by far the nearest to him in age. She was born in 1734, six years his senior. A somewhat neurotic character, she bore the brunt of looking after her father in his old age, long after her sisters had married; then at the age of 40, when it must have appeared to all around, and even to herself, that she was destined for the barren life of an old maid, she married John Pounsett, "Lord of the Manor of Cole" but a working farmer like so many of the Woodfordes' relations and friends. They had one child, another Jane, who turned out considerably more neurotic than her mother. It was, of course, at Cole that Parson Woodforde and Nancy spent their holidays, from 1782. The then recently built house, Cole Place, survives apparently little changed; while just across the road is the much older Manor House, where Pounsett's widowed mother lived in the diarist's time.

John Woodforde, the youngest of the siblings, has also acquired notoriety, if not exactly fame. The diary is full of his escapades: drinking bouts, accidents when he was thrown from his horse, unbridled swearing (his brother wrote once that he never heard anyone ever swear for so long without stopping) and generally undesirable behaviour. His father once tried apprenticing him to a merchant in Bristol, even going so far as to buy him a partnership for £700, but that did not work. He then had a try at farming, but that failed too. At last he sobered up, but not before he had spent most of his money, so that it was "hard times" with him. In 1775 he married Melleora (this is the way she spelled her name on her marriage certificate, but there are five other ways to spell it) Clarke of Evercreech. Dr. Woodforde in the *Family Book* calls her father Captain Clarke, but he appears to have been an innkeeper. They had no children.

As we watch the life of James Woodforde unfold, many of these people will be seen in some detail, and in more than one aspect. If we try to study him in isolation, ignoring his familiar environment and the people who were part of it, we risk seeing only a blurred and imprecise picture of the man; just as, in his later years in Norfolk, we cannot really understand him until we know something of the village life which surrounded him. [6]

CHAPTER 3

-EDUCATION-
FROM MARTHA MORRIS
TO WINCHESTER

James Woodforde was born at Ansford Parsonage on 16 June (Old Style) 1740, and baptised three days later, "being very ill". With healthy infants the baptism was often deferred for weeks, or even months. His godfathers were John Collins, his mother's uncle, who died three years later and bequeathed to him the tiny "estate" at Sandford Orcas[1] and a ring which was handed over to him on his 22nd birthday, by then kept on the New Style date; and his uncle Thomas Woodforde who was represented at the christening on 19 July by a proxy; his godmother was a Mrs. Joan Randolph, about whom I have no information.

His arrival probably caused little stir. Whatever parental raptures the coming of Sobieski in 1725 may have brought to the young parents, now, sixteen years later, the birth was no doubt taken as a matter of course. There are no available anecdotes about his early childhood. James himself, when as a grown man he was writing the diary, never showed any marked interest in children. Perhaps his epoch had not much of that to spare, in any case. It was the Age of Reason, so called, and there was a considerable pressure on children to mature as quickly as possible and reach the state where reason could be an active quality. This is reflected in the adult clothing into which children were so speedily put. Everyone has seen that portrait of the infant Mozart in an 18th century court suit, with a tiny sword by his side. He was of course a child performer, a *Wunderkind,* which explains the need to dress him up like a miniature adult, able to perform in public, while his size proclaimed him still a small child. But to a less striking extent this was done to all children.

It is, therefore, unavoidable that this part of the diarist's biography should be limited to listing the schools he attended. At the same time, thanks to some surviving primary documentation, and research carried out by members of the Parson Woodforde Society, we have an unusually complete record of his education. So much of his childhood and youth was spent in various boarding schools that he must over a long time never have seen his parents, and brothers and sisters, except in the school holidays. However, even before he went to the first of the schools, he does appear to have received some tuition while still living at home, even though we are by no means clear as to what it could have consisted of.

In 1767 Woodforde met a middle-aged woman whom he had not seen for a long time, since she had been living in London for the last 20 years. He referred to her in the diary as his "schoolmistress". Her story has been gradually pieced together and is very unusual indeed, for she ended up as the victim of a murder, and Woodforde was called as a "character witness" by the defence in the trial of her husband in 1775 for killing her.[2]

Martha Widdows was a native of Ansford, where she was born in 1722. As a young girl she went, probably working, to the village of Queen Camel, where she is said to have married a John or James Morris. The marriage is not recorded in the register of Queen Camel, although a "James Morris" and a "James Morris Junr." both died there in the course of the year 1744. Two years before this, Martha had reappeared at Ansford with a baby, whose baptism Samuel Woodforde had entered in his register as "Martha, Daughter of John and Martha Morris of the Parish of Queen Camel". He made one mistake, over the name of the child, which was really Frances. If he made another and wrote "John" for "James", it is possible, even likely, that Martha was married to one of the two men who died in 1744, after which she no doubt returned to Ansford where her parents still lived. James would have been four or five at the time, the right age for such elementary tuition that she could have provided. She was perhaps employed as a nursemaid or, in the modern term, a "nanny". Conversely, she could possibly have run a "Dame School", although this seems less likely.

Whatever the teaching was, James could not have received it after midway through his eighth year. We must now turn to a special volume of accounts, still in the ownership of the family, in which Samuel Woodforde entered various expenses incurred on behalf of all three sons, with a great deal of other material as well.[3] The accounts book reveals that James was shipped off to a boarding-school by the time he reached the age of seven and a half. There seems a general belief that the real heyday of the English boarding-school did not begin until the 19th century. Indeed, I have heard it called one of the booming by-products of the railway. This notion does not square at all with the great numbers of such schools found in Woodforde's time, and even earlier. Mary Woodforde's 17th century diary, already mentioned, describes how her youngest son, "little Willy", was sent away to a school in Winchester, at about the same age as James was now despatched to one at Compton Pauncefoot, no more than a mile from his home and, incidentally, a quiet and wholly delightful place today. The account book tells the story as directly and lucidly as possible:

1748 .... pd. Mr King for half a years Boarding	5 0 0
To Do for my Son James to Mr King's School at Compton Pansford	

Jan 12: 1748/9 paid Mr King for half a Years Boarding &c.	5 0 0
To Ditto for pens, ink & paper &c.	1 10
To Ditto for a New Year's Gift	10 6

July 28: 1749 paid to Mr King for half a Years Boarding &c. due 12th inst.	5 0 0
Do for books, pens, ink &c.	6 0

Nothing could be clearer. The six-monthly bills were paid in arrear - I never heard of an 18th century purchaser who paid for anything in advance. James spent two complete years at the school, from January 1748 to December 1749. The next item records a change of school, and reads:

January 5: 1749/50 Then sent my Son James to Jacque's School at Urchfont gave for entrance	1 7 0

The school at Urchfont, near Devizes in Wiltshire, has left no mark on the page of history. It is just mentioned in the *Victoria County History of Wiltshire* which does, however, emphasise the large number of private schools in the county at that time. It must, all the same, have been a bigger place altogether than Mr King's village school. When James Woodforde went up to Oxford he found at the University a sufficient number of Old Boys to support an "Urchfont Clubb", of which he became a member, though seemingly for only a short time. The costs and payments made to Urchfont are not easy to interpret. Samuel paid 8 guineas on 2 July 1750, six months after his son had gone there, and on 14 January following he sent £10.13.0 "for Board, books &c.". On 17 June there was a further payment of £7.4.0. for "board" only. At the end

of the year 1751 he made only new year gifts, amounting to
£2.12.6. in all, so that by the next summer he owed the school quite
a considerable sum, which he paid off in two instalments:

> June 15: 1752 paid to Mr Gibbs for boarding,
> Books, &c. by Jn Coleman   10 6 8
>
> July   1752 paid to Mr Gibbs for boarding
> &c. by Jn Coleman   9 7 0

I do not know who Mr Gibbs was, but at a guess he was Jacques'
successor at Urchfont, and the payments recorded above were to be
his last, for we have reached the year 1752, a most important one in
the boy's life. His father supplies the first details of the move:

> Sep 6: 1752 Enter'd him at Winton School, &
> paid for things there   10 0 0

This next educational step was to take him to a place to which
Compton Pauncefoot, or even Urchfont, could bear no sort of
comparison. 18th century Winchester, that amazing and in many
ways horrifying place, demands and must be given a chapter of its
own.

CHAPTER 4

A CHILD OF THE FOUNDATION

The College of St. Mary de Winton, Winchester, commonly called Winchester College, to give the place its full formal title, was founded in 1379 by William of Wykeham, bishop of the diocese and former chancellor of England. Like other charitable foundations of its type, such as Eton and Rugby, it aimed to take selected boys of poor families and train them to be monks and secular priests, an intention reflected in the buildings of Winchester, with their close similarity to those of a monastic house. After completing their time there, the boys were to go on to the sister Foundation (opened 1382), another St. Mary's College, situated in Oxford, which soon had the appellation of "new" tacked on to it, retained today after 600 years of existence. With an Oxford degree to crown their efforts, at least some of the brighter students might attain the higher echelons of church or state, in emulation of the Founder himself, eminent in both. William drew up the rules and commands for the running of both Foundations in the extremest detail. He expressly stated in the first of the Statutes laid down for Winchester that the boys were to be poor and without means ("pauperes et indigentes"). Therefore both tuition and accommodation were to be free. There was a Warden ("Custos"), ten Fellows ("Socii"), and three Chaplains ("Capellani"). To do the teaching a Head Master ("Informator") was appointed, and given as an assistant the Under Master, or Usher, or "Hostiarius". (The originally humble nature of the latter post is indicated by the name, which means gatekeeper). The boys wore a gown, not unlike a monk's habit, of a "dusky" colour, the Founder having forbidden black, and white, and powder-blue. This gown is shown on a 15th century brass in the Hampshire church of Headbourne Worthy, in memory of a boy named John Kent, who died while at the school, and its survival into a time long after James Woodforde's schooldays is shown by its presence on Flaxman's fine monument to Joseph Warton in Winchester Cathedral. It was also after he left that the term Scholar, by which the boys on the Foundation were known, came into use. The term which he would have known was Child: "puer", hence the use of the phrase "Child of the Foundation". In addition to these, there was a second group, the Quiristers who, as their name implies, were brought in chiefly to sing at the chapel services. They were taught together with the Scholars in the great School Room, the Head Master at one end on his throne and the Hostiarius at the other. As soon as their voices broke most of the Quiristers left and were then usually apprenticed to various tradesmen in the city. Only a few lasted long enough to be admitted to the upper forms, and none was eligible for admission to New College. [1]

At first, there must have been little or no prestige value attached to belonging to a charitable foundation of this kind. But, as time went by, schools like Winchester began to attract a different class of entrant. People who were both willing and rich enough to pay to have their sons educated there, even without any prospect of going on to New College, began the process that was to turn Winchester and the others into the great "Public Schools" - a long-term total misnomer, since they were nothing if not exclusive. So, long after the other two groups, the Commoners ("Commensales") appeared, the word standing for the pupils who paid for their own food-allowance, or commons. It was the Head Master of Woodforde's time, Dr. John Burton, who did most to encourage them, building "Commoners' Hall" outside the school premises for their accommodation. [2]

All the above resembles the kind of information about the school that one might derive from a guide-book. It does not even begin to do justice to the realities of that remarkable place. Winchester in James Woodforde's time was run on an elaborate system of "double think". The pretence was that nothing had ever changed there since the Middle Ages. Every word written by William of Wykeham - his Statures were solemnly read aloud in New College Chapel three times a year - was held in the greatest reverence. To accommodate his regulations to the changes which had inevitably taken place over the centuries, the most devious subterfuges were practised. A good example may be seen in the matter of the stipends drawn by the Head Master and Usher. These had originally been set at £20 and £10, no doubt handsome enough salaries at the end of the 14th century. By 1776, long after Woodforde had left, they were still no more than £42 and £32. To bring this into some kind of perspective, it is necessary to have something to which it may be compared. As a young curate working for his father, James received £35 - £20 for Cary and £15 for Ansford. £20 was, in fact, the going rate for curates with a single church throughout the second half of the 18th century.

The Masters, however, had two other useful sources of income, apart from such incidental bits of preferment that they had been able to pick up here and there. One was the Commoners. Contemporaries said of Joseph Warton, one of the best remembered Head Masters of Winchester, that the foundations of his renown had been laid by his first wife, who ran Commoners' Hall like a first rate boarding house, greatly adding both to the popularity of the school and the profits derived from this source. There had also grown up a custom by which the teachers were allowed to collect money from the parents or guardians of the Scholars, although this practice had been expressly forbidden by the Founder. I do not suppose that there will exist a single reference to this in any Winchester source, for very obvious reasons. Fortunately we have Samuel Woodforde's invaluable accounts book, which reveals that, throughout the time his son James was at Winchester, he sent, every half-year, 3 guineas to Dr. Burton and 2 guineas to the Hostiarius; and, while James was a junior, 1 guinea to a senior boy named Thomas Nicolls, who acted as his "boy Tutor". The full tally of 70 scholars was never attained in the 18th century. In 1752, the year of James' admission, it stood at 61. A reasonable, perhaps rather conservative estimate of average numbers would come out at about 50-55. If Burton was receiving 6 guineas a year multiplied even by 50, he was doing very well for himself, at the currency values of the time. It is not at all surprising that when in 1764 it was proposed to raise the salaries to £250 and £150 a year respectively, and do away with the "ex gratia" payments, both teachers at once turned the offer down.

There was a certain logicality in the actions of these men. They were defending their own standard of living, and if they could do this by playing off one Statute against another, or otherwise bending the rules, it is hard to blame them. Other manifestations of the dead hand of William of Wykeham cannot be defended on any principle of reason. Heard of in any other context, they would be dismissed as absurd fiction. Associated with 18th century Winchester, we accept them without demur.

If one reads the Winchester historians, who have with varying degrees of aptitude written of Wykehamist life and customs, the main impression left on the mind is of the sheer awful discomfort of the place. The traditional Winchester bed was no more than a wooden frame with strips of iron nailed across it. Bed linen and other articles collectively named "Chamberstock" were either supplied by a boy's own family or could be hired from the school, but were not issued free. It would appear likely that most of the things most needful to and in use by a schoolboy were private property. Woodforde owned a set of these essential articles and when he left Winchester he parted with them to a boy named Bedford who had just been admitted, and who later sold them to

Uncle Tom Woodforde for the use of his son Frank. The diary lists them as:

> ..... a bed, Bolster, Sheets, Scobb, Chest, Bands, Towels, Toys,
> Desk, Gowns, Blanketts and Ruggs and Surplices. [3]

But all manner of things could be charged up to the boys' parents or relatives. "Causeway money" was exacted after Dr. Burton had spent £60 of his own cash on road repairs outside the school. "Nutting money" was collected for a picnic supposedly held in the autumn. Most bizarre was "rod money", for the cost of implements used for the endless beatings - at Winchester given the special name of "tunding" - which were a very unattractive feature of school life everywhere. They were provided from a special kind of apple tree found only in Herefordshire. These must have been either very hard-wearing or frequently replaced, because fustigation was a way of life. Anthony Trollope boasted that he had received "five scourgings" in a single day at Winchester. [4] He was probably exaggerating, but a mid-Victorian Head Master said that during his boyhood, when he was a pupil there, there might be 20 floggings in a day, "and all for slight offences". [5]

But to appreciate even vicariously the full horror of the experience, we must go with the Winchester Scholars through the whole of a working day. It was, to begin with, inordinately long, even when it is remembered that in all aspects of 18th century life long working hours were the rule. It began at the inhuman time of 5 a.m., or just possibly 5.30 by the time Woodforde arrived there. If the boys were up at the earlier time, roused by the cry of the prefect on duty in each of the dormitories or Chambers with the cry of Get Up! ("Surgite"!), they had to be in chapel by 5.30. At 6.00 a.m., still fasting, they were herded into the great Schoolroom, and the morning lesson lasted 3 hours. Only after that came breakfast, which consisted of dry bread and cold beer. At one time this had apparently been reinforced by "Broth sav'd" from the meat of the day before; but this had plainly disappeared by the time Woodforde arrived at the school. At the Election Scrutiny of 1766, after he had left, a suggestion was made that the school should "allow Butter and Cheese to the Children to their Breakfasts". It is not known whether this was acted upon; but tea did not replace beer until 1838. [6] After breakfast the boys were dismissed to their Chambers, to "meditate" until 11 a.m. The next hour was again spent "in School". Dinner ("prandium") was at 12 noon, and after it the pupils were set to work all through the long afternoon, four days a week, broken by a snack which, strangely enough, was allowed only in summer time. At 5 p.m. came supper ("cena"), after which the boys were supposed to study in their Chambers until 7.30, when there was a second chapel service. After that a drink was handed out, and as soon as they had taken it, they were despatched to bed. Half an hour after they had entered the "Chambers", the doors were locked by the prefects.

The above time-table comes mainly from a list dated 1647. There is another in the Winchester archives, covering the years 1825-9. The two are practically identical except that by the early 19th century the midday meal was called lunch and the evening meal dinner. This was now served at 6 p.m., and evening chapel did not begin until 8.30.

Let us look rather more closely at the meals. They were characteristic of an age which did not minister to the comfort of schoolboys. But they are far more than this, having an especial staggeringly uninviting quality that is all their own. Friday and Saturday were meatless days. On the other four weekdays, dinner consisted of 40 lbs. weight of boiled beef. On Sundays there was a smaller quantity, but it was roasted, and may have been marginally less unappetising. In the absence of any real supervising authority, the duty of seeing the food shared out devolved on the Prefect of Tub ("Praepositus Ollae"), who presided over the division of the meat into large chunks or "ferculae". These were then subdivided by the junior boy at each table into smaller lumps called "gispers". A gisper was each boy's individual portion. As if dinner had not provided enough heavy animal protein, supper was a meal of precisely the same kind, but was mutton instead of beef. Thomas Trollope writing of the 1820's mentions potatoes with the evening meal, but by then the dietary had in some ways improved, by comparison with the diarist's schooldays.[7] There is no mention of green vegetables of any kind, or of fruit - but this last item the boys would have provided for themselves, whenever they had any pocket money. It is significant that almost the only comment Woodforde ever made about Winchester, as distinct from mentioning people he had known as schoolfellows, concerned the "Huckster's Shop" (we should call it a tuck shop) where he "ticked", or bought goods on credit, and which had "many a Shilling" from him.[8] At the same time, Samuel Woodforde's meticulous listing of the expenses incurred over James' time at Winchester makes no mention of pocket money. A rather vague statement in one of the books about Winchester life holds that some, presumably very rich boys, did not eat the school meals at all. They must have managed somehow to have their supplies brought in from outside, for the rules forbidding egress from the school premises except for the prescribed outings were very strict.

On Tuesdays and Thursdays, all the year round, the scholastic routine was broken by what were doubtless intended as recreation, but a description of the practices makes it clear that they could became ordeals for the Scholars. The outing, always the same, was called "Going on Hills", and took the form of an expedition to St. Catherine's Hill, outside the city. Originally there were two of these, "Morning Hills" and "Middle" or "Afternoon Hills", to which a third was added, surely in the summer months only, "Under Hills", to the village of Tunbridge at the foot of the hill; also called "Evening Hills". The pleasure to be derived from all these jaunts must have varied sharply according to the time of year. One description of "Morning Hills" begins:

> ..... in the earlier years of the nineteenth century, when the
> start was made about 6 or 10 shivering breakfastless juniors
> ..... would huddle together at what was fitly called "Misery
> Corner" from 7 to 9 on a February morning. [9]

There were, of course at the time Woodforde was a schoolboy, and for long after, no sort of organised compulsory games, and once arrived at their destination, the boys were free to enjoy themselves in any way they wished, supervised only by the prefects. We hear in the various Wykehamist literature of "bird-slinging,pole-jumping,tree-climbing,mouse-digging, adventurous mountaineering in the chalk-pit". [10] I take it that the first of these pursuits would be aiming at passing birds with a catapult. For "mouse-digging", Trollope says there was a special implement for this, a sort of miniature pick-axe for gouging out field mice, afterwhich the captives were taken back to the school and kept in cages. A very popular "sport" was badger-hunting. The animal was brought in a sack, and chased about by the boys, no doubt terrified like all nocturnal creatures when exposed to the light of day. At different times tame badgers and foxes were kept in the school.

More conventional games included football, quoits and a bat-and-ball game which, it being Winchester, had to be played with a "pila" and a "bacillum", evidently a primitive form of cricket. "At the periods, no doubt there were boys who did nothing whatever", or at least restricted their activity to strolling and lounging about. William Whitehead (adm. 1718), later one of the succession of limp 18th century Poets Laureate, "would seek a sequestered nook, and read some book of poetry". But even the recreation periods could be turned into a hell for some unfortunate boys. With only two masters in charge of 50 or more boys, it was inevitable that discipline and order had to be enforced by the prefects, who often abused their power, in the manner of young males free to tyrannise over those smaller and weaker than themselves. Bullying was rife, and there are some horrible tales about it in the annals of Winchester. [11]

It is not at all surprising that many boys cracked up under this Spartan regime, and the Great Register is full of the names of those Scholars who either fell ill and had to be taken away, or died while at the school. It is clear that boys who were in poor health to begin with had little chance of survival. A boy who was admitted in Woodforde's year, Richard Fisher, of the city of Gloucester, aged 9 (this was the lowest age at which a Scholar could come in), did not last long. Afflicted by the "stone", he was forced to leave, and died soon afterwards. The long and indubitably fatiguing lesson periods, the inadequate and unbalanced diet, lacking in many of the essentials for healthy living, the exhaustion and cold in the leisure periods, all must have contributed towards ruining the health of the weaker boys. It had been no doubt much worse, in the Middle Ages when they all had to be poor to be admitted. By James Woodforde's time most of the boys on the Foundation, who were receiving free tuition and board, must have come from middle class families as well-off as those of the Commoners who were paying for both. But for those who were really poor, and unable to buy any of the sweeteners of existence, life at Winchester must have been very rough.

One question remains - what did they learn there? First, the Wykehamist was given a "classical education" in the fullest sense of that word. It was based entirely on Latin, to a rather lesser extent on Greek, most repetitively discussed, analysed, and paraphrased. It contained a huge and quite disproportionate amount of sheer rote-learning. Woodforde's friend Henry Bathurst is supposed to have said that he learned by heart sixteen thousand verses while he was at Winchester. [12] But there was also a good deal of improvisation. By the time they arrived, most Winchester boys would have already had some training in Latin, from preparatory schools or private tutors although, as we have seen, since boys as young as nine were taken, the lowest class must still have been learning the language in its grammatical forms. Those who had already gone beyond that basic stage were at once put to being trained in the use of argument and persuasion by means of Latin. This was the function of the declamation. A "theme" was given out, and the boy who was being tested had to speak on it extempore. We can tell quite accurately the nature of the exercise, since James Woodforde continued to do the same kind of work as an undergraduate at New College, and noted the themes in his diary. They tended to propound some question in aesthetics, such as "Whether all the arts have a common link", or are moralistic in tone: "Whether a slanderer or a thief is the more detestable"; or to deal with some question of ancient history.[13] A more complex and elaborated form of what essentially was the same exercise, called disputation, was described by Lord Selborne (at Winchester 1825-30) in terms that show it as derived with little change from the wit-combats of the 16th century: [14]

> Three boys were appointed, two to maintain or contradict, and
> the third to leave in doubt, a thesis proposed to them, in Latin
> prose of their own composition, which they recited publicly in
> the school.

He added "a dull performance it nearly always was". When we come to discuss Woodforde's academic career at New College we shall have occasion to note some ways in which the task could be rendered easier.

There was another but cognate kind of exercise, in which again the element of extemporisation was decisive. This was known as "Varying", the term restricted to Winchester. Even the junior boys were expected to be able to make up Latin verses, and such a composition was called a "vulgus". Varying came at Winchester to mean a vulgus composed in class, without the help of books and not written down. In other words, it was the production of a sort of epigram, spoken "off the cuff". As we shall see, whether or not a Winchester Scholar found his way to New College depended less upon intelligence or his performance as an examination candidate than upon the amount of influence his family possessed; but varying formed the last part of the examination and was considered to be important.

Then there were "Gatherings", copied-out extracts of poetry or prose. Selborne again wrote of them as an interesting exercise, which "led us to search for information on the subjects of which we had been reading". "Collections" appear to have been an abstract or summary of given passages out of books, chosen by the boys themselves.

In 1756 the Under Master, Samuel Speed, left and was replaced by Joseph Warton. The new Usher was given on arriving a complete list of the Greek and Latin writers studied throughout the school, compiled for him by Edward Holloway, the Senior Prefect. This document was lost for a long time, and discovered by accident only in the 1930's. Woodforde was a senior boy in the Fifth class, and a glance at the list will show the range of his studies in that year. Homer and the Greek Testament; Virgil, Horace, Paterculus, Sallust and Juvenal, all are there. It looks like a formidable programme. It is also, by comparison with any modern educational curriculum, absurdly narrow and over-specialized. With the exception of some incidental knowledge of divinity, ancient history and geography that might have emerged from it, nothing was taught except the texts themselves. At Winchester the classics were to maintain their predominance until the middle of the 19th century. There is no record of a modern language being taught there until 1821, and although mathematics had by then made their appearance, it was as an optional "extra" not taught by the regular masters.

Any first-year student at a College of Education could produce a satisfactory essay tricked out with all the most approved clichés, to show what was wrong with it. Without raising the point that such a curriculum did somehow manage to produce well-educated and highly literate people, we may admit all the deficiencies of a system so alien to all established notions about education, even while we wonder if our wholesale abandonment of the classics is not as clear an example of total onesidedness as was the 18th century's devotion to them.

In the context of this book, the most serious objection to Winchester must lie in its effect upon James Woodforde himself. Certainly he went through all the motions and learned enough to take him on to New College. But having got there, and secured the qualifications he needed by a repetition of what he had already studied at Winchester, he made not the slightest use of classical literature ever again. He had been crammed for five or six years, given the sort of one-track education that could have produced in him either a devoted love of the classics or profound indifference to them. In this case, it was the latter. In his diary, written day after day for so long, there is scarcely a hint of an allusion to the languages he had spent so much time and energy gaining a proficiency in. Very late in his life he took to putting down an occasional schoolboy Latin tag. Once he wrote English words in Greek characters when he had occasion to jot down something uncomplimentary about his niece Nancy. It seems a very small return for a great deal of effort.

At Winchester in his time there were three forms, each called "Classis" or "Book" - the last was another term exclusive to Winchester. They were Fourth, Fifth and Sixth, with a vestigial lower form called "Second and Fourth", into which the youngest or most backward boys were placed on arrival. The Fourth and Fifth were each divided into Senior, Middle and Junior parts. The class position of every boy was listed on the Long Roll drawn up at the time of the Election, at the end of the school year. Boys moved up

34

or down in class, according to the correctness or otherwise of their answers. [15]

If, armed with this information, we examine the scholastic career of James Woodforde, we find that he was very much an average pupil, neither spectacularly bright nor outstandingly dull. He was placed when he first arrived in the Middle part of the Fourth class, and never failed at the end of each year to move into the Class, or part of a Class, just above his, although he never jumped over one, as some boys did, and his final placing in some years was low. By 1757 he had reached the Sixth Class but was occupying a very inferior place in it, which suggests that the high-fliers had totally out-distanced him. We might also notice that he was never made a prefect or chosen to deliver one of the ceremonial addresses, in Latin of course, such as the speech "Ad Portas" which greeted the examiners from Oxford at each Election. On the other hand, there is no evidence at all that he was ever in any kind of trouble.

Winchester College Entrance with the Warden's House
(from R Ackerman's History of Winchester College, 1816)

Winchester College Chapel taken from the Warden's Garden
(from R Ackerman's History of Winchester College, 1816)

A Winchester College Scholar
Although of a later date, the scholar's gown had not changed since Woodforde's time.
(from R Ackerman's History of Winchester College, 1816)

School Room of Winchester College
(from R Ackerman's History of Winchester College, 1816)

CHAPTER 5

ELECTIONS AND BRIBERY

The Founder had laid down that the annual Election, which governed both the intake of new pupils to Winchester and the arrangement by which those who went on to become Scholars and Fellows of New College were chosen, could be held at any time between the Feast of St. Thomas Becket (17 July) and the beginning of October. In James Woodforde's time it was held early in September, with the actual date varying slightly from year to year. This date was fixed by New College, and the message handed, by virtue of another weird medieval practice, to a foot-messenger who walked with it all the way to Winchester. He was known as "Speedyman" or "Speeding man", and he also performed the same journey whenever a vacancy occurred among the Fellows of New College. On arrival he had to mount a ladder and affix a copy of the missive to each of the two school gates. This form of peripatetic survival or animated fossil was still around when Thomas Trollope was a boy at Winchester. Long afterwards he wrote in his autobiography:

> How well I remember the look of the man, as he used to arrive
> with all the appearance of having made a breathless journey,
> a spare, active-looking fellow, in brown cloth breeches and gaiters
> covered with dust. Of course letters telling the facts had long
> outstripped "Speedyman". But with the charming and reverent
> conservatism, which in those days ruled all things at Winchester,
> "Speedyman" made his journey on foot all the same. [1]

It might be added at this point that among the college dues paid by Woodforde on his arrival at New College as a freshman was an item recorded as "Speeding man - 0 4 6d", not much short of £25 in our money. This was presumably the cost of the walk to Winchester to proclaim the vacancy later filled by James Woodforde.

The Election was presided over by six people: the Warden of Winchester, his sub-warden for the year, and the Head Master; and three from Oxford, the Warden of New College and two Fellows, the "Posers" (a corrupted form of Latin "Praepositus"), who were drawn in a rota system, and each of whom served twice. Woodforde was "Junior Poser" in 1769 and "Senior Poser" in 1772. This is fortunate for us. He may have left no recollections of his experiences when taking the Election as a boy, but in return his diary provides us with by far the clearest and most detailed picture of the event that we possess.

One of the tasks of the six academics was to carry out the kind of Visitation which centuries ago bishops and their representatives had conducted in monastic houses. They held a "Scrutiny", and sent for the boys, to know if they had any complaint of any kind about any person or anything else [2] - to which the boys, if they knew what was good for them, would have meekly replied in the traditional form: All Well ("Omnia bene"). But the main business was the production of the two lists. The "Roll ad Winton" contained the names of boys newly admitted to the school. The "Roll ad Oxon" had those seniors who aimed at a place at New College. The Election was the vital preliminary to a Fellowship, and everything depended upon securing a place as near as possible to the top of the list, since the Roll was valid only to a date seven weeks before the time of the next Election. The names were taken in strict rotation to fill the vacancies created within that period. The first two places were given to the especially favoured "Founder's Kin" candidates. There could be up to eighteen of these in the school at any one time, and their intake was carefully controlled so that two were due to leave at the end of each school year. Of course, the pedigrees drawn up to prove lineal descent from William of Wykeham were in every case spurious, but none the less extremely useful. [3]

This competition for coveted places, while it cuts right across the belief, which appears to be widespread, that promotion from Winchester to New College was automatic, can quite easily be explained. William of Wykeham no doubt intended his 70 Fellows of the Oxford foundation to balance exactly the 70 Winchester boys; but when the Fellowships began to be held for life this balance was destroyed. When Woodforde finally arrived, he found one Fellow who had been there for 43 years, and two more who had each been there over 30. This meant that there were never enough places for all the Wykehamists who sought after them. We can, I think, clinch this argument by citing a little statistical evidence.

1752, the year Woodforde entered Winchester, was in no way unusual, except that the number of entrants was smaller than in many years. He was put down as the last of 11 names. George Wickham the first on the list, failed to make any use of his favoured position. He left in January and, obeying the second injunction of the famous "Aut disce" which stood by the Head Master's throne in the schoolroom, went into the Navy.[4] The other Founder's Kin entrant, William Hearst, went on to New College. The next in order,

John Oglander, was Warden of the college 1768-94. William Willis left as early as 1756. Edward Loggin went to New College and remained there until his early death in 1772. John Phillips left, no date being inserted in the register. Benson Bennett, whom Woodforde meeting in later life called "Mr. Benson Earle", almost certainly signifying that he had changed his name upon inheriting money or property, took both the 1757 and 1758 Elections with him, but was unlucky. He was in ninth place in a year which produced only eight vacancies. Thomas Middleton went absent and was expelled in 1766. Thomas Brown went on to the University but was at Corpus. That leaves Fisher, whom we have already noted as having fallen ill while at school, and Woodforde himself. The total amounts to 4 out of 11 who made it to New College, odds of slightly better than 3 to 1 against getting there.

The Statute No. 2 had decreed that all pupils who were not Founder's Kin had to leave upon attaining their 17th birthday. The school register listed these as "Superannuate". If, however, a boy had by then already taken an Election, and as a result obtained a place too low to give him much hope of a Fellowship, he was allowed to stay on and take it again. This is precisely what James Woodforde did. In September 1757 his undistinguished place in the Sixth Class, at 15th out of 18, was capped by a hopeless listing on that year's Roll ad Oxon, 19th out of 24. Vacancies among New College Fellows could occur only through death, resignation or, in the case of the majority who were or intended to be clergymen, the acceptance of a church living or other preferment worth more than a certain annual sum. At that time it was fixed at £70. The likelihood of there being as many as 19 drop-outs in little over 10 months must be estimated as practically nil.

At this point many left and went no further with their education. In the case, however, of those aiming at a career in the Church a degree from Oxford or Cambridge, although not absolutely vital, was a considerable help, and New College was extremely wealthy, its profits shared out each year among its Fellows; and it had the agreeable prospect of 46 tied benefices. So, while taking the advantage of an extra year at Winchester, they were in most cases enrolled at another college. If their second Election produced a higher placing on the Roll than their first had provided, they were in line for a vacancy turning up at New College. If not, they stayed at the other college and made the best of it.

On 8 May 1758 James Woodforde was matriculated from Oriel, paying £8 "Caution money".[5] This deposit was a kind of primitive insurance policy, to guard against a student leaving in debt to the college. Having done this, he returned to Winchester, where he stayed until the time of the next Election in September. He was now a Superannuate, and this was absolutely his last chance. It is worth while looking at what he had to do. The reader need only transpose the examiner of 1769 and 1772 who described the procedure of the Election in his diary into the aspiring pupil of 1758, to have a clear enough picture of what went on. The Election was held over three days. A good deal of time was spent on ceremonial speeches and general jollification, with the mutual giving of symbolic presents.[6] The actual examination of the candidates took two days. On the first day:

> ..... After Chapel we went into the Election Chamber and heard
> the Young Gentlemen say their Election Tasks - 27 in Number.

Only the Sixth Class and part of the Fifth could take the Election. These boys were divided into three groups, called "Fardels" - Senior, Middle and Junior. There originally must have been four, since the word comes from German "Viertel", a fourth part, a quarter. The next day:

> ..... After breakfast we dressed ourselves & went into the
> Election Chamber and examined the Senior Fardle -
> The Middle & Junior Fardles brought up their Tasks also
> The Senior Fardle made a very good appearance .....
> After Dinner we retired to the Wardens Rooms and drank a
> Glass of Wine or two, and then went into the Election
> Chamber where Senior Fardle translated some out of one of
> the Spectators - And then all three Fardles came up into
> the Chamber and varyed -

All translation, sight-reading and extempore delivery, was from English into Latin; and "varying" inevitably played its part in the examination. Woodforde wrote down the quotation chosen from his "Theme", from Horace. After the test was completed, they "made up both Rolls - but not till ten". On the last day he with the others signed the Rolls just before they all dispersed. Three years later, the procedure was exactly the same; but the account has a particular interest because of an altercation over the making up of the Oxford Roll. There could be no argument over the two Founder's Kin candidates; but Warden Oglander wanted a particular entrant named Boys or Boyce to be placed next. All the others opposed him, and another name put down. The Warden tried again, and this time Woodforde supported him; but no-one else agreed, with the result that Boys was given no higher than fifth place. Now we know that his family and Oglander's were friends and neighbours in Dorset, and the incident highlights the immense importance of personal recommendation in determining the position of a given candidate on the Roll, and hence the value of his chances of getting to New College.

Having taken the Election for his second time, Woodforde finally left Winchester with 7th. place on the Roll ad Oxon. This gave him a reasonable chance, but by no means a certainty, of getting to New College. A month later, at the beginning of the new Academic year, he went into residence at Oriel.

Back at Ansford, Mr. Woodforde senior reached for his accounts book:

> Sep:8 1758 paid Bills at Winchester when
> he left the College & Expences
>   10 paid for a Superfine Suit
>   of cloaths & Making for James W   5 5 0
>   12 paid for a second Suit
>   of cloaths & for shirts and
>   stockings   9 0 0
>   gave him cash going to
>   Oxford to keep term   7 10 0

The new clothes must have been special garments made to provide sartorial chic, and allow James to cut a dash as a freshman. The "superfine" suit; i.e. the best quality broadcloth, would cost over £200 in our depleted money. When on 30 February next year his father paid Mr. Owens, the Castle Cary barber, 13 shillings for a "scratch-Wigg" (defined as a wig covering part of the head only), it must have been a very dressy undergraduate who strolled through Oriel College gates.

There is a paradoxical situation here. Literally hundreds of diary entries describe the minutest details of his personal life, particularly the pleasures, enjoyments and pastimes of the New College years; but there is little about the academic work he did, possibly because most of the exercises on the way to his degree were orally delivered. On the other hand, while we know nothing about his life at Oriel, and that college is mentioned in the diary only in connection with a handful of Oriel men he continued to see after he had left there, the Bodleian Library has no fewer than 173 written Latin themes, supplied with an index classifying them as "Declam". (25), "Prose" (49), "Verse" (66) and "Metre" (33). This is dated 26 June 1759, right at the end of his Oriel year.

Meanwhile, that year had slipped away. Autumn, when he had first gone up, merged into winter, winter into spring, spring into summer. If James was enjoying himself and not worrying, the same could not be said of his father:

> June 4 1759 Going to Winton, London, Hornchurch
> Essex, Oxford &c. to procure a resignation for my
> son James & at Bristol -   10 0 0
> July 5 paid the proportion of the money for
> Bingham's resignation   34 5 0 for Reynell

The exact sequence of events cannot be understood without some explanation. As already stated, the Roll ad Oxon was not valid beyond the end of July 1759. Evidently Fellows who had made up their minds to resign could at this late stage be expected to gain something from their successors, if they agreed to go while there was still time. That is clearly what Samuel meant by "procure a Resignation". Now in 1759 a Fellow, Isaac Moody Bingham, did resign on taking two benefices. But the money was to go, not to him but to a man named Reynell. A glance at the Roll shows that a Harry Peckham stood in 5th place, Woodforde was 7th. and this same Reynell 8th. When Bingham resigned, it was Peckham who was due to move into his vacant place. Samuel Woodforde was willing to give a large sum of money, in the currency values of the day, to induce him to waive his claim and let James fill the vacancy. This arrangement may seem like a very poor bargain for Peckham but, although he did become a clergyman, his earlier career was in the law, and in those circumstances New College was less important to him than it was for anyone intending from the start to enter the Church. As Reynell was behind Woodforde on the Roll, he could not have been directly involved, but he and Peckham were friends and he was apparently quite ready to act as a go-between. [7]

But now another factor intervened. Mr. John Risley, a Fellow since 1748, picked up the living of Tingewick, Bucks. His palm well oiled, he obligingly resigned his Fellowship, with about a week to spare. Now the Woodfordes had no need to persuade Peckham to stand aside, so he took Bingham's former place. Finally there was a third resignation, that of Robert Bathurst. His place went to Reynell as Risley's to Woodforde. So in the end all three young men were elected Scholars of New College on the same day, 21 July 1759. [8]

Six weeks later, James Woodforde and his father both summed

up the situation. The accounts book states tersely:

> Sep: 6 paid Doctor Bridle for Mr Risley's Use 45 0 0

The diary entry for the same day corroborates this and, in addition, sets out the entire transaction.

> Septem: 6 Doctor Bridle and his Brother at Bristol (the Sugar
> Baker) dined at our House at Ansford.
> My Father gave Doctor Bridle, 45, for Risley's
> Resignation; July 5th My Father gave young Reynells
> 35: to get Peckham of, which makes 80£ in all.

It had cost Mr. Woodforde £80 in good, honest Georgian money to pull it off; but it had all turned out satisfactorily in the end and everyone, I presume, was pleased with the result. For James Woodforde, at least, 21 July 1759 was a great red-letter day in his life. He must have felt that he needed to signalize it with some especially distinctive token. It was on that day that he began to write his diary, with the words:

> Made a Scholar of New-College

CHAPTER 6

NEW COLLEGE AND THE EARLIEST DIARY

The visitor who goes down New College Lane, with its sharp turns and air of grey antiquity, is rewarded by the sight of the splendid gateway which is a fitting preliminary and introduction to one of the great architectural masterpieces of the Middle Ages. All one has to do is to will away Gilbert Scott's hulking Holywell block of the 1870's, and a few later innovations such as the new library built in the 1930's, to see a congeries of buildings already ancient in James Woodforde's time. It is true that, on a closer inspection, many of the medieval glories are seen to have been damaged by later hands. The chapel suffered restoration by Wyatt in the 18th century and by Scott again in the 19th, while the huge reredos, "intended to give the effect of the original, ... is not an entirely convincing substitute". [1] All the same, a good deal of what was familiar to James Woodforde has survived.

We can stroll in the garden where he often played bowls, in the shadow of the ancient city wall. Here he once went scrambling, and frightened himself very much by a near-fall. Even some of the rooms he knew are still identifiable. We can still go into the "Chequer", a sort of common room which could also be hired out for private parties, often mentioned in the Oxford part of the diary.

Woodforde could not have been in Oxford on the day the college accepted him. We know this because the elaborate printed form (it cost him 3/6d.), signed by the notary public, by which that acceptance was ratified, lacks the details of his birthplace, county and diocese. He must, of course, have been familiar with New College long before he joined it. On certain ceremonial occasions boys from the Winchester Foundation were invited there, and during his Oriel year he surely must have visited friends a year or two older than himself who had already made the transition. But even if he had not made its acquaintance before, he was not the kind of excitable and fervid youth who would have been impelled to rush off and see the goal to which his six year stay at Winchester had led.

Instead he stayed quietly at home, as the diary shows, until the new academic year began. Then for the first time he wrote down what was to be one of the features of his mature diary: the detailed account of a journey. Setting out from Ansford on the morning of 1 October, he reached Everley, where he stayed overnight at the *Rose and Crown*. The next day he went on, through Hungerford, Farnborough and Abingdon, to reach Oxford in the evening. Most of these place-names were to reappear in subsequent accounts of the same journey. In college he stayed the night in the room of Nicolls who had been his "Boy Tutor" at Winchester.

The system by which rooms were allocated was intensely complex; but at all times some rooms were empty. This came about because, although the rules about residence were very strict for undergraduates, once a Fellow had graduated (the academics of that time saw no anomaly in Fellowships being granted two years before graduation, and given immediately to the Founder's Kin entrants) he could leave college, and stay away, while retaining the right to his room which, provided he had not let it off to a collegiate sub-tenant, would be unoccupied. For the first few weeks the diarist moved from room to room, sometimes vacating it if its rightful possessor returned, until he finally managed to take over one which he soon began to call his own. It belonged to William Burland, from Wells, an acquaintance of the Woodforde family, a non-resident who was perhaps already afflicted by the ill-health from which he was to die three years later.[2] Woodforde uses the terms "room" and "rooms" quite impartially, often of the same apartment. A set of rooms at New College consisted of a bedroom and a study, but some undergraduates may have had single rooms only.

In his first few weeks we see him preoccupied with settling in to his new surroundings, and in particular finding and stocking comforts which he appears not to have had in his time at Oriel, probably having regarded his residence at that college as a short-stay event only. He bought furniture:"a new Norway-Oak Buroe,[3] which I am to pay for, at a Convenient time, two Pound, five Shillings to one Mr Badcock Cabinet-Maker by Christ-Ch Coll:" (15/10/1759). And again: "Had of Mr Ward the Upholsterer, a Round Table, a Picture of Our Founder, and a Sett of Chairs. He lent me a large looking Glass". (25/2/1760) Other purchases included "a new Grate, fire Pan, Poker, Tongs, & 2 brass Candlesticks, of Reynolds at the Back-Gate". (14/12/1759) Rather than buy them, he had some bedclothes sent from his parents' home: "a Bed, 3 Blanketts, a Quilt, Bolster & Pillow". (10/11/1759) At the same time he purchased clothing : "Had a new Shaggy Coat & a new flannel Waistcoat, & New Trencher-Cap & Tossle".(13/11/1759) [4]

He appears to have been keenly aware of the advantages of

social accomplishments. He began to learn to play the "Spinnett" under the tuition of Philip Hayes, son of the Professor of Music at Oxford. He was later Professor himself and organist at New College and Magdalen, by which time he had become "a man of enormous size and exceedingly bad temper". Woodforde paid at the rate of 12 lessons, or "Lectures" as he called them, for a guinea. He was also taught dancing by E.C. Orthman, dancing-master and musician, principal cellist at the Music Room in Holywell. Woodforde stayed a long while with him, the last "Lecture" having been received on 19 November 1761. Orthman reappears, as Steward of the "Catch Clubb" that used to meet at the "Mitre", in High Street, as late as 1775. 5 Woodforde mentions only two kinds of dance, "Country Dances" and minuets, neither of which should have taken very long to master. Perhaps he was not a very apt pupil!

On 7 May 1761 he noted: "I went in the Evening to a Private Hopp", organised by the dancing master at his home in the High Street, near the "Angel Inn", opposite Queen's College. The entry lists the men, all "gownsmen" from various colleges, paired off with girls who were "well to-do tradesmen's daughters".6 Living in a wholly male, celibate community, where only the Warden was allowed to marry, (and for the Fellow matrimony meant an immediate rescinding of his Fellowship, without formal resignation being necessary), one of James' few opportunities to meet girls of his own age socially must have been in such parties as this.

There was also his friendship with the Bignell sisters. They were very likely related to John Bignell, a New College servant, described in 1773 as "our Comm: *(sic)* Room Man". He had a brother William and a son Jack, "our Common Room Boy", all three working in the college at the time of Woodforde's second period of residence at the University. The first we hear of the relationship is on 24 November 1760 when he wrote: "Gave Nancy Bignell six white Handkerchiefs to make for me". This at once raises the supposition that she was in a lower social class than his own. There is no record of his paying for this service. Some time before he had given two yards of blue ribbon to "Bett Robinson at the fruit shop". Now, on 28 November, he wrote:

For a Steel Twizer Case -	pd - 0. 8. 0
For 5 Yards of 7d Ribband	pd - 0. 2.11
For 3 Yards of 8d Ribband	pd - 0. 2. 0
Gave Nancy Bignell 3 Yards of the sevenpenny -	
Gave her Sister Betsy 2 Yards of the sevenpenny -	

That was the preliminary to a series of meetings. James went walking once with Nancy alone, but several times with both sisters. He walked them round the Parks, he invited them to coffee in his room at New College. On 21 December he gave Nancy "a silver Thimble", but on Christmas Day he made the same present to her sister.

It is to be remembered that Oxford was not the bustling, industrialised place it is to-day but, the University apart, a small and not over-prosperous market town where, as the saying goes, everybody knew everyone else. Relations between the University and the city had never been cordial, and it was only to be expected that James' being so often in the sisters' company would be noticed and commented on, particularly by representatives of "Town" as opposed to "Gown" On 2 January 1760 he noted:

> For Ale in a House in Holliwell where
> I took some Verses from a Man, made
> upon Nancy Bignell and myself - pd - 0. 0. 4

The sequel may be read in the entry for 7 January:

> Peckham, Loggin, & Webber went with me to Halse's the Sadler,
> where I threshed his Apprentice Crozier for making Verses on me -

But before this, on 3 January, one day after he had seen the verses he so much objected to, there is a mysterious one-line passage:

> Had a Lecture from John Bignell -

As we have seen, he used this word to mean a lesson, but he apparently knew no man of that name except the servant, and it is not likely that he would have been in any position to give lessons of any kind to an undergraduate whom his business was to wait on. There is another possible explanation: that John was the girls' father and the "Lecture" was a telling off he gave the young man. The dictionary definition of "Lecture" as "An admonition, esp. by way of reproof" was, of course, current at the time, although there is only one other place in which the diarist uses the word in that sense.

Woodforde continued to go out with both girls, although rather less frequently than before. The last reference to them is dated 4 May 1761, when he wrote: "Took a long Walk this Evening with Nancy and Betsy Bignell for 3 Hours". His direct allusion to the time spent might indicate that the occasion was a special one. Perhaps they discussed his friendship with the sisters, and he told them it had to come to an end. At all events, he never mentioned them again.

And perhaps some time in the late 1820's, there were two very old ladies living in Oxford, both cherishing a silver thimble, and both believing that if the young man, who had grown handsome and more dashing through the distortions of a long memory, had not married either of them, it was only because he was unable to decide between them!

On one of his walks with the Bignells he had brought along his friend John Geree, perhaps the closest of his Oxford friends and his regular correspondent in the years he spent away from the University between 1763 and 1773. Geree and Woodforde formed part of a group who spent a lot of time in each other's company. Some of them were no doubt more intellectually inclined than others, but we see them most often when they are enjoying themselves with a great variety of different games. It was an easy-going life by any standard, with a great deal of spare time to be filled. An overwhelmingly large number of entries in this part of the diary are devoted to showing how he filled this time. He played a number of card-games: quadrille and brag (a form of poker), cribbage, loo and "Lambskinnet". [7] Billiards was frequently played, most often in a billiard room he calls "Capillaire's" or "Cap's"; probably a nickname, for the term meant a kind of syrup. On 23 April 1761 he indulged in a veritable marathon of games:

At Billiards with Bennett [8] from Eleven in ye Morn
till Eleven at Night for Games I owe   0 .. 8 .. 4
A Betting with Bennett - lost   0 .. 1 .. 6
Had some Bread & Cheese at ye Billiard Table
from the Coff: House for Bennett & myself -
Went with Bennett afterwards into ye
B C R where we sat up and played Cards till
8 the next morning - had a Bottle of Wine -
Won of Bennett at Cards -   0 .. 1 .. 6

Even after this, he invited his antagonist back to his room, where they breakfasted on "Lamb, Bread & Cheese", and went on playing cards. This time he lost 7/6d. Possibly by now he was overtired. He always played competitive games for money, and sometimes the amounts won or lost were surprisingly large.

Out of doors he liked to play "Crikett" on Port Meadow;

sometimes as part of a team, at others one against one, like Mr. Jingle and Quanko Samba. As we have seen, he played bowls in the garden beneath the city wall, and skittles or "skirls" or "skeels". Occasionally he went shooting "in Stanton Woods". In the very cold January of 1763 he went day after day to skate on the frozen Isis, on one occasion not coming off the ice until 7 in the evening. He invested in some new straps for his skates, of a kind devised by Mr. Halse the saddler, whose apprentice he had "threshed" two years before. And all this sporting activity reveals a trait which was constant with him. He would be struck with a "craze" for some pursuit, indulge in the enjoyment of it many times - and then as suddenly drop it and never take it up again. He went on doing this for the rest of his life, with people as well as things, as the diary witnesses.

But with all this, he was a B.A. student reading for a degree, as we should phrase it today. I have left discussion of this until last, since while looking over his life at this period, I have the distinct impression that his academic work meant less to him than the manifold enjoyments of his leisure hours. And this was by no means because he did not care about taking his degree. He certainly did, if only to please his father. In a way, his attitude was rather like that towards his parish work, in the years when he was a beneficed clergyman. In each case, he did what was required of him, but without enthusiasm. The fire and spirit that come from a sense of vocation were missing.

In the case of his academic studies at least, he can hardly be blamed for his somewhat lack-lustre approach to them for they were little short of farcical. There can be no dispute that Oxford was intellectually at a low ebb during his time there, although some of the stories adduced to prove this surely must have begun their lives as jokes, most of them in Cambridge. It is not easy to believe, for example, that the sole history question asked of a student supplicating for a degree was: "Who founded University College"? The right answer, of course, was King Alfred!

The reality was bad enough, and had been getting steadily worse for some time. Something more than a century before, Laud had thoroughly reformed the curriculum, with the intention that no-one should be awarded a degree without a proper course of study leading up to it. Had the Laudian Statutes been obeyed in the spirit as they were in the letter, there would have been little room for criticism. According to their provisions, the student was bound to go through a series of exercises for the Bachelor's degree which should have tested the continuous steps of his progress, and finally to pass a comprehensive examination. Three public tests were obligatory: first, what was called "Disputationes in Parviso", and commonly as "Generals" or "Juraments". Then there was a test called "Answering under Batchelor", with a B.A. to act as "Moderator". (The word survives in our "Moderations"). Finally there was the degree examination itself, taken after four years or twelve terms. Its subjects were supposed to be geometry, natural philosophy, astronomy, metaphysics, history, Hebrew, Greek and Latin. Although it would have been impossible to test average candidates in all these subjects to anything more than a low standard of proficiency, in fact it was only in the last two that Winchester had provided any training or preparation. The only reason why everyone who stayed the course and did not get into trouble with the authorities ended up with a degree was that the discipline had "degenerated into a series of meaningless formalities".[9] There were no grades, so that one pass was as good as another; and "Honours" had not yet come in.

As Woodforde is our subject, we must endeavour to find out how he coped with the not very exacting programme of his studies. The only statutory requirement was the declamation, given aloud, so far as New College was concerned, either in the Hall or the ante-chapel. The students were obliged "to declare a prepared discourse on a theme set by their tutor". Woodforde had been doing this kind of thing for five long years at Winchester; and the giving out of the theme beforehand took away any need for extempore speaking. His first declaration, on 26 October 1759, was on the subject of: "Pompey achieved a triumph while still an adolescent". He affirmed this. On 9 November he "read a Theme" on: "Whether fortitude in war or unceasing justice in the courts is more praiseworthy in the citizen". He argued for the first proposition, but it is hard to believe that he had any real opinions about the question, one way or another. His next declamation was on the notion that "Time changes opinion". Undergraduates were not called upon to declaim more than three times in a term, and when they did so, the whole thing must have been almost as dull to them as it sounds to us. As for the disputations, these were described by the satirist Nicholas Amherst, a Whig who could never resist a dig at Tory Oxford, as being no more than the formal repetition of a set of syllogisms "upon some ridiculous question in logick, which they get by rote, or perhaps only read out of their caps, which lie before them with their notes in them".[10] Yet on one occasion when James disputed with his friend Peckham, he found the arguments of his fellow-collegian "very low, paultry, and false", which at least shows that some feeling occasionally intruded into these arid and futile pseudo-academic quibblings.

A good example of the way he managed to combine his studies with the more pressing business of enjoying himself is to be found in the diary entry for 4 November 1761. He was "doing Generals", which , as already stated, was the first of the formal examinations for his B.A. The day the test began he says he was in "the Metaphysical School" for two hours, "from one till three - being the usual Time", and "came of very well". But he was clearly more interested in what happened in the Common Room after he got back: "Dyer laid Williams 2s 6d that he drank 3 Pints of Wine in 3 Hours, and that he wrote 6 Verses out of the Bible right - but he lost. He did it in the B C R, he drank all the wine, but could not write right for his Life - He was immensely drunk about 5 Minutes afterwards - ".11

On the evening before the last day of the test, he sat up with four other New College men, including the inevitable Peckham, and Lieutenant Rooke. This last was the only son of an old family friend, and a sort of "Rake's Progress" character who ran through all his money and came to a bad end at last.12 He had five sisters, whose charming "pet names": Miss Molly, Miss Sally, Miss Kitty, Miss Priscy and Miss Nancy, conjure up pleasant daydreams of 18th century drawing rooms and Mozart on the harpsichord, and gives the impression that they must all have been of flower-like grace and beauty. At length all but one of the revellers staggered round to an inn called the "Bear". Most people to-day tend to think of the 18th century as the age when the customer was always right, and every whim could be satisfied, so long as he had money to pay for what he wanted. It was not so, indeed. On this occasion the landlord refused to serve them with a late meal, and "they would not give us one bit - After we had took our Leave of Rooke, and found we could have no Victuals, we went about 6 o'clock to Baggs's Coff: House 13 where we eat some Pork, and I paid for it 0. 0. 6.". Then "I went immediately afterwards to bed and laid till 12 o'clock". It is typical that the account of the examination that follows is nothing like so vivid as the picture of the carousing undergraduates.

On 2 March 1762 he completed the "answering under bachelor" test. However the names of these various exercises differed, the same features prevailed, for this was another round of disputations. "Mr. Adams was so good as to oppose me". Oglander, he who later became Warden, "was my Father, and I was his Son". What this means was that his friend was a "Praelector", a public orator or reader, and it was his responsibility to present Woodforde for his degree. The examiners were the Senior Proctor and one of the Pro-Proctors. This was very nearly an all day affair: "We went up at 9 and stay'd until half an Hour after tea".

After that he had no more to do, although he did not take his degree until over a year later, when his twelve terms were almost completed. The final arbiter in this matter was the college, which could refuse "grace", or permission to supplicate for the degree, if the "Thirteen", the Senior Fellows who ran its administrative life, saw reason to do this. Together with the three men who had been admitted on the same day as himself, and one other, with two more who were taking the degree of Ll. B., he took part in "a grand Procession from N: College: to the Convocation House". After that: "I sat up in the B C R this Evening 'till after twelve o'clock, and then went to bed, and at three in the Morning, had my outward Doors broke open, my Glass Doors broke, and pulled out of Bed, and brought into the B C R, where I was obliged to drink and smoak, but not without a good many Words - Peckham broke open my Doors, being very drunk, altho' they were open, which I do not relish of Mr Peckham much".

A little over a week before he had taken another important step in his career. On 23 May, at Corpus Christi College, Woodforde was examined for Minor Orders by "Mr Hewish the Bishop of Oxford's Chaplain, ... and I came off very well - ". He continues:

> I was set over in the middle of the fifth Chapter of St. Paul to
> the Romans, and construed that Chapter quite to the End - I was
> quite half an Hour examining - He asked a good many hard & deep
> Questions, I had not one Question that yes, or no, would answer ..
> Mr Hewish is a very fair Examiner,
> and will see whether a Man be learned or no - .

The chaplain must have found him sufficiently learned, for on the morning of 29 May he was "ordained Deacon ... by Hume Bishop of Oxford" in Christ Church Cathedral, one of a batch of 25 deacons and 13 priests.

Although there is nothing about it in the diary, he must have already been looking about for possible curacies. Newton Purcell is on the Oxfordshire-Buckinghamshire border, about 20 miles from Oxford. The church, not identical with the building Woodforde knew, for it was restored or even partially rebuilt early in the 19th century, is very small and plain.There is a picture of this church on the cover of the Quarterly Journal of the Parson Woodforde Society, Vol. XVIII, No. 1. The patronage was held by Mr. Trotman, the nominal rector, who was non-resident, being also the incumbent of another living in the county. The official curate was George James Sale, one of Woodforde's best friends among the older Fellows of New College. He, however, had become a Proctor at Easter, and no doubt could not spare the time to make the journey to Newton Purcell once a week; and so called our newly made Parson to stand in for him. It was at Newton Purcell that Woodforde's career in the Anglican church began.

He was quite proud of this, calling the place "my Curacy". On 5 June he wrote: "At eleven o'clock went to my Church, and read Prayers and preached my first Sermon". As a deacon, he was not yet allowed to do more. He served Newton Purcell for six weeks. He says eight, but on one of the Sundays he swapped churches with another temporary curate, and on another he did not go out of the college. All the same Sale paid him four guineas, half a guinea a time. This was of course a mere stop-gap appointment, and was followed by others of the same kind: at Ardington near Wantage, Berks., Great Chesterton, Oxon., and Drayton, two miles from Abingdon. But while during the summer of 1763 he went about taking these services, it was with the comforting knowledge that he had been offered and accepted what he really wanted, a long-term curacy in Somerset. On 12 September he went down from the University, ending his first phase of residence there, and journeyed home. When on 8 October he arrived to take up his new position, a phase of his life opened, which was to endure for the next ten years.

NOTE TO CHAPTER 6 - THE M.A. DEGREE

The academic exercises which the diarist was obliged to carry out in order to obtain his second degree were accomplished during the first half of the time he spent working as a curate in Somerset; and therefore belong chronologically with the events described in the next chapter. At the same time I have thought it best to deal with them here, as part of the section on his University life, rather than cause ungraceful breaks in the narrative dealing with the years of the Somerset curacies. His periodical returns to Oxford during that time seldom took up more than a few days.

The M.A. course officially began in 1764 with a disputation, in which all the recently made B.A.s were expected to take part. They were based on "nine Logical Questions" which he had sent in "to the Scholars" in the previous December for them "to compose Epigrams upon again in Lent". On 2 March, in the Hall of the College: "I went thro' the nine Questions first with a Batchelor .... wherein I was Respondent, and then immediately with an Undergraduate .... upon the same nine Questions upon which I was Opponent - I was up in Hall disputing from five o'clock this afternoon 'till eight".

This may be regarded as a sort of rehearsal for the real thing, which started on Ash Wednesday with another "Grand Procession", from St. Mary's Church to the Schools for all the Determining Batchelors", led by the deans of their colleges. One could employ a helper, called an "Aristotle", to argue with the dean. Woodforde's own Dean was not present, and another Senior Fellow stood in for him. The diarist read his nine epigrams which, as we saw, had been made for him by others. All this took up four hours, and there was another stint on the following day. He had rather more to do then, as he was disputing for an hour and a half. Again a "son" assisted him. His opponent suggested that their labours might be refreshed by some wine, so Woodforde bought a pint from his bedmaker, which the latter "carried to the Schools". It cost him ninepence. On the following day, 9 March , he was again determining for three hours, from 9 until 12, and the same man was his "son", although seemingly without the wine. He had paid a fee of 16/8d, besides a half a guinea for the dean and incidental expenses. After these intellectual efforts, he must have felt he needed a rest, for he did not start on his journey back until 22 March.

He returned just over a year later, on 30 April 1765. His purpose was now to read the "Sex Solennes lectiones" decreed by the Laudian Statutes and expressively termed the Wall Lectures, since they were read to the walls of an empty room! There were five of these to give, not six, which the diarist says he delivered on 9, 10, 13, 14 and 17 May. Woodforde never offers us a single word in explanation of the subject or subjects, how long they lasted or, indeed, anything about them at all. They must for him have represented some mechanical routine task to be got over as soon as possible. But they were "for my M.A.". He also had to declaim twice. The first time was before one of the Proctors on the subject of:"Alexander said he owed more to his tutor Aristotle than to his father Philip". He does not tell us what his second declamation was about. Two other students were with him to accomplish the same task, and a beadle walked before them from St. Mary's to the Schools. Two days later he got up at 3 in the morning and walked to the "Starr Inn in the Corn Markett", where he "took Coach & set forth for Bath" on his way home. "There were only two more in the Machine beside me - One was (I believe) a dissenting Minister, and the other an Oxford old Lady who is going to Cirencester". Once released from the meaningless grind of the disputations and all the rest of the musty medieval lore, his natural interest in the real, living world about him quickly reasserted itself.

After a further two years he arrived in Oxford on 22 April 1767 for the final stage of the proceedings. He still had some work to do, if that is what one may call it. On 9 May he took part in the "Disputationes apud Augustinienses", so called because in the Middle Ages Oxford scholars had disputed with the Augustinian monks there. In University slang the exercise was called "doing Austins". On 20 May it was the turn of the "Disputationes Quodlibeticas", known as "Quodlibets". In this a candidate was supposed to answer any sort of question put to him by anyone. In reality Woodforde was as usual examined by members of his own college, answered three questions and spent two minutes over them. Next day he appeared before the heads of the college, "the Thirteen", to ask for permission to take his degree, which was granted at once. "I shall take my Degree I believe next Saturday". He was right to the day. On 23 May he went to the Schools and "had a Masters Degree conferred on me by the V. Chancellor &c. &c.". His expenses amounted to £3.16.0, and in addition a dozen bottles of port wine sent in according to the usual custom to the Master's Common Room. However, "there was but little drank all day in the M C R".

CHAPTER 7

THE SOMERSET CURACIES

The Anglican Church that Woodforde knew and worked in was, like Georgian Winchester and Georgian Oxford, full of anomalies that would make it the natural target of serious-minded, conscientious and energetic 19th century reformers who eventually changed it out of all semblance of its former self. The highest in status of the professions, above the law and armed forces and immeasurably superior to medicine which was only just freeing itself from its ancient associations with barbers and horse-leeches, the Church was immensely rich; but the wealth was so badly and unevenly distributed that its ranks showed the extremes of riches and poverty. At one end of the scale were sees like Winchester and Durham ("St. Cuthbert's Land", as its vast possessions were called); on the other were the poverty-stricken Welsh dioceses with their dilapidated churches, such as Tremeirchon, which so shocked Dr Johnson's friend Mrs. Thrale when she first saw it.[1] The same imbalance was seen in its personnel, wealthy incumbents side-by-side with the possessors of livings so inadequately endowed that they hardly afforded a bare subsistence to those who served them. At the bottom of the clerical pyramid was the large number of priests who could never obtain a benefice of their own, and eked out an existence as ill-paid curates doing the work of some rich absentee. One of the root causes of the trouble was the long-established custom whereby bishops licensed far more ordinands than there were livings for them to fill. This was exacerbated by the practices of simony and pluralism, for the more benefices a minority of favoured people could accumulate, the fewer were left to go round. All this made the Church an overcrowded and highly insecure profession for a man who was without influence and powerful friends. We must admire the foresight of Samuel Woodforde in making such efforts to ensure that his son reached New College with its tempting array of well-endowed livings. He himself never held any such, and his own two were, added together, a good deal less valuable than the single benefice that James afterwards held. But we must not anticipate. Woodforde was at the beginning of his clerical career, and had no reason to expect that he would have a benefice of his own for many years to come.

Among the alumni of other colleges he had got to know in

Oxford was a young man named Henry William Fitch, of Queen's, whose father, the Rev. Henry Fitch, had in his gift the Somerset living of Thurloxton, between Bridgewater and Taunton, of which he was the absentee rector. On behalf of the patron, young Fitch had offered the curacy to Woodforde, at a salary of £40 a year, about double the going rate for curates at the time. That was back in May 1763. Woodforde played for time, said he would have to consult his father; then finally accepted the offer on 29 June, agreeing to take the curacy "at Old Michaelmas" (5 October). Three days after that deadline was reached, he arrived there.

Thurloxton today is a pleasant enough place. It is true that the main road is the usual roaring hell of noise and danger that the motor-car has fastened upon us; but one need only turn off along Thurloxton's single street to be enveloped at once in an aura of ancient peace. On the corner where the two roads meet is an old house which used to be the *Green Dragon Inn*, where James Woodforde stabled his horse on that October day long ago. The church has a fine Carolinian screen and pulpit, dated 1632, and an altar table believed to be Elizabethan. The Victorians built an aisle on to the church in 1869, supported on brick pillars, but without seriously damaging the proportions of the building. Woodforde was, like most of his contempories, totally indifferent to the aesthetic appeal of medieval churches, but if he did not appreciate the charm of Thurloxton, at least he was enjoying the novelty of his position, as he wrote of "My Church", "My Clerk", "My Parish".[2]

At first he experienced some difficulty in finding accommodation for both himself and his horse. "The Widow Nowel", recommended by Mr. Fitch, turned out on investigation to have been dead for the last year; and two others were unable or unwilling to oblige. But he soon found what he was looking for:

> .... I afterwards
> went myself to the Esquire of the
> Parish whose name is Cross, and
> he took me at the very first Word,
> and likewise my Horse; which I
> ordered down immediately to his
> House, and there I supped, spent
> the Evening and laid in the Best
> Room ....

He and his landlord at once came to an agreement. He was to have room, board and washing, and provender for his horse, for £21 a year; and 1s.1¹/₂d deducted for every day he was absent. He was clearly satisfied with the deal, not remarking that the rent was over half his salary. Mr. Cross was married, with three young children and "another coming". Mrs. Cross was very good natured and looked like the diarist's sister, Mrs. Clarke. Next day he sounds even more pleased with his bargain, remarking that "Mr. Cross has a most noble House, good enough for any Nobleman ...."

Where can one place Mr. Cross, who lived in a house good enough for any nobleman and yet took in a lodger and was not above bargaining over the rent? The answer is that he was not really the squire, although perhaps the nearest thing to one that Thurloxton possessed. The actual Lord of the Manor was Viscount Portman, one of a family of permanent absentees. Cross' house, so much admired by the diarist, was known as the Manor Farm House, the name borne by its successor on the site today. He and his wife were named John and Elizabeth. A namesake of his had been rector, and signed his name - Johannes Crosse - at the beginning of one of the register books in 1698. Woodforde's acquaintance was born in 1726: "John Son of Mr. Thomas Cross and Elizabeth his Wife was bapt. April 6th".[3]

James wrote his handsome tribute to the house on the Sunday evening. Early the next day he mounted his horse and set off for Ansford, staying at home until Friday, when he went back in time to take the church service at Thurloxton on Sunday. He also carried out another clerical task that had come his way:

> Preached and read Prayers this Afternoon
> at Newton Chapel, about a Mile and half
> from Thurloxton, & which Chapel I hope I
> shall service - I shall send to Morrow
> a Letter to S[r] Thomas Acland, [4]
> concerning my serving the Chapel at Newton
> as it is in his gift; and as there is no
> one to serve it besides myself, I am in
> hopes of getting it ....

During the short time he was to stay at Thurloxton, James got on very well with his host. They discovered that they shared a common interest in coursing, and when the diarist found himself unable to keep up with Mr. Cross as a toper, he could always retire to his own room, as we see he did on 6 November, the day of a marathon drinking party, after he had christened the latest arrival in the Cross family. But in spite of incidental amenities, the situation could not really have been to his satisfaction. He could hardly have enjoyed the twice weekly journey to and from his home in winter and on roads, the bad condition of which he mentions more than once.

He was, therefore, probably glad enough to hear of another vacant curacy, much nearer his home. At Babcary, only 6 miles from Ansford, the incumbent was no longer able, through infirmity, to carry out his parish duties. That is not surprising, when his age is considered. According to *Alumni Oxonienses*, first series, William Hite or Hyte had matriculated from Wadham as long ago as 1705, and had been at Babcary since 1735, five years before Woodforde was born. Now, evidently feeling his age, he had left the parish to its own devices and gone to live with a cousin, Mr. Blake of Padnoller Farm. Meanwhile Mr. Bower, a farmer who was one of the leading parishioners at Babcary, was very worried about church affairs in the parish and anxious to find someone who would stand in for the absent rector. Woodforde acted at once. From his home he rode over to Babcary on 11 November. It was unlucky that when he arrived he found that Bower had gone "to Yeovil market". Yet, to his relief:

> the curacy was not disposed of yet; and in my
> return, Monday, from Thurloxton to Ansforde,
> I promised to call on Mr Bower, and to talk with
> him about Babcary -

Three days later he managed to catch the farmer at home, and events seemed to be leading to a favourable conclusion.

> .... I believe that I shall have it; but I must
> call upon him next Wednesday sennight and then I
> shall have a definite Answer -

But Mr. Bower's decision had to be ratified by the absent rector. Padnoller Farm was out to the west of Bridgwater, and he could make a visit there on his way to Thurloxton. It actually needed two before he could reach an agreement with Mr. Hite, "a very aged and infirm Man". But at last he was able to write down the details in the diary:

> That I should be paid Quarterly - 5 - 0 - 0
> That I should have all the Surplice Fees.
> That I should have the Easter Offerings,

the free Use of the Parsonage House, &
Gardens & Stable, and likewise to
have the Use of Mr Hites Furniture in
the Parsonage House, 'till disposed of -

From then on, he had very little interest in Thurloxton. He continued to spend the absolute minimum of time there, until his first and last quarter was up. As for Newton Chapel, when he learned that the incumbent, Mr. Abram or Abraham, was prepared to make him only the stingy offer of £8, he had no qualms about dropping that appointment also. But he had been on such good terms with Mr. Cross that he worried about having to approach him with the news that he was leaving. But Cross after all got in first, saying after supper on 20 December that "he could not afford boarding me and my Horse, any longer than this Quarter, for the Mony we agreed on, being £21 Per Ann:".

There was, however, a kind of "gentleman's agreement" prevailing in these cases. One who, like Woodforde, was breaking his agreement, was really obliged to find a replacement, so that the church services should not be interrupted. Woodforde now went to his cousin Thomas, apprenticed to an apothecary in Taunton, and it was he who discovered Mr. Boon.

The son of a Taunton couple, Boon had so far led an adventurous life. He had been "Chaplain to the 86 Regiment", now "broke", or disbanded; whereby, as Woodforde commented rather enviously,"he received per Annum clear, for doing nothing - 56 - 0 - 0". It would seem more likely that he had been invalided out of the service and in receipt of what we would today call a disability pension for, as the diarist tells us, "while at Senegal" he lost "his left Arm, in shooting of an Eagle, the Gun bursting in his Hand, which carried away all but his little Finger - It was very agreeable to hear him give an Account of that Island". Boon did not only take over at Thurloxton but spent the rest of his life there, dying over 40 years later, in 1804. Examination of the bishop's register shows that he was once given a living of his own, but soon renounced it.

On 7 January, two days before his single quarter was up, Woodforde rode to Thurloxton "for the last time". He had in his pocket "an Order" made out by Fitch, authorizing his tenant, a Mr. Warren, to pay the curate off. But Woodforde received only £7.10.0, showing that his salary was not the £40 he had been promised, but £30. Meanwhile Mr. Bower was insisting upon two services each Sunday at Babcary, for which he apparently had the support of the bishop. Woodforde thereupon wrote to the ancient Hite, saying that this demand was "by express Order of the Bishop". Therefore, "he must make an annual Addition to my present Salary of 10 - 0 - 0". This meant that he would earn as much as he had got from Thurloxton, and at the same time enjoy all the advantages that Babcary had to offer.

This quiet phase of the diarist's life lasted for something over a year. Mr. Hite died on 1 June 1764 and Woodforde bought some articles of furniture and household goods at the sale of his effects a fortnight later. There was a dispute with Hite's executors. Woodforde had been engaged on 29 November in the previous year but, tied up by his duties at Thurloxton, was obliged to call on his clerical friend Mr. Gapper, 5 who took the services at Babcary until Woodforde became free early in the new year. If I understand the position rightly, he thought he was entitled to be paid for the time Gapper had been officiating, as well as for the later period from 15 January. But there was also a previous curate, the Rev. Mr. Hopkins, still officially employed down to the end of 1763, who claimed for all the time worked by Gapper, leaving Woodforde with only 20 weeks payment for himself, which amounted to 10 guineas. Maybe he was compensated for the loss by the amusement he derived from having made the acquaintance of Hopkins:

> I never saw so bold a Man in my Life as
> Mr Hopkins is, and very droll he is -
> I thought I must have burst my Sides by
> laughing at hearing him talk -

Woodforde was admitted to Priest's Orders at Wells in September 1764, and on 4 December was able to write in his diary:

> Farmer John Jukes of Meer, aged about 80 was married
> this Morning at Ansford Church to Mrs Simpson of
> this Parish aged about 70. by me Js Woodforde -
> Mem: This is the first Couple I ever married -
> I recd. for marrying the above Couple -   0 - 5 - 0

He was already helping his father in this way, by taking occasional services. In the spring of 1765, however, there was a change in his affairs. We last saw Samuel Woodforde in 1759, running about the country in his efforts to see James safely made a scholar of New College. Full of energy then, six years later he had greatly slowed up. He was now verging on 70, an age none of his sons would reach. Feeling his years, he had lately taken on a curate.

A comparison of the registers of the two churches shows that the assistant served Castle Cary, leaving Ansford,the smaller place and near his home, to Samuel.

The new curate was Robert Penny. His family came originally from Milborne Port but had settled at Clanville, a hamlet to the south-west of Cary. He was a Fellow of Oriel, to which college he owed his swift rise to affluence, since it was there he met the Duke of Somerset, to whom and to whose successor he became Domestic Chaplain, while enjoying all the preferment the Beaufort connection brought him.[6] But in 1765 he was still at the beginning of his career, the first steps being chronicled by Woodforde in his diary entry for 18 April 1765:

> M[r] Penny is presented to the Living of Evercrech,
> to hold it for a Minor (Justice Rodbard's Son of 12 Years old)
> and therefore is going to quit my Father's Curacy at C.
> Cary, which I am to undertake for him, & Babcary too,
> but I cannot serve Babcary but once of a Sunday

For some months he managed to look after both churches, although this involved a 12 mile ride every Sunday. Hite's eventual successor at Babcary, the Rev. Richard Cheese, was vicar of Alton, Hampshire, by no means far from the places where James' most distinguished ancestor had lived and worked. He was a pluralist who had no intention of ever coming to reside in Babcary, and was delighted to find parish affairs in the hands of a steady and reliable curate. Woodforde now had a good deal of work to do. He arranged for the "farming out" of Mr. Cheese's tithe and the letting of his glebe, and represented him in the inevitable discussion about "dilapidations" with Mr. Hite's estate. This phase of the diarist's life did not end until his father went by degrees into what was in practice full retirement, although he remained the titular incumbent of Castle Cary and Ansford for the rest of his life. This meant that James had to give Babcary up. Just as he had done at Thurloxton, he provided his own successor, Mr. Denys Colmer, a middle-aged man with grown up children. Not very long afterwards, Colmer died, but by then the affairs of Babcary no longer affected Woodforde. On 6 October 1765 he "went to Babcary for the last Time". Next Sunday he assisted his father in the administration of the Sacrament at Cary in the morning, and "read Prayers and Preached this Afternoon at Ansford being the first Time of my serving Ansford for Papa" - he means officially, for he had several times done this in the preceding months.

He made another kind of change also. His experience of looking after himself and "housekeeping" at Babcary Parsonage had clearly given him the desire not to go back to be an ordinary subordinate family member in his father's house. He arranged to go into residence at the other Woodforde property in Ansford, the Lower House; also, to take along with him the housekeeper at Babcary, Mary Chrich, or Creech, and her daughter Betty. He calls Mary Chrich, rather ungallantly "my old Woman"; and once, by way of a really handsome compliment, "my old and honest Women". She was only in her 50's, but working women aged quickly in those times.[7]

The life-style he now adopted was to continue with virtually no change until his father's death in 1771.

CHAPTER 8

LIFE AT THE LOWER HOUSE

With their lives shaped by the modern tendency towards dispersal and movement from place to place, in an age in which one marriage in three ends in divorce, and the country is full of "one parent families", our contemporaries must find it no easy task even to comprehend the closely integrated community life of the Woodfordes. Most of them lived within easy reach of one another. Ansford Parsonage, the "Old Parsonage" of today, lies on the flat topmost part of Ansford Hill, which was a turnpike in Woodforde's time and is still a main road. Not much more than a hundred yards away is "Ansford Lodge", the home of the Whites, where one of the windows shows the signatures of Brother Heighes and other members of the family, scratched with a diamond on the pane. A little farther along, just before the turn-off to Castle Cary, is what used to be the Ansford Inn, still recognisable from the large windows of the room in which so many parties and "Hopps" were held. Running off from the side of the Parsonage is Tucker's Lane, commemorating Reginald Tucker, who in 1775 killed his wife, that Martha Widdows or Morris whom we have seen as James' former "Schoolmistress", by striking her on the head with a sledgehammer, a blow which broke her skull in three places. In the lane Sobieski Clarke lived with her husband "in Dr. Clarke's new Hospital", set up for the accommodation of his better-off inoculation patients. The lane skirts the churchyard, where at its edge his two aunts, whom he calls "Aunt Parr" and "Madam Anne", lived; and then becomes "Lower Ansford, dropping down to rejoin Ansford Hill at a lower point in its course. Not far short of the junction is a grassy rectangle, the site of the Ansford Lower House. Burned down in 1892, it was not rebuilt and the site has never been reoccupied. It was not so old as the originally medieval parsonage but Tudor or Elizabethan, and so of respectable antiquity.[1]

In this house, the property of his mother, James Woodforde lived from 1765 to 1771, together with his two brothers, Heighes and John, the latter of whom owned it as an inheritance from his mother. The life he led there stresses the point already made, about the close relations the Woodfordes maintained with one another, which was to survive even the great quarrel over the church living and its mutual bitterness.

The detailed fulness of the diary allows us to see these family relationships with very great clarity. At his parents' home open house was kept. James "lived" at the Lower House, in the sense that he was domiciled there for several years; but very often he is seen as only sleeping and having his breakfast there, while he ate the other meals and spent a great amount of his time at the Parsonage. There, of course, he would constantly be meeting his two brothers, his sisters and their husbands and children, his cousins, James and Richard Clarke, the two elderly aunts, even uncle Tom, not yet transformed into "my greatest Enemy", and his wife and son. The reader of Woodforde knows well that whenever he went out and met "Company", or entertained friends in his own home, he was impelled to put down the name of everyone present. Here is a whole short entry, taken at random and even containing a trifling purchase, another hall-mark of his peculiar way of writing a diary:

> Breakfasted, and laid again at the Lower House -
> For Cruttwells Sherborne Paper this Morning pd - 0 - 0 - $2^1/2$
> Dined and spent the afternoon at Parsonage
> Aunt Parr dined and spent the afternoon with us -
> Supped and spent the Evening at Parsonage -
> Ned Coleman have [sic] been at Work in the Garden below all Day
> (15/11/1765)

Yet this period of his life was not, by and large, a happy one. Not until the onset of his final illness many years later was he to write so many depressed entries. And he did have a great deal to worry about. His father, who had given up work as soon as James assumed responsibility for both his churches, was beginning to show signs of breakdown in his health. His mother was very ill with some condition involving her breast; possibly some kind of external cancer, although the only commentator who has made that diagnosis was Dr. Woodforde in the *Family Book*. James also mentions another symptom which could have been a metastasis of the same disease:

> .... Mama was taken very bad again this Afternoon, with
> a sudden pain in her Hip, which makes her a Cripple -
> (8/9/1765)

The progress of his mother's illness, her good days and bad days, and his determination to cling to an obstinate belief that she was getting better, are chronicled in his diary. He undoubtedly loved his parents; indeed, it is difficult to find any other people in the diary to whom he gave such unstinted affection. Thirty years later, when the mother of his young clerical friend Mr. Mellish died rather suddenly, he wrote:

> .... Pray God that she may be happier,
> and send Comfort to her much distressed Family -
> as so good a Parent must occasion on her decease
> such sorrow as is not to be described or felt
> but by those that have experienced it - The
> Loss of my dear Parents I feel to this Moment, and
> never can forget during Life - 2

Finally his mother became so ill that he could no longer delude himself. On 6 February 1766 he wrote: ".... Poor Mama grows weaker and worse daily - The Parsonage is a very melancholy House now indeed - ". On the next day he wrote down:

> .... Poor Mama sent for me and Jack this Afternoon up into her
> Room and very solemnly took her Leave of us: therefore I do not
> believe she can exist very long in this World -

Jane Woodforde died next day, aged just under 60, and was buried four days later. Added to the long account of her funeral - and Woodforde was a great connoisseur of funerals, very critical of those which failed to meet his high standards of funereal propriety - is a note stating that she had left to her unmarried children "all her whole Estate .... by Appointment in Fee". This was the usual way of bequeathing property in families at this time, the interests of the others having been taken care of upon their marriage.

James' unsatisfactory relations with his brothers were also a cause of anxiety. They were people of very different temperaments from his own. By comparison with them he appears a very quiet, reasonable young man, even a trifle priggish. They may have resented him, seeing him as their father's favourite son who alone had been given the chance of a career in the church. In reality, Samuel Woodforde must have seen that Heighes would never make a satisfactory clergyman before James was born and had thereupon ruled out Winchester and Oxford for him. Again, it is not the case that a lot of money was spent on James that had been denied to the others. Being on the Foundation at Winchester, his tuition and board were free, except for the surreptitious payments made in defiance of the Founder's orders, and some part at least of his incidental expenses were met by James' receipts from the little "Estate" at Sandford Orcas.[3] The money that had been spent on trying to make Heighes into a lawyer and John into a merchant must have greatly exceeded what James cost his father. But of the three investments in the future, James' was the only one that had paid off, and that was perhaps what the others could not forgive. James also was, I think, a timid young man by nature, and also restrained by his status as a clergyman. His brothers recognised his weakness and played upon it. Although it was for him so unhappy a life, it is characteristic of him that he did nothing at all about it except complain mournfully to his diary, and characteristic also that his devotion to the family, as a family, remained unimpaired.

Both his brothers drank heavily, were quarrelsome in drink and, John in particular, were prone to flashes of aggression. Most of all he deplored their habit of coming back late at night, after he had gone to bed, and waking him up with their noisy, drunken humours. So badly did they behave that he was once driven to calling the Lower House "the worst House in the Parish, or any other Parish". At the same time we can detect in him a censoriousness, a holier-than-thou attitude, which also reveals a part of his nature, and which they must have found intensely annoying.

In June 1769, over three years after the mother's death, her possessions were divided with scrupulous fairness and equality between the three unmarried children. The long and very detailed entry about the share out may be read, like so much else, only in the Parson Woodforde Society's edition of the diary. It must be of interest to everyone who is curious about the social and financial arrangements of this vanished 18th century world. It was accomplished without friction, and with no need for the armies of solicitors and estate agents and bankers that would be required to felicitate such a transaction today; and, by the same token, done without expense to anyone. Three people made the survey: Woodforde's two brothers-in-law, Dr. Richard Clarke and Robert White, and a third man, William Clarke, always called "Painter Clarke" in the diary. He was indeed a house-painter, but also a merchant, auctioneer, undertaker and, possibly maker of musical instruments, which he certainly sold as a sideline. Here was a person who fulfilled the 18th century ideal of "the ingenious man". No small town and village was complete without one of his kind, and although his actual status was no higher than that of skilled workman, he was on familiar and equal terms with all the notabilities and leading citizens of Castle Cary.

Woodforde accompanied the trio as they moved "over all the Estate" and formed three lots which were then drawn for. He was the second to draw and chose the third lot which is listed as:

The Farm House, Garden, Barton & outhouses,
and the Orchard behind the Farm House -
All the Poor Houses - Worthies, Little Field
and West Field -

By the "Farm House" he did not mean the Lower House, which was formally the "Mansion House" and became part of John's share, but another house always occupied by the tenant of the farm land which constituted the greater part of the estate. The "Poor Houses" were rented by the parish for the accommodation of paupers, and the last three items were, of course, field names.

There now ensued for James the unhappiest part of his stay at the Lower House. At the Parsonage his father was beginning to fail. Jenny, to whom fell the traditional unmarried daughter's task of looking after him, bore the brunt of it. His temper was sometimes bad. James spent evening after evening playing backgammon with him. The weaker he grew, the more scandalously two of the three sons behaved. The diary adds up the occasions, in October 1770, when Heighes was drunk, "quite full", "quite merry", for eight successive nights, and stopped then only because he developed "the bleeding piles". Woodforde added, with the air of one experiencing the triumph of hope over experience: "Therefore I hope he will not drink so much". Early in the new year his father was persuaded to go to Bath in search of medical advice. Taking the Ansford Inn chaise, he left, with the family servant Elizabeth Clothier. James went along with them on horseback, found lodgings for them and was there when an apothecary came, and then the consultant, who delivered his expensively bought opinion:[4] "My Fathers Disorder is thought to be an irregular Gout" - that is, the famous "flying gout", which was supposed to wander through the body and be fatal if it touched a vital organ. James went home next day, but as soon as the week-end was over he was back again. He took out a circulating library subscription: "I subscribed that my Father may divert himself in reading a little". In the intervals of tending his father he went out by himself, bought "a walking Cane with a Sword in it, at Mr. Evils great Shop the finest Shop I ever saw - paid 0:10:6" and went to a ball, where he ran into Captain Poore, one of his former Oriel friends. But his father weakened still more ominously. A Dr. Dixon from Taunton was brought in. The local specialist, Dr. Richard Clarke, also weighed in with advice, and prescribed ipecacuanha, an emetic, but this not surprisingly only made the patient sick. He took half the quantity the next night, Woodforde

71

reflecting philosophically that "it cannot hurt him much as they give that much to Infants". Only once did he seem willing to admit to himself that his father was dying, and prayed: "Grant Him O Lord an Easy and happy Exit - ". For most of the time he wrote no more than "My Father near the same", or "not so well as Yesterday", or even "seems rather better", just five days before his father died.

On 15 May 1771 Samuel's sister Elizabeth, the unobtrusive "Aunt Parr", four years younger than himself, died. Woodforde reported this with an unusual display of emotion:

> My poor Aunt Parr departed this miserable Life,
> to God for a better, about one o'clock at Noon
> The latter part of her Life was most miserable, and my
> poor Fathers Illness shortened her Days I believe much -
> No Woman could like a Person more than she did
> my good Father, & she daily prayed to depart this Life
> before him, & it pleased God to hear her Prayers & take her -

His father died at nearly the same time on the next day. The lengthy account of the funeral, in which no possible detail, even the most inconsiderable, is left out, testifies eloquently enough to his grief. In February Samuel Woodforde had insisted on making a codicil to his Will, with a number of bequests, to his family and to Elizabeth Clothier:

> .... And that he would have no people invited to the
> Funeral to make a Show, but that he is carried
> to Ansford Church by six of his Poor Neighbours.
> Robin Francis & his Brother Thomas were mentioned
> and that they had half a Crown a piece ....

The direction was carried out, and Robert and Thomas were there, but only as "Under-Bearers", and the others who attended in that capacity were all servants. These nuances of social class feeling are often illustrated in such a way in Woodforde's diary.

What followed bears out Proust's cynical dictum that a death in the family always makes things easier for the survivors. After his father died, James Woodforde was able to move back to the Parsonage and was liberated from the enforced companionship of his rowdy brothers. It is very plain that he now considered himself the effective head of the family.

Heighes Woodforde 1726 - 1789
Parson Woodforde's brother

CHAPTER 9

AN INTERLUDE - JUSTICE CREED
AND THE CARY SINGERS

We are in the year 1768, and it is 5 November, the day on which "the Papists had contrived an hellish plot in the reign of King James the first, but by the Divine Hand of Providence fortunately discovered", said James Woodforde, writing up his diary that night. In the morning he had commemorated the event by taking the obligatory church service, in its origin less religious than political, which in later times, when he had his own living, he dropped from the list of his obligations. Then he recorded that:

> The Effigy of Justice Creed was had through the Streets
> of C. Cary this Evening upon the Engine and then had
> into the Park and burnt in a Bonfire immediately
> before the Justice's House for his putting the Church-
> Wardens of Cary into Wells Court, for not presenting
> James Clarke for making a Riot in the Gallery at
> Cary Church a few Sundays back - The whole
> Parish are against the Justice, and they intend to assist
> the Church Wardens in carrying on the Cause at Wells -
> The Justice is now at Lord Pawletts at Hinton -

The reader of Woodforde may well experience an unexpected shock of recollection upon encountering this, for it is surely a variant of Thomas Hardy's "skimmity" or "skimmington" ride, as recounted so vividly in *The Mayor of Casterbridge*. Castle Cary and Ansford are at no great distance from Dorchester and Stinsford. Hardy was born exactly a century after Woodforde, and he is a witness that, at least in his youth, certain customs known to Woodforde's time had survived.[1]

The occurrence should also caution us against the historiographer's tendency to simplify matters by treating any historical epoch as very much of a piece. There were in reality profound differences between place and place, between one kind of society and another. Woodforde was to spend nearly half his life as Rector of Weston Longville, which was what might be called a traditional eighteenth century parish, with a resident squire who

74

took seriously his duties and obligations and owned most of the land, a parson but no other professional man, farmers of varying degrees of prosperity, the usual craftsmen and a crowd of labouring families. By contrast Castle Cary, of which Ansford, although a separate parish, was really a part, was a market town with a quite complex social structure, even then partly industralized by virtue of its position in the great West of England broadcloth area, with shopkeepers, doctors and lawyers, and even one small entrepreneur who may be called "a business man" in the modern sense of the term. Power here was not all in the hands of one, but tended to be shared among a number of wealthy and influential people. Although "Squire Creed" was one of Woodforde's alternative names for the Justice, and although he was undoubtedly rich and well-connected, with friends among the aristocrats and the greater landowners of the West Country, he was certainly not a squire in the sense that Mr. Custance was one. Custance could have done virtually what he liked at Weston, so long as he did not break the Common Law. Creed had no such autonomy, and any attempt on his part to act in what the townspeople were sure to consider a high-handed way inevitably must arouse strong opposition.

Cary Creed, who lived in the building called "South Cary House", now much altered and used as a retirement home, was born in 1708. [2] He was the grandson of John Creed, who had taken over the living of Castle Cary in 1664, as soon as the Anglican Church had been restored, and lived until 1720, when he was succeeded by Samuel Woodforde. The vicar had a son, also Cary Creed, born in the same year as Pope and the English Revolution; this was Woodforde's "Old Mr. Creed". His wife had been dead for ages, and he lived with his son, the younger Cary Creed, now approaching 60. In recent years Creed had become friendly with Woodforde. The diary shows that from time to time he treated the young man in rather a patronising way; but on other occasions he was kind and generous. He indeed practised the hospitality on which the time so prided itself.

There is one story in the diary which, apart from being exceptionally vivid in itself, brilliantly shows the contrasts in this society; as it were, the extremes of civilisation and barbarism meeting. January 1768 - this is actually not long before the great dispute began - was very cold. Woodforde was getting ready to go out and dine with Mr. Creed when the churchwardens sent him a message that he was needed to bury an unknown man found dead in the snow. And, says Woodforde, "the Justice was so kind as to put off Dinner half an Hour", so that after conducting this unceremonious funeral he could scramble out of the bleak, snow-covered churchyard and relax in the warmth and comfort of Creed's home. As for the dead man, no-one ever found out who he was. Woodforde kept a place in the diary for his name, but it is left blank. Creed, then, was prepared to show a certain consideration to his young friend. He was also valuable to the curate through his wide acquaintance with people of influence. For example, Woodforde owed to Creed his one experience of dining out at Stourhead, as distinct from merely trotting about the gardens like everyone else. [3]

But what really happened to set Creed and the parish by the ears, and at one time threatened to damage the friendship between Creed and Woodforde? Most parish churches at this date had an upper gallery, usually situated at the western end of the building. It was by immemorial custom the rightful place of the village choir. At Cary, the only other person allowed free access to it was a Mr. John Tidcombe or Titcomb, who ran a private school and could take "his Boys" into the gallery. The trouble began when Creed wanted his servant to sit in the gallery. We do not know how long the quarrel had been brewing. The first intimation of it we have is on 4/9/1768:

> .... Justice Creed & Mr Hindley made a short
> Visit this morning at Parsonage - Mr Creed
> desires that the Door leading to the Gallery
> in Cary Church might be taking [sic] down on
> account of the Singers keeping out his Servant
> there this morning - Tom Davidge - The Singers
> have made disturbances before now and like to
> make more ....

Woodforde's entry for 5 November, cited earlier, names only one person, his cousin James Clarke, as though he had been the ringleader. We know, again from Hardy, that these choirs included instrumentalists. By a most felicitous irony, in March of this year, before the trouble started, Woodforde had written: "Justice Creed made me a visit this Morning, and my brother gave him a Song, while James Clarke performed on the Base Viol" - that most Hardyesque instrument, beloved of old William Dewy. It is to be hoped that James Clarke was able to "rozzum away" with the best, and that Mr. Creed enjoyed the concert. There was to be no harmony between them eight months later.

On the Sunday after the riot, 11 September, not only was the door still in place but, to add insult to injury:

> .....The singers in C.Cary Church kept out
> Mr Creeds Man again from coming into the
> Gallery - Mr Creed therefore is determined
> to seek for redress -

It so happened at this time one of the regular Archdeacon's Visitations was due. This institution, which went back in origin to the Middle Ages, had been established mainly for the purpose of keeping a check on the day-to-day running of the parish church and the state of its property. Burn's *Ecclesiastical Law*, article on "Visitation", says:

> The Archdeacons in the visitation shall see that
> the offices of the church be duly administered; and
> shall take an "account in writing" of all the
> ornaments and "utensils" of the churches, and also
> of the vestments and books: which they shall
> cause to be presented before them every year for
> their inspection, "that they may see" what have
> been added, and what have been lost.

In earlier times the archdeacon had been expected to travel round to each of the churches in turn, and carry out a personal survey of them all. By the 18th century it had become customary to hold the visitation at one only of the churches in the archdeaconry. Nothing can be more expressive of the somnolent condition into which the system had fallen in Woodforde's time than his casual remark in the diary on 27 October 1768, the date of the visitation, that not only were "the Clergy excused coming by sending in their Fees by their Church-Wardens, but "The Archdeacon also absented himself". It is true that this was felt to be going too far in the direction of latitude, for he added a final line to his entry: "N.B. The Church-Wardens don't like the Clergy not attending".

Now the traditional duties of the churchwardens at these visitations were not limited to rendering accounts of church services and church property. To revert to *Ecclesiastical Law*, this authority explains that churchwardens and other lay officials had the duty of informing the diocesan authorities of any irregularities or misdemeanours taking place in, or associated with, the church: and this was called "Presentation". The times and occasions when this could be done are explained. Then, in an opaque and strangulated terminology, canon 117 recites their responsibility to "present" offences committed in their parishes, and that if they "willingly or unwillingly" failed to do this, they were to be prosecuted in the ecclesiastical court.

Creed had, I imagine, a legalistic mind, sharpened by his activities as a magistrate. Two "riots" had already taken place in the church, and there was "public fame" that this was so. The visitation, an opportunity for this kind of complaint to be made against parishioners, was coming. Creed must have ordered the churchwardens, Seth Burge and David Maby, both prominent diary characters, to "present" James Clarke and others.

This put them into a very awkward position. It is clear that Creed's original decision, to force his man into the singers' gallery, was unpopular; and the more stubbornly he insisted on it, the more disliked he was likely to be. If the churchwardens obeyed him, they would share in the general disapproval his actions had provoked. On the other hand, he was a man of some power and influence, able to make his wishes respected.

It is here that the Melliars come into the story.[4] If Mr. Creed was the most important man in Castle Cary, William Melliar, who lived in the big house near the church, was the second. Now the Creeds and the Melliars had been on bad terms even before the row over the gallery blew up. Woodforde was on a friendly footing with both families; yet his diary practically never shows both together. The Melliars are mentioned often enough in the earlier parts of the diary, but hardly at all just in these months, when Woodforde was spending a lot of his time with Creed. Melliar's second wife, Joanna Check, was an active and managing woman, who had some kind of unexplained relationship with the Fox-Strangways family, which granted her the entree to the mansions of both Lord Ilchester and his brother Lord Holland. On 9 August the Melliars threw a most elaborate party, called "Mrs. Melliar's publick Breakfast". It spilled right over into the adjacent unoccupied vicarage garden, where the guests danced in the open air until 3 in the afternoon. They then moved to the Ansford Inn, where there was a ball that went on until very late. All this was in honour of "Lord Stavordale's coming-of-age". He was Ilchester's heir, who would assume the title himself in 1776. It is true that the young sprig of the aristocracy did not grace the festivities arranged for him:"His Lordship is on his travels abroad". But even without his presence, it was a memorable affair. Everyone in Cary and Ansford who was anybody was invited, with a single exception. Mr. Creed had not received an invitation, because of "a misunderstanding between the Houses", as Woodforde tactfully put it. This was a slap in the face, a public insult. It is not at all surprising that, when the quarrel over the singers broke out, Melliar put himself at the head of the popular or anti-Creed party.

Creed, however, was not the man to be defied by a pair of mere churchwardens, whatever support there might be for them in the town. He at once brought an action against them in the ecclesiastical court at Wells.

He wasted no time. On 14 September 1768, only three days after the second disturbance in the church, he turned up at Ansford Parsonage with his friend Mr. Hindley, and asked Woodforde to go with them to the cathedral city, "to wait upon the Bishop". The diarist now became acutely embarrassed. Throughout his life, he tried to avoid being entangled in this kind of dispute, which had all the signs that it might drag on for years and bring satisfaction to no-one. He wrote plaintively in his diary that Creed was trying to force him to take sides; and his uneasiness caused him to make a hash of the grammar in this entry:

> .... but I shall not go (I believe) nor interfere
> at all concerning it, but to live peaceably with
> all men - It is a little unreasonable to
> desire it, as I must then fly in the face of all=
> =most all my Parishioners - Great & many are the
> divisions in C. Cary and some almost ireconcile=
> =able -
> Send us Peace O Lord with thee all things are
> possible -

Creed, however, wanted supporters, and this tepid response on the curate's part led to a temporary breach between them. Although the diarist was asked to dinner with the Creeds three days afterwards neither Creed nor Hindley would say a word about what had gone on at Wells. However, he says they behaved "very respectively" towards him. But things got worse; tempers became frayed. On 1 November Woodforde wrote in the diary:

> .... Justice Creed has put Mr Seth Burge and
> David Maby Churchwardens of C. Cary into the
> Court of Wells, and they are cited to appear
> the 9, Instant, for not presenting at the

last Visitation, some People for making
Disturbances in C. Cary Church &c -
I am really sorry that there is so much
Likelihood of endless quarrells &c. in the
Town of C. Cary.

The "skimmity ride" took place on Guy Fawkes Day, as
recounted. By 11 December Creed and Woodforde were barely on
speaking terms, for "N.B. M[r] Justice Creed was at Church and
behaved very shy to me".[5]

The churchwardens must have appeared at Wells on 9
November, and there was a preliminary meeting and the case
adjourned until later. Meanwhile the English genius for
compromise was asserting itself. We can only guess at the
conversation and diplomatic manoeuvres carried on about the turn
of the year; but by February 1769 things had progressed so far that
actual negotiations could start. On the 7th of that month Dr. Clarke,
probably willing enough to have the matter hushed up, as he may
not have been happy about the part his son had played in it, called
at the Parsonage "to desire my Father or me to meet some
Gentlemen at the George Inn [6] at Cary this Evening, to endeavour to
compromise Matters with regard to a Law-Suit that is now carrying
on between Justice Creed on the one Part and the Church-Wardens
of Cary on the other; accordingly I went with the D[r] down to the
George as my Father would not".

Samuel Woodforde, indeed, appears to have ignored the whole
business and would have nothing to do with it. His vitality was
exhausted and he had only a little over two years to live. James,
however, kept the appointment and found a crowd of the little
town's most prominent men assembled. Melliar was there, old Mr.
William Burge, uncle of the churchwarden Seth Burge, Dr. Clarke
and Woodforde's other brother-in-law Robert White, his uncle Tom
and the ubiquitous "Painter Clarke" had all turned up. They all got
round the table to argue the matter out:

.... It was proposed that as the Gallery at Cary
Church was large enough to contain between 3. and
4. Score People, and the Singers not being above
30. in Number, that there should be a partition
made in the Gallery for the Singers, and the other
part open to any Body, and also for M[r] Creed to

pay his own cost, the Parish the other but the
Church-Wardens would not come into it, therefore
Hostilities are likely to be very great indeed -

Woodforde paid a shilling, his contribution towards the cost of
the supper, and walked home, probably thinking he had spent a
wasted evening. But only two nights later, a kind of agreement was
reached. Once again the venue was the George Inn, where:

We met again to make up the approaching Law-
suit, between Mr Creed & the Cary Church-
Wardens - and it was proposed the very same
as at the last meeting there and agreed to
by all parties.
Which Proposals will I hope be agreeable to
each contending party, which will prevent
such Strife

It is a little difficult to see what he meant by "all parties",
because Creed was plainly not present, either at this or the previous
meeting. No doubt one of the others, old Mr. Burge or Mr. Pew,
were there to represent him, and afterwards he must have honoured
the agreement made in his name. By next Sunday things had
quietened down:

.... Every thing in Cary Gallery was quiet -
Mr Titcomb & his Boys &c. sat in part of
the Gallery & the Singers in the other Part -
& very harmonious -

It was inevitable that this compromise peace should have left a
residue of ill-feeling. We are not told of Creed's reaction to the
agreement which he may have accepted against his will, because
Woodforde and Creed were not meeting. The Justice vanishes from
the diary for much of this year, and once when they did meet, on 26
July, Creed greatly worried the diarist by announcing that he
intended to claim the Sandford Orcas estate, which James had held
since he was a small child.
It was not until early in 1770 that peace finally reigned, and
then it appears largely to have been thanks to the efforts of
Woodforde himself. The entry for 12 February described how he

went successively to call on Melliar, Creed and Dr. Clarke, to ask them to come up to the Lower House, drink "a Dish of Coffee", and "if possible to reconcile all animosities in Cary and to stop and put an end to all Law Suits now subsisting". There were enough of these: Creed's original prosecution of the churchwardens, their counter claim, on the grounds that he had tried to have a door in the gallery removed, and lastly the case at issue between the churchwardens Burge and Maby and their successors in the following year. None of these actually came to a hearing, and consequently they are merely noted in the records of the Ecclesiastical Court, as being adjourned from week to week.[7]

In making up as they did, the principals, who at the end of the last meeting "hobbed and nobbed in a Glass of Wine and drank success to Peace", were doubtless sincere in their intention that "all animosities between the Houses of Creed and Melliar should from that time cease, and be buried in the Gulf of Oblivion", as Woodforde put it, obviously quoting from what was actually said on the night. Creed and Melliar ceased to bicker openly, and are even found occasionally in company with one another. Woodforde stayed on reasonably good terms with both of them, for the short time they survived, (Melliar died in 1772, Creed early in 1775). But it is too much to say that they ever really became friends.

CHAPTER 10

UNCLE TOM AND THE ANSFORD LIVING

One of the difficulties of writing biography is that life, unlike art, cannot be shaped into conscious and easily recognizable patterns. All sorts of quite heterogeneous actions are performed within the time-scale of a day, an hour, even a few moments, which the biographer must arrange into a single narrative thread, giving the sometimes misleading impression that one followed another at a distance, like railway trains on a time-table. In James Woodforde's life what I have called the Lower House phase lasted from 1765 to 1771; the machinations of Uncle Thomas to divert the reversion of Ansford Rectory to his own son Frank went on from 1766 until Frank became rector in 1773; the romance, if such it may legitimately be called, of the diarist's "dear Maid of Shepton", began in 1770 and ended only on the day in 1775 that his niece Jenny Clarke told him Betsy was about to become Mrs. Webster. These events and the emotions they engendered were referred to alternatively, as in turn each became uppermost in the diarist's mind. That is why a personal diary is the most "natural", in the sense of unstudied, spontaneous form of literary composition; and indeed the jumble, the inchoateness, the unconscious proclamation in every line that the writer does not know what will happen next, constitute one of its greatest charms. But that will not do for the biographer, who must always be aware of the end in the beginning, and has to impose a sense of literary progression on to what is in reality the disorganised ragbag of a human life. So here, Chapters 8 and 9, the present one and its immediate follower all deal exclusively each with its own topic, although as part of James Woodforde's life they were anything but separate.

Thomas Woodforde was born at Elvetham in February 1705/6. He was the youngest son of his parents and, unlike his two brothers, did not go to Winchester. He seems to have settled in Ansford at the invitation of his brother Samuel, the rector of the parish. James indeed wrote that his father had been the "making" of Thomas and his family. Samuel's invaluable and already much consulted accounts book tells us that, back in the 1750's, Thomas was the tenant of the Lower House. It has never been possible to discover what he did for a living; but in that rural community, in default of positive evidence to the contrary, it is natural to assume that he was a farmer. But there were other ways of making money. One was moneylending, at a time when the boundaries between a moneylender and a banker were still blurred. We know that Samuel Woodforde lent money out at interest, and at his death over £1000, a huge sum in the currency values of the time, was found at the Parsonage, in the form of "cash, ... Mortgages, Bonds, and Notes of Hand".[1] The garbled story which Samuel R.A. either told to his acquaintance Joseph Farington or the latter mixed up when copying it into his famous "Diary" says that the painter's rise began when Mr. Hoare of Stourhead, who became his patron, was shown some drawings made by young Samuel, through the instrumentality of "an Uncle of his ...". That certainly sounds like Thomas, who was Samuel's great-uncle. But at once Farington adds that he was "an Attorney", and no evidence that Thomas Woodforde was any kind of lawyer has ever come to light. But however his money was made, it is plain that he was quite well off.[2]

He married Sarah Adams, of whom all I have been able to find out was that she was "the sister of Dr. Adams", and that does not get us very far. Francis, or Frank, was their only child, rather than just the one who happened to survive, for the register has no record of other children born to the couple. There was a niece, Miss Jordan, whom James admired because she was so good a dancer, "the best in the Room", as he informs us after dancing every dance with her from 10 at night until 4 the next morning. But when he fell out with his uncle she disappears from the diary. He quite liked his "Aunt Tom", until he began to suspect that she was a schemer like her husband. She comes through vividly in a comic scene from the diary. It was May 1772. Mr. Melliar was ailing, and "Very bad Accounts to day rec^d of him". What was worse, he had gone to London and no-one knew where he had got to or what had become of him. Woodforde wrote:

N.B. The underwritten is a great Deceit of Mrs Thos. Wood =
=forde of Ansford.-She was Yesterday at Sally Francis's
with James Clarke & Painter Clarke where Mr James
was saying before them that he would go with all
his Heart with Painter Clarke to London, upon which
Mrs Thos. Woodforde said to him, what should you
go for Mr James - what good can you do &c. &c.
which kept James from going - and then went home
and undoubtedly advised her Son to go, for he is gone.[3]

It remains to be stated that he eventually suspected the Melliars of conspiring with Thomas and Frank against him in the matter of the living.

Clearly Thomas Woodforde wanted to put his son into the church, perhaps originally for no more than to show that he could do as much as his brother. It is natural in the circumstances that he should make use of the family association with Winchester. Frank, born 1750/1, was duly admitted on the Roll ad Winton in 1762. We know a good deal about this because James, as an Old Boy of the school, was invited along to show his young cousin the ropes, Thomas paying his expenses there and back. It so happened that four years later, in 1766, the diarist and his brother Jack took a trip to Winchester, and on the way overtook Uncle Tom. When they arrived, "Uncle Tom went to the Warden's House as usual". This suggests that, when each Election came round, the only time of the year when the school was open to visitors, Thomas seized the opportunity to do some handy canvassing on behalf of his son.

But a bad shock awaited him. Frank was no great scholar, yet had worked his way through the school and on the 1765 Long Roll had been placed second in the Middle part of the fifth class, by far his best placing. By now, a year later, he was entitled to take the Election for the first time. But instead of that:

> Cousin Frank was determined to leave College, and there=
> =fore resigned this morning which made my Uncle very uneasy - 4

The notion of a schoolboy "resigning" from his school, while his father looked on, must strike us as irresistibly odd and hilarious. But it is clear that Frank took no part in the Election, which began on the day after he handed in his notice, and his name does not appear anywhere on the Long Roll for the year. We can do no more than speculate on his reasons. It could hardly have been that he left because he was afraid of failure and a consequently low place on the Roll. We have seen how much the positions depended on personal recommendation rather than ability; and in any case Frank was not yet 16, and his baptismal date meant that he could have taken the Election twice more before he was forced to leave as a Superannuate. And with a father who had no doubt been assiduously pushing his claims for four years, he would seem to have an excellent chance of a high place on some future Roll. And if it had been his personal dislike of the school that moved him it is strange that he had endured it so long without protest.

However "uneasy" Thomas was made by his son's decision, it did not make him abandon his plans for him. At once he took him to Oxford and enrolled him at Pembroke. This was Dr. Johnson's "nest of singing birds", but at the same time a poorly endowed college, lacking the wealth and the tied livings that made New College so attractive to aspirates for a career in the Church. And Thomas was no great magnate whose riches and influence could have bought his son a living anywhere in the country. If Frank was to be the fortunate possessor of a benefice or, with even more luck, two, the only benefices within his father's grasp were the local ones at present held by Samuel Woodforde.

Thomas acted without delay. The Lady of the Manor of both Cary and Ansford was Anne Powell, living at Harpenden in Hertfordshire. ("Harding" in the diary). She had once been the companion of Rachel Ettericke, who had inherited from her father, and in turn bequeathed, the advowson or right of presentation to the two churches of which she was the patroness.[5] The position of her Steward was held by Brother Heighes. I have no information about what his duties were, or how much he was paid, but should imagine that it was a honorific sort of job and limited to periodical attendance at a Court Leet or something of the kind.

Frank discharged himself from Winchester on 3 September 1766. In less than a month Thomas had edged Heighes out of the post and taken it over. On 1 October Woodforde for the first time mentioned his uncle in an unfriendly and disapproving tone:

> I desired my Uncle, as he is appointed Steward to Mrs Powel
> and Mrs Etterick, which he got by very shabby Means, to let
> Brother Heighes have the full Profits of the Stamps as he sup=
> =planted him in the Stewardship; and it was denied me
> Nothing was so scandalous to be sure -

Obviously it was not these profits, which are unlikely to have been substantial, that had attracted Thomas; but rather the opportunity of ingratiating himself with Anne Powell and so getting himself in a favourable position with a view to buying the advowsons. It is hard here to be certain whether the diarist's protest was only on behalf of Heighes, or if he could foresee his own position being undermined. The possibility of this had sunk in by 15 March next year:

Uncle Tom who came from Oxford, London & from Mrs. Powels
at Harding near St. Albans in Hertfordshire his Lady
with whom I am afraid he has been endeavouring to
supplant my Interest in the Livings here for his Son, as
he told my Father positively that he should not go to her ...

Three days later Thomas, perhaps aware that he had made his intentions too clear, was attempting to smooth things over: "Uncle Tom came to Parsonage this afternoon and wanted to set matters right which he could not do to me I'm sure".

His father was no longer the man he had been in 1759, when he went racing about the country on James' behalf. But now he did rouse himself, and on 20 April set out for London. His "chief design is to see Mrs Powel at Harding near St. Albans in Hertfordshire, about these Livings here". The diarist himself was about to leave for Oxford, for this was the trip on which he obtained his M.A. When his father returned, back at Ansford by 30 June, not a word was spoken on the subject of the livings, at least not one he thought worth putting into the diary. So his father's appeal to the patroness must have been inconclusive.

After that everything died down, for so long as four whole years. No doubt James took the line of "Don't worry - it may never happen". And, in the lifetime of Samuel Woodforde, nothing could happen. It was not until March 1771, two months before his father's death, that James wrote about the livings to Anne Powell. Her answer brought the dispiriting news that Castle Cary had been "promised" elsewhere.[6] "Some Person had told her I do not want Cary". A second letter, in April, elicited the reply that for Ansford she had been offered "14. Years Purchase", (i.e. 14 times the annual value of the living, the usual way of estimating the value of real property at this time) an offer she could not afford to turn down. The would-be buyer was of course Thomas Woodforde.

With the death of his father James' position became highly insecure. He even found himself driven, to his intense chagrin, to petition the Bishop of Bath and Wells so that he could continue unmolested in the curacy of Ansford until Frank was old enough to be ordained. Frank had taken his B.A. from Pembroke in 1770, but still had some time to wait, as 23 was the usual age for ordination, the age at which James himself had entered the church. Thomas took good care not to ask him to hold the living ("keeping it warm" as it was called) during the intervening time, since that would have entailed making James the nominal rector for two years, at the end of which time, since these transactions held only by a verbal agreement and were not recognised in law, he might have broken the compact and refused to leave. Instead he called on a distant relation of the Woodforde family, Mr. Dalton, the rector of Cucklington. Perhaps James did not have a very acute eye or ear for the finer points of irony; otherwise he would have appreciated the joke that Dalton himself was an extreme example of father-to-son succession in a church living. His father and grandfather had both held it before him.

Although Frank was once heard boasting in Castle Cary that he had been given both livings, in the end he had to be content with one. The right of presentation to a benefice was in theory vested in the bishop of the diocese, but ever since Henry VIII had plundered the monastaries which had themselves for hundreds of years been appropriating church property, and promptly sold off much of the land to lay owners, the practice had grown by which the bishops on the one hand and the lay patrons on the other shared these rights by alternately providing the incumbent to fill a vacancy. Where there were two benefices, as here, the most acceptable compromise was for each to take one.

In this way the bishop abandoned Ansford to Thomas Woodforde, but maintained the right of presentation to Castle Cary. He gave it to Thomas Wickham, the vicar of Shepton Mallet, who had the best of all claims to a second benefice, since his wife and the wife of the dean of Wells, Lord Francis Seymour, were sisters. As he had no more wish to reside in his new benefice than Mr. Cheese had to live in Babcary, he was happy enough to let James Woodforde carry on as curate there. At the same time Dalton left him alone at Ansford, while two years passed.

But finally there came that day, 19 July 1773, which signalled for him the parting from his birthplace, the church he and his father had served, and much else in his life:

> I breakfasted, dined, supped & slept again at Parsonage
> Mr Frank Woodforde was this morning in=
> =ducted into the Living of Ansford, and he imme=
> =diately sent me a Line that he intends serving
> Ansford next Sunday himself, which notice of my
> leaving the Curacy is I think not only unkind
> but very ungentlemanlike - I must be content -
> Far be it from me to expect any favour at all from

that House - All their Actions towards me are bad -
I intend to quit the Parsonage House when my
Year is up, which will be at Lady Day next, and
to take up my residence once more at New-College -

But he had also quite another reason for that decision.

St Andrew's, Ansford

CHAPTER 11

"A MERE JILT"

Robert White (b. 1715), a farmer, married in 1753 James Woodforde's second sister Mary. He had three brothers, James, Samuel and Richard. James was an attorney at Shepton Mallet. Woodforde calls him "Lawyer White" whenever he wanted to distinguish him from his relations, the Whites of Ansford.[1] In later years he took as a partner his nephew, another James White, who had been named after both him and James Woodforde, his godfather. But the young man was another of the short-lived Ansford Whites, and died at the age of 29. "Lawyer White" was married to Margaret Hole, of Shepton, and they had only one child, a daughter named Elizabeth, now well-known as Woodforde's "Betsy White".[2]

She was born at Shepton in January 1755, and was thus between 14 and 15 years younger than the diarist. She first appears in the very early diary at the age of seven, as "Little Miss Betsy White, a Daughter of Lawyer White" (18/6/1762). But Woodforde was not much interested in small children, and to find the occasion on which he first noticed her, as it were, we have to look at the diary of several years later. On 23 January 1770 "Betsy White of Shepton Mallett, a very fine Girl" dined and stayed on to supper at the Parsonage. She was now just 15.

Although Ansford and Shepton Mallet are only some 10 miles apart, the two had generally the chance to meet only, as in the visit just recounted, when Betsy came over to spend some time with her relatives the Ansford Whites. A week later: "Betsy White went home this afternoon, and on her way called & took Leave of us at Parsonage". It was well over a year before she was back at Ansford, together with her mother and Mrs. Farr and her daughter. These last were distant relations of the Woodfordes, rich people who lived in a big house just over the Dorset border and were on particularly friendly terms with the diarist's sister. "Mrs Whites House is pretty full of Company at present". On 23 July he went to Shepton with his youngest sister Jane and, as part of a round of visits, called on Betsy and her mother. On 26 August he drank tea at Ansford Lodge with Mrs. White of Shepton and her sister. This lady, whom he calls with unusual familiarity "Phylly Hole", kept a haberdashery shop at Shepton Mallet and also had an odd kind of sideline, that of buying worn or "clipped" or otherwise damaged gold and silver coins at discount prices. On 8 September Betsy was again at Ansford and "spent the latter part of the Evening at Parsonage".

So far there is no sign that he was paying the lawyer's daughter any particular attention, but by the middle of the month the relationship was in its first brief flowering. Betsy had returned home in the meantime, but on 17 September Woodforde ordered out the chaise he had inherited from his father, to take his ailing nephew "Jacky" White over to Shepton for an outing. When the boy returned, Betsy was with him. There now began a fortnight of visits and parties.

Betsy was clearly enjoying herself. When the diarist went to Shepton Mallet on 25 September to dine by appointment with the new vicar of Castle Cary, Thomas Wickham, whose curate he had now become, Betsy accompanied him there. She was supposed to be going home, but Woodforde, after much pleading, prevailed on her mother to let her return to Ansford with him. It was at the end of this happy day that he wrote words that had never appeared before in his diary:

> .... She is a sweet tempered Girl indeed and I like her much,
> and I think would make a good Wife, I do not know but
> I shall make a bold stroke that way -

One might be permitted to wonder, on reading this, whether bold strokes of the kind were very much in our diarist's line; still, many men have been transformed out of their old natures by the power of love. But now, reading on, we become aware that things had gone disastrously wrong:

Betsy was in Ansford once again, and on 23 January of the new year, 1772, Woodforde wrote:

> I went up to Sister Whites this Evening to desire Betsy
> White to spend the Evening with us, but she would not.
> She is highly affronted with me or Sister Jane I believe.

And although Betsy relented far enough to visit the Parsonage for supper on the next evening, she returned home on the following day "on Horseback", without having seen James again. We have no information as to the cause of the quarrel, but the mention of Jane having been implicated prompts speculation. Jane was a neurotic woman. She was in her late 30's and Mr. Pounsett had not yet come along to rescue her from the unenviable fate, in this society, of the "old maid". Had she jealously resented the attention shown to her favourite brother by a pretty 17 year old girl or his attraction towards her? We cannot tell, and know only that Betsy vanishes from the diary for the space of a year and a half.

At this stage of his life Woodforde's actions were being very much dictated by external events, and the two years after the death of his father constituted a period of "marking time". As already pointed out, it suited the absentee Wickham to retain his services at Castle Cary, while his appeal to the bishop had left him, in spite of Uncle Tom, unmolested at Ansford until Frank was old enough to be ordained. This gave him the excuse, if he had needed one, not to make any radical change in his way of life, but to soldier on and hope for the best. But it was no time to be thinking of marriage, as he must have realised. He did not even go to Shepton for nearly six months, and when he finally did revisit the town, to see Mr. Wickham, he managed to avoid mention of Betsy, writing merely: "I called at Miss Paynes, Miss Holes and Mrs. Whites at Shepton".

But all prudent considerations vanished when he finally saw Betsy again. It was 24 August 1773, not long after he had lost the curacy of Ansford, his cousin now having taken over the control of the benefice. He took a ride to Shepton Mallet to dine with a friend, Mr. Figgus, lately married to the Miss Payne mentioned in the last quoted entry, one of a number of Woodforde's acquaintances reported some time before as being "out of her Mind" - but now presumably cured. "We had a Goose for Dinner - Gave the Maid - 0: 1: 0". The replete diarist now strolled round to pay a call on Mrs. White. He may not even have known that Betsy would be at home - but there she was, having returned from London a few days earlier: "She is greatly improved and handsomer than ever". The sight of this new and even more beautiful Betsy was enough to revive with a bound all the emotions of two years before. He stayed with her until 8 o'clock and, love lending wings to his respectable plodding Parsonage nag, polished off the 10 mile journey and was home by 9 - "but we went a smart Pace", he remarked with modest satisfaction.

Two days later he received interesting news from Oxford. On a recent visit there, he had met George Bridle, Master of the Charity School at Bedford, in the gift of New College.[3] Now Bridle was dead and his place vacant. The newly appointed vicar of Alford, a few miles from Cary, was John Phillips, not only a Wykehamist and former schoolfellow, but also a native of Bedford, "born and bred", his father being"one of the Alderman there".Woodforde did not, at first, go to Alford himself, but sent his cousin Richard Clarke to

THE OLD PARSONAGE, ANSFORD.

M.F.PECK

The Old Parsonage, Ansford

interview Phillips. Dropping in afterwards at Ansford Parsonage for supper, Richard filled in the details:

> He told him that it was the third best thing in
> the Gift of New-College a new built House
> with an exceeding handsome Garden - 50. Guineas
> paid the Master every Quarter - Fuel, Candles,
> & all kinds of expences about the House and
> Gardens paid for the Master & no Taxes whatever.
> An Usher also found & paid for by the Charity -
> About 12. Boys to teach - by the Master and Usher.
> The only bad thing belonging to it, is, being a Borough
> Town, and there is no such thing as being neuter -
> Upon the whole I like it well and I believe
> shall accept of it, if it comes to me - 4

He then added a long prayer, about how good God had been to him. Although we should not doubt his sincerity, it reads somewhat oddly after all the calculations. Two days later he rode over to see Phillips, who gave "a very satisfactory and pleasing account" of the school, and lent him a copy of the Act of Parliament that had set it up -"an amazing Charity indeed -".

He seems to have thought that it was within his grasp, which explains why, no doubt feeling that he had burned his boats, he handed his notice in to Mr. Wickham, giving up the £20 which was now his only regular earned income. On the same day he paid another visit to "my dear Betsy White". On 16 September he was again at Shepton: "I drank Tea this Afternoon at Mr. Whites, with him, his Wife and my dear Betsy White". Near the end of this entry comes the most romantic utterance in the entire diary:

> I carried my dear Maid of Shepton some Peaches &c. &c.

There was another meeting, and then on 25 September Betsy and her mother came to Ansford again, escorted by a Mr. Berry, "who is much a Gentleman", and slept as usual in the house of Woodforde's sister. A day or two later, as the ladies wanted to see the gardens of Stourhead, he ordered the Ansford Inn chaise for them, and borrowed from Mrs. Melliar her private keys to go through Lord Ilchester's park, the most direct route there.

One might now have expected James to make what he had called "a bold Stroke", and propose to Betsy. But no declaration came. The trouble may have been that when he was actually with Betsy, her good looks and nice manners charmed him to the point that he could have desired no happier lot in life than to be married to her. When she was absent, all sorts of other considerations crowded into his apprehensive mind. To be fair to him, all this was happening at a time of personal crisis because he knew that, married or single, Betsy or no Betsy, he would eventually have to make a career and a new home in some strange place, perhaps far away from all the familiar things he so appreciated and prized.

On 4 October, he left for New College, "to hear about Bedford". But what he heard when he arrived there was the reverse of encouraging. Preferment was handed out on a system not dissimilar to that of the "Roll ad Oxon" by which the Fellows had all been admitted. The order on the list was based on the date of ordination. Only if a Fellow refused the church living or other preferment then on offer could it be passed down to another person. The news was that "Hook intends taking Bedford School". John Hook, or Hooke, of Gloucester, had been one of James' friends in their undergraduate time, but they had not met for years. Woodforde stayed in Oxford for 10 days, and then went home. The day before he left, he took part in a "Meeting of the House" - that is, of all the Fellows then in residence - "at which I attended":

> Hooke was nominated to be Master of Bedford School
> & he is to have a Year of Grace from the Day that he
> takes Possession of it till that Day twelvemonth - And
> in case he should relinquish it before, he is to re=
> =ceive what shall become due to him from it - 5

There can be no doubt that a return to New College must have been in his mind ever since he had lost Ansford, and that he was certain of it by the time he discharged himself from the curacy of Castle Cary in September. He made that formal return on 14 December, spent Christmas in college but went back home on the first day of February, 1774, staying until 22 March.

In the early spring of that year it could fairly be said that matrimony was in the air, so far as the Woodforde family was concerned. Brother John had gone through a stormy relationship with Miss Nancy Watson of East Pennard who, encouraged by her mother and sister who did not trust him at all, finally threw him over in 1773. He had now found a new inamorata, or "Dulcinea", to use the diarist's term, and he mentions in an incidental passage "my

Brother John who pays his addresses to the eldest Miss Clarke of Evercreech", or in other words the charming Melleora, to whom he would be married in the summer.[6] Then there was Jane, who at 40 was courted by John Pounsett, a working farmer who was styled "Lord of the Manor of Cole", a hamlet well remembered by readers of the diary since it was there that Woodforde used to pass his summer holidays in later years. But the wooer went about his task so tepidly and with such a lack of the necessary ardour that James, who took himself seriously as head of the family, intervened to prod him forward. The diarist "talked to him pretty home", or, as we should say, gave it to him straight. At this intimation of family displeasure Pounsett collapsed at once, and the marriage was quickly arranged. Another trip back home was made for the purpose of marrying Jane on 24 May. It was the last time Woodforde ever officiated in the church he had been accustomed to think of as his own.

Three days after his sister's wedding he went to Shepton Mallet and brought Betsy White back with him. The next day they both dined at the Lower House with John:

> I went home with Betsy White & had some talk with her concerning my making her mine when an Opportunity offered, and she was not averse to it at all -[7]

How far this may be called a serious proposal of marriage is uncertain. He would have thought it no more than simple common sense not to tie himself down to a definite obligation to marry while his prospects were still uncertain. That is why he was so offended and called Betsy a jilt when he learned that she had married someone else. On the other hand Betsy may have thought she was being offered no more than a conditional half-promise that committed her to nothing. Her disclosure that she was "not averse" from the idea of marrying him tells us more about the passive and submissive role allotted to women in this society, in which men made all the running and the female's part in the transaction was limited to a mute acceptance or refusal, than it does about her feelings in the matter.

Of course, one is entitled to think that all this was just a classic example of Murphy's Law, and that the timing was simply inauspicious. If Woodforde, suppose, had gone back to New College earlier, and picked up a living or some other preferment before he had renewed his acquaintance with Betsy, then when he made his guarded proposal he would have had something tangible to offer, and all would be plain sailing in the future. I find this impossible to accept. I believe it far more likely that James Woodforde, in his heart of hearts, never wanted to marry at all. I think also that to charge her with having jilted him was the best way to absolve himself from all blame over the debacle. What he would have done with a steadfast Betsy, regarding herself as plighted to him and resolved to keep faith, can never be known. But I am convinced that, if he had after all found himself in a position where he must honour his pledge or be disgraced, he would have approached the altar as reluctantly as any of the unwilling bridegrooms whose enforced "compulsatory" marriages he occasionally celebrated in later years.

It is difficult otherwise to explain away the awkward fact that the day after Betsy had expressed herself "not averse" from the idea of becoming Mrs. Woodforde was the last time he was in her company until her final appearance on the turnpike road in 1775 as Mrs. Webster. Even before this it had become rather painfully clear that he was by no means the kind of lover who cannot live without frequently seeing the beloved. When, at a time when his attentions to her must already have been known, he made one of his calls on Betsy and her mother, "they wondered not to see me before".[8] Returning to Oxford two days after his talk with her about marriage, he was promptly immersed in his concerns there, a life in which she could have had no part. As he was there in search of an income which would allow him to marry, one would expect to find a record of letters to her, to keep her abreast of developments. Perhaps he did write to her, and perhaps she answered his letters. But if so, it is strange to find no mention of them in the diary, given his lifelong habit of referring to letters received and sent. Even after he had received the preferment he had been angling for and solved his financial problems, his ability to support a wife and family now unquestionable, he appears to have put off telling Betsy until the next time he went home.

Four months went by before he next went to Shepton only to be told that she had gone to Bristol with her father. When on 28 January 1775, with the Norfolk living safe in his possession, he again made the journey it surely must have been to give her the good news. The diary, here as nearly always so completely unemotional in tone, gives no indication that he was doing any more than paying a routine social call when he arrived at the home of the Shepton Whites. They, looking at the situation from the standpoint of parents concerned for the welfare of their child, may have regarded him with less than enthusiasm as a prospective son-in-law, considering him altogether too cautious and unwilling to commit himself. It may have been rather coldly that they told him Betsy was once again not at home, having gone on a visit to Devonshire, "at Mr. Troitt's". It must have been while she was there that she met Mr. Webster and his brilliant prospects.

When his brother was rejected by Nancy Watson, he had got roaring drunk and behaved "like a Madman". Although that is scarcely to be called admirable conduct, from the biographer's point of view it has its advantages. By contrast, James tamely trotting back to Ansford, we may be sure breaking no speed records this time, has us guessing. If he was hurt and disappointed, he never confided his pain to the diary. We should feel more sorry for him if Betsy's marriage had followed at once, too soon for him to do anything about it. As it was, the rest of the winter, the spring and the early summer went by, and August had arrived before his niece Jenny Clarke, who had herself been visiting in Devon, told him that "Betsy White of Shepton is to be married in a fortnight to a Gentleman of Devonshire by name Webster, a Man reported to have 500 P$^{d.}$ per annum, 18,000 P$^{d.}$ in the Stocks, beside expectations from his Father". Also "300 pd. per Annum" had been "settled upon Betsy" by this Devonian Croesus. This alone was over three quarters of the value of Woodforde's newly acquired Norfolk living, and shows us clearly how he had been outbid in the marriage market. Yet even if Webster and his loads of money had not existed, we must still have serious doubts that James and Betsy would ever have become man and wife. In the Shepton Mallet register which records the marriage on 6 September, he is named as Charles Webster, bachelor, of the parish of Uplowman - it is near Tiverton. Very little is known about him and his family; but among his and Betsy's children was a son James who married his cousin Elizabeth, another "Betsy White", the only one of the large family of the Ansford Whites who ever married.

The tailpiece or anticlimactic coda to James Woodforde's one and only romance came a few weeks later. Newlyweds of the time did not go on honeymoon; that was a Victorian invention. Instead, it was the custom for a just married couple to pay social calls upon their friends and relations, almost as though in a way asking their approval of the union. This was thought particularly important when one of the parties, as here, was a stranger. So it was inevitable that Mr. Webster should be toured round Ansford, that he would be taken to the home of the Ansford Whites, and that Woodforde's sister would invite him to meet the happy pair. It is noteworthy that no-one in his immediate family seems to have had any notion that he had been badly treated. It is most likely that he had told them little or nothing about Betsy anyway.

James himself had made his own plan. He would carefully time it to arrive after Betsy and her husband had left and were safely away, before entering his sister's house with many insincere expressions of regret that he had missed them. But he was unlucky in his timing. He started out too early and ran into them on the turnpike road, before they could get clear of the neighbourhood. Ironically, it was on this road that he and Betsy had enjoyed a happy walk, some months ago.

Women are much better than men, in handling this sort of ticklish situation. On Woodforde's own account, Betsy wanted to be friendly, but he, as he says, was "shy". We may imagine that he escaped as soon as he could. When he recounted the episode, and the whole story, at no time is there expressed real sorrow; only a kind of irritated pique. She has, he wrote in the remark that is now famous, "behaved to me like a mere Jilt".

He never mentioned her again.

CHAPTER 12

NEW COLLEGE AGAIN
AND WESTON LONGVILLE

James Woodforde's immediate reaction to the prospect of once again living in college was one of dismay. On 16 December 1773, the day after his arrival, he gloomily informed his diary:

Exceeding disagreeable to me yet Oxford seems
being so contrary to my old way of Living -

But, as we know and everything about him proves, he was an adaptable man. By the next day he was in a mood that led him to revise his first hasty verdict. He took part in a meeting of the "Thirteen", called "to pass the Bursars Accounts" of the previous year. Then, sitting at the High Table, he attended a supper in Hall at which the Warden and all the resident seniors were present, and the Bursars provided the treat of "Oysters and Wine". Writing up his diary at the end of the day, and clearly as an afterthought, since the last passage is placed in the box with the date of the entry and must have been written after he had drawn the customary line at the conclusion of the day's entry, he noted:

things seem something better
to day - & hope will more so
daily - when I get to College

By that he meant actually living with a room at college, for he was still staying overnight at the Blue Boar inn to which he had gone on arrival. Next day he had more college business to attend to. From 11 in the morning until 3 in the afternoon he was "in the Audit House with the Warden &c.", passing the college accounts for the whole of the year. He also managed to find accommodation for himself in the college:

.... I sleep this night in one Mr Bowles's Rooms - He
is a Gentleman Commoner & just gone from College
for the Christmas Holidays - very good Rooms -

For a shilling he got the "Hostler" at the inn to carry his "Trunk

& Portmanteau" to New College, a fair distance for anyone weighted down with two pieces of heavy luggage. Another shilling went to "Mr. Bowles's Servant George who formerly lived with Warden Hayward".[1] Two days later he was at another meeting, "to put the finishing Stroke to the Bursars Account, and to swear in the proper Officers for the Year ensueing". It is very clear that this was a kind of work he enjoyed. It was at this meeting that he was made sub-warden, an annual office which all the Senior Fellows in turn became entitled to hold. Characteristically, he noted it down without any sign of gratification or pleasure. We may ask, but without any expectation of an answer, whether he was surprised or whether, on the contrary, he had been told earlier of his promotion and knew what to expect. However, we may guess that he was happy enough in his new office, even though its responsibilities were, except in the absence of the Warden, largely honorific and ceremonial. On the next day, having received some of the profits of his Fellowship and £20 from the last sub-warden, John Webber, he wrote down, perhaps with some degree of complacency:

> I dined in the Hall and took my Place there as
> Sub-Warden for the First Time -
> I went to Chapel this Evening and took my Place
> there as Sub-Warden for the first Time also -

He helped to pass "the building Chest Account" and, as sub-warden, was given one of the keys to the chest in which the documents were kept. That was on 23 December, "our Founder's Commemoration Day", when "a handsome Dinner in Hall", with port wine and madeira, was put on.

On Christmas Eve he was able to write:

> I got into my own Rooms this Afternoon and there
> slept for the first Time - they are very good Rooms
> in the Lower Court the second Stair Case next
> to the Chequer, one Pair of Stairs and the Door
> on the right Hand [2]

On Christmas Day Woodforde did justice to the occasion and himself, prompting the suspicion that the Fellows may have made him sub-warden because of his expertise in the matter of meals. The diarist's account both of the dinner itself and the elaborate ceremonial which accompanied it deserves extended quotation:

We had a very handsome Dinner of my ordering
as I order Dinner every Day being Sub-Warden
We had for Dinner two fine Codds boiled with
Fryed Soals round them & Oyster Sauce, a fine
Surloin of Beef roasted, Some Peas Soup & an
Orange Pudding for the first Course, for the
Second we had a Lease³ of Wild Ducks roasted,
a fore-Qr. of Lamb & Sallad & Mince Pies -
We had a Grace Cup before the Second Course
brought by the Butler to the Steward of the Hall
who was Mʳ Adams a Senior Fellow, who got
out of his Place & came to my Chair and there
drank to me out of it, wishing me a merry Xmas
I then took it of him & drank, wishing him the same
& then it went round, three standing up all the time.
From the High Table the Grace Cup goes to the
Batchelors & Scholars -
After the Second Course there was a fine Plumb
Cake brought to the Senʳ· Table as is usual on
this Day which also goes to the Batchelors after -
After Grace is said there is another Grace-Cup
to drink omnibus Wiccamisis, which is drank
as the first, only the Steward of the Hall does not
attend the second Grace-Cup - ⁴

Soon after this he experienced a loss. On 8 January he wrote of
the mysterious death of one of the bedmakers' assistants occasioned,
or so he believed, by the man "having had no Stool for a great while
and what was given him had no Effect whatever ...." Only
three days later "a report went about of the death of my Good
Friend John Geree".

Geree, who came from East Ilsley, near Newbury, Berks, was
very close in age to Woodforde (baptismal date 19/8/1740).
Admitted to Winchester the year after him, Geree's places as they
advanced through the school were generally higher then his own.
Geree appears as one of the more unobtrusive members of his
undergraduate society. He was probably hard up (we know that he
had a widowed mother, and after his death a sermon, preached by
"Penrose of Newbury", was published for her benefit) and seldom
took part in the gambling at which Woodforde won and lost so
much money. In the time when the diarist was seeing the Bignell
sisters, he once took Geree along to make up a foursome. After

Oxford from Headington Hill (early nineteenth century)

graduating he stayed on at New College until 1772, when he exchanged his Fellowship for one of the more valuable Fellowships at Winchester. In 1773 he was awarded the tied living of Milborne Port in Somerset, but his death came about before he could be inducted into the church there.

Ever since Woodforde had left Oxford in 1763 Geree had been his most assiduous correspondent, and looked after his interests there. They last met in 1772, when the diarist was carrying out his duties as "Senior Poser" at Winchester. Geree must have been popular with the boys, since Woodforde commented, perhaps with some pique, that his friend "had a great deal of young Company with him, as usual". After that, nearly a year went by before he received a letter from Geree, "in which he tells me that he is very bad & is going to Bristol" - almost certainly to the Hot Wells, so famous all over the West country for its supposedly beneficial effects in cases of pulmonary tuberculosis, and other chest complaints. There were no more letters, but Woodforde must have been kept informed about his friend's condition, as he expresses no surprise, but an unusual depth of emotion on hearing of his death:

> ... He had been in a very bad way a long Time,
> and his Life despaired of for some Time, being in a
> Consumption. - "How great is the Loss of a sincere Friend".
> Pray God that his Change (if true) might be happy.
> He was deservedly esteemed by all that knew him,
> and most universally is his Death lamented -

14 January was officially the first day of a new term. The Warden invited the Fellows up to the Senior Common Room, and gave them "some Sack Wine and some Bread and Butter", as he was taking his D.D. that day. Then they all went off in a procession to the Convocation House. Woodforde loved processions, and never failed to describe any he took part in. He also had a job to do there, to act as sponsor for "Cooke Junr.", who was to take a Master's Degree. "I scio'd for him there". [5]

And here is another Oxford scene, outside the walls of the college but typical, as skating and sliding in the meadow were so popular.

> I took a Walk after Prayers up the Hill and round
> Christ-Church Walk with Cooke Senr. and saw many
> People skating in Christ Church Meadow, we saw
> one Man fall into the Water - the Ice giving way, but

the Water was not much deeper than his Middle
therefore did not receive much damage only wet.
We saw a Battle between 2. Boys, a very good one (21/1/1774)

Woodforde's awareness that he had reached the end of an era in his life, which had already begun to take a new direction, is clearly shown by what happened on the occasion of his first visit home, already referred to in the previous chapter. The immediate reason for this was the settling of some family accounts. It was now that his late father's real property was divided, as the mother's had been, between himself, Jane and Jack. On 24 March he formally handed over the tenancy of Ansford Parsonage to Pounsett,[6] just before he started back to Oxford. The parting from his relations was painfully emotional, especially by comparison with that when he had left them to go back to the University in the previous October. Then he had written no more than: "I left my whole Family rather dejected this morning". Now it was:

I got up very early this morning, packed my Things
settled all Accounts with my People, dined at 12.
& at one set of in Ansford Inn Chaise with a very
heavy Heart for Oxford thro' Bath - ...
I left all my House in Tears & I could not refrain
myself from the same - Pray God Bless them all -

He had not long been back when a new honour came his way. The Proctors of the University began their term of office at Easter. This year John Webber was to be Junior Proctor. The two Pro-Proctors who assisted each of the Proctors were invariably of the latter's college. Woodforde, together with Washbourne Cooke ("Cooke Sen[r]"),[7] was nominated. Rather irritatingly, he tells us nothing about the way the post was conferred upon him, and the first we hear about it is when he attended a dinner given by Mr. Shackleford of St. John's, the outgoing Junior Proctor, on 9 April: "it being usual on this Day for the Jun[r]. Proctor to give a Dinner to the present and future Proctors". A similar meal two days later was hosted by Edward Bowerbank, the Senior Proctor.

Woodforde may, in this second period of residence at University, have only been "dressed in a little brief authority", but there can be no doubt that he enjoyed exercising it. In New College we find him quite often "sconcing", or fining, certain of the staff: two of the "bible Clerks", for not waiting at table, and the "Sexton" for the same omission. As sub-warden and in charge of the proper provision of meals, he fined the Manciple [8], and two of the cooks for sending in a "rump of Beef" not heated through. In superintending the declamations and other undergraduate exercises, he penalised those students who failed to turn up. This was no doubt customary among the Fellows, but they may not all have been so pertinacious in carrying out this part of their official duties. There seems about all this punitive activity a distinct sign of the "new broom" and the stickler for discipline. This may indeed be one of the reasons why so many of the Junior Fellows voted for his opponent in the disputed election over Weston Longville at the end of the year.

As Pro-Proctor he seems to have taken his responsibilities more seriously than either Webber or Cooke. Throughout his term of office we catch sight of him prowling the streets of Oxford at night, picking up stray undergraduates and escorting them back to their colleges, often with an "Imposition". At the same time, let us not forget that when he and Webber encountered "a common strumpet", it was Woodforde who intervened to save her from being arrested and sent to the "bridewell".

His two official posts having given him a higher status in the academic world then he had previously held, he was for a time on more or less equal terms with some eminent people in the University. In April he met at dinner "at D^r. Burrows's Rooms at Magdalen College" several of these high-fliers, including Bowerbank the late Senior Proctor. The biggest gun there was Dr. Thurlow, "Master of the Temple in London", later Bishop of Lincoln (1779-87) and of Durham (1787-91). Another, Richard Woodeson or Wordeson, was Vinerian Professor of Common Law from 1777 to 1793 besides holding other prized legal and academic honours.

After dining out in the company of some of these top-drawer individuals, Woodforde evidently thought the time was ripe for him to reciprocate, so he issued invitations to a special party to be held in the Chequer on 27 July. One of the guests was Mr. Hindley of Twickenham whom we have already met in connection with Justice Creed and his struggle with the townspeople of Castle Cary, and who was on a visit to the University town. The others were Thurlow, Burrows, Bowerbank and William Brickenden of Magdalen, all of whom no doubt seemed more imposing in their lifetime than they do today. Woodforde had dined on the previous day with all but one of the same company in the rooms of a Dr. West, another Magdalen man.

The host plainly went to a good deal of trouble to entertain his distinguished guests. Two identical accounts of the menu exist; in

New College, Oxford. The Chequer which featured much in Woodforde's social life at Oxford, is to the right of the arch in the background
(From an engraving by Michael Burgers, 1708)

The Chapel, New College, Oxford

the diary and in the New College "Dinner Book", an odd volume of which survives in the archives, covering this period. The latter is preferred, as it gives the price of the ingredients. 12¼ pounds of "Chine Mutton" (providing approximately 2 pounds of meat for everyone present) cost 4/1d. There was a goose for 3/6d., and a "Codling Pye" which cost 1/2d., besides "Bread and N Coll Puddings", a "Colliflour". "Pease" and a quantity of soup. The total dinner bill came to 18/5d., but the sum is wrong and the diarist was overcharged a shilling. The much more modest supper bill came to 3/3d. It is a hard business trying to understand 18th century culinary tastes, for mutton was again served up, now cold, together with lamb and cucumbers. The host won playing whist after dinner practically the amount the feast had cost him.

In addition, he provided "Madeira & Port Wine to drink, after & at Dinner, some strong Beer, Cyder, ale & small Beer". Also: "I had a handsome Dish of Fruit after Dinner". At 7 o'clock they all trooped over to Woodforde's rooms for coffee and tea, served together as was usual. After supper "I gave them to drink some Arrac Punch with Jellies in it, and some Port Wine". Dr. West dropped in during the afternoon and stayed for the rest of the proceedings, although he seems to have been the only guest not to enjoy himself: "I made all my Company but Dr. West quite merry". Brickenden "went forth from us soon after coffee, and did not return again".

Writing in the immediate aftermath of the party, his summing-up was that everything had gone off very well: "We were very merry and pushed the bottle on very briskly". As we see in his remark about having amused all the guests except Dr. West, he must have considered himself the veritable life and soul of the party, and the last line of the entry carried a note of slightly immodest self-satisfaction: "I carried off my drinking exceedingly well indeed".

Perhaps the reaction set in fairly soon, for only the day afterwards he was writing: "I have not seen or heard anything of my Company that dined &c. with me Yesterday". And they vanish entirely from his circle of acquaintance, and from the diary. Dr. Hargreaves-Mawdsley has a rather uncharitable comment on his behaviour at this party, to which he was obviously referring when he wrote: "Woodforde's drinking seems to have reached such a height that he perhaps even shocked some of his companions, for some of them never came near him again". However, he dated this wrongly, confusing it with another but entirely different sort of convivial meeting, when the diarist, after drinking 6 bottles of wine with three college friends and an undergraduate, Grattan, a notorious breaker of rules, went with the latter into the Music Room where, as he admits with disarming candour; "We were both merry and were taken notice of".

Woodforde possibly came to realise that, on the day of his special party, he had, to use the phrase common to his contemporaries, "exposed himself much" or, as we should say, made a fool of himself. He may also have felt slighted by the non-appearance of his late guests. When a few days later Brickenden turned up at New College "to desire me to serve his Church this Vacation", he replied in tones that no doubt sounded as curt as the words look unfriendly in print, that he "did not chuse to do it".

For those who stayed up during the Long Vacation, the division between it and term-time was far less marked than it is today. Woodforde was much concerned with the conferring of degrees and supervision of the examinations he had himself taken in his own student days. On 3 July he should have been in the Schools for the "Austin Disputations" of a Mr. Wells, but forgot to turn up. Other entries, such as that for 25 June ("I presided over Austin in the Schools to day, but one Set") show him as carrying out this kind of work. "I set on several Sets to day doing Generals" and "I granted a Liceat for Generals for the first Time - 0. 0. 6". This permission consisted of handing the candidates papers which were stuck on each of the two main gates. They then went over to St. Mary's and had their names inserted in a book kept there. Woodforde had described all this in detail when as an undergraduate he went to take "Generals" himself. Now, as Pro-Proctor, he was one of those qualified to conduct the examination.

He was present at the Encaenia of this year, or "Grand Gala", as he called it, when Handel's *Hercules* was put on in the Sheldonian Theatre, where he had an altercation with Mr. Peddle, an insubordinate student. He put the man's name in the "Black Book" or record of student misdeeds kept by the Proctors, with the result that Peddle was rusticated. On 4 September Woodforde took a service for one of his fellow-collegians in Headington Church. Then, probably feeling that he had earned a rest, he went home for the last month of the vacation, but returned for the start of the new academic year in October.

All this time, he must have kept an eye open for any preferment that might come his way. But he never so much as breathes a word of his hopes in the diary, any more than he mentions Betsy White, to whom he presumably considered himself engaged. No vacancy had appeared since the previous autumn, when Hook had snapped up the Bedford school and was now working through his "year of Grace", before he must resign his Fellowship. And then, only a month after Woodforde's return to Oxford, a day came along which was second in importance only to that other day when he learned of his acceptance by New College. On 5 November 1774, news arrived of the death of Dr. Gloster Ridley, the holder of "one of our livings in Norfolk by name Weston Longeville - worth it is said 300. Per Annum". This cleric, who owed his unusual first name to having been born on board the "Gloucester" East Indiaman, although the Winchester register puts him down as from the London parish of St. Alban, Wood Street, was a pluralist, with church livings in London, also a prebendary of Sarum, and chaplain to the East India Co. At Weston he had been a part-time resident, spending only the more clement season of the year in the parish. He had a married daughter, Mrs. Evans, and a son James, or "Dickey Ridley", mentioned occasionally by Woodforde until 1762, when he "married a fortune".

Woodforde was at once interested. But here, just as at Bedford, someone else was before him. William Master came from Broughton, Hampshire. He was "Founder's Kin", very near to Woodforde in age, but had started both at Winchester and New College a year ahead of him. During the diarist's long absence Master had sometimes collected his share of the Fellowship money for him, and paid odd debts on his behalf to tradesmen. It could be said that they were fairly close friends, and plainly came to an agreement by which Master, who had the first option on the living, should tell Woodforde as soon as possible about his own decision. With that on 14 November he went off to inspect the vacant living.

The diarist's term of office as sub-warden was nearing its end, but we still see him wielding his authority and keeping things in order. On 1 December he was having supper with his fellow Pro-Proctor Washbourne Cooke, who "treated me with some Fish", preparatory to their starting out on a proctorial ramble through Oxford, when they were alerted by sounds of revelry by night:

> Bingham had a good deal of Company at his Room
> this Evening and at 11. o'clock they being all merry
> made such intolerable Noise by hallowing that
> myself & Cooke went to Binghams Room, called him
> out & gave him a Lecture which made all quiet -

Afterwards he encountered outside the college "some of Mr Binghams Company, who are to wait on us to Morrow Morning". Woodforde, apparently with little else on his mind that evening, went to the trouble of writing down the names and colleges of those he "took to". Only after he had completed the day's entry did he add, a certain sign of an afterthought with him, an extra note on the blotting paper opposite the page:

Rec^d. a letter from Master Senr.
from Norwich this Evening who is there looking
at a Living lately become vacant - He
does not seem to approve of it at all -

The letter outstripped his friend by only a day:

Master Senr. returned this Evening from Norfolk
he makes many objections to Weston Longville -

In the next few days he must have discussed the situation with his friends, but he could make no move while Master was still in the running for the benefice. At last, on 6 December:

Master Senr. publickly declared this Afternoon in M C R*
his Intention of not taking the Living of Weston I
therefore immediately being the next Senior in Orders
canvased the Senior Common Room, and then went
with Master Senr. into the Junior Common Room, and
canvassed that - The Junr. Common Room pretty full -
(* *Master's Common Room*)

It might be thought that, as this was simply going through an established routine, nothing could possibly bar the diarist's route to the vacant living. In the many cases in the diary of presentation to benefices, there is not one in which two candidates and a disputed election form part, although a year later there was a contest between two Fellows for the post of college steward, and even there one of the candidates withdrew before the vote was taken. But, ahead of the diarist, Mr. Hook, who had seemingly begun to vacillate about the Bedford School, put in a rival claim, although not in person:

M^r. Caldecot presented a Petition or rather a Case this
Evening to the Senr. Com: Room in favour of M^r.
Hookes Claim to the vacant Living, but it did not
answer the Gentlemans Expectation so much as
was thought therefore I believe he will not succeed -

Woodforde's rather cryptic remarks here suggest, I think, that

John Oglander, Warden, New College, Oxford, 1768-94.
Warden Oglander supported Woodforde's election to the College benefice of Weston
Longville, Norfolk, in 1774

Hook had primed one of his friends to force matters by this sudden announcement, but that it had failed of its expected effect. It would all the same appear likely that there was no precedent that could be called on to decide the question, since no-one advanced to a preferment by the College had claimed another while his "Year of Grace" was still running. However, it made a disputed election and a vote inevitable.

"Hooke came to College this Evening, he looked rather dissatisfied concerning his claim to Weston". Next day: "Hooke came into my Room this morning & talked a good deal with Masters [sic] concerning Weston". Whether or not his dissatisfaction came from a well-founded suspicion that he was going to lose, it is impossible to say.

But that was the way it turned out. There were 36 Fellows available to vote in the election on 15 December; almost exactly half the number of those entitled to vote if they had all been present. Woodforde says that "Many learned & warm Arguments stated & disputed", which sounds a bit of an overstatement, since the only question open to debate was the propriety or otherwise of Hook's applying for a second place of preferment. All the same, it lasted for two hours, which suggests that a good deal of hair-splitting enlivened the proceedings. As everyone who knows anything at all about Woodforde is aware, he won the contest by 20 votes to 15; a respectable margin but no landslide. As he took the trouble to put down the names of those who voted on both sides we can see that he was brought home by the votes of his near contemporaries: the two Oglanders, Webber, Lucas, Master and others, and one or two younger people such as Henry Bathurst, the later Bishop of Norwich, with whom he had always been on friendly terms. Conversely, most of the Junior Fellows voted for his opponent, and these included people with whom he had fallen out during his term of office as Sub-Warden. Peregrine Bingham, whom he had not long since told off for making too much noise, was one of these. But there were also a few men of his own age who sided with his antagonist. One of these was William Milton, the grandfather of Anthony Trollope, and a friend of Hook. Woodforde, who could not really have been expected to appreciate his eloquence, said that he "talked nothing but nonsense".

Immediately afterwards an order was made "& agreed by the whole House & entered in the Sub-Wardens Book", to the effect that it was:

Resolved that any Gentleman already pre=
=sented to a College Living or other Preferment shall have the Li=
=berty of quitting that Living and making his
Option of any other that may become vacant
during his Term of Grace, of which Term the
Day of taking Possession shall be esteemed
first Day - John Oglander, Warden.

This may be regarded as a justification of Hook's action in applying for the living. Not that Woodforde had anything to complain of. He had won, and his victory assured him the life-tenure of a well-endowed Rectory. His financial troubles were over, and with them the insecurity and frustration of the last few years.

His victory also meant that, from that time henceforth, his life would be fixed in a particular mould that did not admit the possibility of change. As he was a man who loved routines, it is unlikely that he was dismayed by this. It is true that, although he was officially Rector of Weston Longville from the moment he was voted into the living, he displayed no enthusiasm for the prospect, and was certainly in no hurry to take possession of his new benefice. Considerably more than a year was to elapse until, in May 1776, he finally went into residence and moved into Weston Parsonage which was to be his home for the rest of his life. But then, as we have already had much opportunity of proving, he was not the man to do anything in a hurry.

CHAPTER 13

A COUNTRY PARISH

The Norfolk village of Weston Longville is situated 10 miles north west of Norwich. All those who make that journey today, at their ease in a speeding motor vehicle, should remember those Herculean furniture removers, by name Abraham Seily and Isaac Warren, employees of Mr. Sudbury the "Upholsterer", who carried a sideboard and "a large new Mohogany Cellaret" all the way from the county town to Parson Woodforde's house. Nothing could more strikingly express the infinite distance between what was expected of working men in his time, and modern conditions of service. It is one more reminder that Woodforde's world was very different from the one we reside in.

The history of "Longuevile's Manor" may briefly be noted here. In the reign of Henry I, Walter Gifford, 2nd. earl of Buckinghamshire, acquired the estate, with "the tithe of his demean, and the church", and gave it as a daughter house to the priory of Longueville in Normandy. During one of the phases of the Hundred Years War it was seized, as an "alien priory", by the Crown, in a sort of rehearsal of the Dissolution of the Monasteries which came about two centuries later. The rectory was bestowed upon the then quite recent foundation of New College, Oxford, early in the reign of Henry VI; to be more precise, on "12 September in his fifth year", 1423.[1] In 1440 its near neighbour, Great Witchingham, was also granted to New College, and both are still in its gift. They are still "tied", and can be held only by Fellows of New College. The manor was purchased in the reign of Henry VIII by Firmin Rookwood, whose family owned it until 1726.

Weston was surely never a "picture postcard" village, or renowned for particular beauty, although it could hardly have been in Woodforde's time so shapeless as it is today, lacking a proper centre. A large part of the village was wrecked by the war-time airfield, and this damage was perpetuated by the turkey farm built on the site of the airfield. Many changes have taken place since his day. Between the church and the site of his Parsonage is now nothing but an expanse of fields. Woodforde's extremely precise language, using the word "neighbour" to denote only those people and families who actually lived near to him, shows that there must

117

All Saint's, Weston Longville, Norfolk
Woodforde held the living from 1774 until his death in 1803

have been a number of dwellings in the area which have gone. In the village today there is no building other than the church, the former Hart or Heart inn just across the road, now a private house, and what is left of the Old Hall, one-time home of the Rookwood family, older than the 19th century. The old Rectory is a charmless edifice that about 1840 replaced Woodforde's own Parsonage, now so famous through the diary. The village pub, once the *Three Ringers* has been renamed the *Parson Woodforde* in his honour. The school has closed down in recent years, one of the vital steps in the progressive decline of a village. All in all, Weston is too near to expanding Norwich for its own good, and one might forecast its probable future simply by looking at neighbouring Ringland, neither country village nor town suburb, but an awful mish-mash of both.

Woodforde, like most of his contempories, was totally insensible to the charm and delight of medieval churches. To him Weston Church was simply the place where he worked: very cold in the winter, draughty, inhospitable, the antithesis of the Parsonage which he made as comfortable as he possibly could. Yet it is a fine building of its kind. By a happy chance it escaped the worst excesses of what H. J. Massingham called "the Gothicizing pillagers of the 19th century", and to appreciate what it could so easily have become one has only to look at the neighbouring churches of Mattishall and Great Witchingham, scraped and made featureless beyond all reason. The 13th century tower is the oldest part of the building. The chancel is good Decorated, with sedilia and piscina, while the nave has octagonal pillars of the same period, or a bit later. The fine tree of Jesse in the north aisle has also been estimated as being of the mid-14th century. Of course Parson Woodforde never saw it, for it was covered in successive layers of whitewash until long after his time. The roomy pew of the Custance family can be seen, and there is a brass, with two kneeling children, to commemorate Rookwood's wife:

Of your charity pray for the sowle of Elizabeth
late wife of Firmin Rokewode, Esq; daughter and
heiress of Sir John Timperley, Kt. who died May 13. 1533. [2]

But today the church is very much a shrine to Woodforde himself. His fame has attracted sightseers and enthusiasts from all over the world, as a glance at the Visitors Book kept in the church shows. A very prominent object there is the head-and-shoulders portrait painted after his death by his nephew Samuel, from sketches made 20 years before; the only likeness of him that exists, except for a silhouette. There too is his grave, in the north west corner of the chancel, and above it the modest wall-tablet, which I am sure he would have called both "neat" and "genteel", and the inscription recording his long stint as "29 Years rector of this Parish".

The materials for a history of Weston Longville in Woodforde's time are almost wholly lacking, except for that unimpeachable source, the diary itself. Even he himself does not tell us anything like so much about the village and its denizens as he might have done, had he been so inclined. There is a reason for this, easily understood. Woodforde came from a farming community. Two of his three brothers-in-law were working farmers, while the third, Dr. Clarke, ran a farm attached to his lucrative medical practice. He himself earned as a young man small but quite useful additions to his income by doctoring horses. His father seems to have been anything but a snob, and round the table at Ansford Parsonage are quite often seen guests from many different social classes; former servants, the turnpike keeper's daughter and, of course, farmers. At Weston Longville it was very different. There, however well he was received by the natives, he would always be a "foreigner". Therefore, it was necessary for him to stand on his dignity as the rector and ex-Fellow of New College. His social circle, as we shall see, was to a great extent restricted to other clerics and their friends. His relations with the local farmers were strictly formal. They very rarely came to his house, except on the annual occasion when he was collecting their tithe contributions, and when they did it was usually on some parish business or other. At all other times there was a social gulf between them, which he took care never to bridge. The one possible exception to this, in Woodforde's early years at Weston Longville, was a farmer named John Bowles, with whom something of a friendship did seem to be springing up. But Bowles died "of drinking", and no-one of his social class ever came to take his place.

Our understanding of the social structure of the village is further impoverished by the lack of the Custance estate accounts, which were presumably destroyed at the time Olive Custance sold the estate and Weston House was demolished (1926). There were at least three other landowners who owned real property in the parish but the squire's acreage was much larger than that of anyone else. There is an entry in Woodforde's diary of a most exceptionally rare kind, in which he records the arrival of two new farmers, Girling and Howlett, and gives the acreage each was to hold. Together with a third holding, Mr. Custance's home farm, of which Girling was appointed Steward, the aggregate comes to over 1000 acres. All of it was Custance property.

The farmers varied a good deal in the size of their holdings and their standard of living. When the diarist arrived in 1776 there were perhaps 5 or 6 large scale farmers identifiable, in the absence of more direct information, by their tithe and Poor Rate contributions. Two of these went bankrupt during Woodforde's incumbency. This may appear strange, in the light of the usual text-book contention that the second half of the 18th century was a good time for farmers, especially in an advanced county like Norfolk, with its modern agricultural techniques. But there was little advanced about the farming practices of Weston Longville, which still kept its traditional open fields, since Mr. Custance resisted enclosure on the grounds that it was against the interests of the village people. A few of the more prosperous farmers would have lived in a style approaching professional standards. Typical of these was Mr. Girling, already mentioned. He had a number of servants and sent his youngest daughter to a boarding school. Her letters leave us with a vivid impression of the way a farming family of this kind lived. Below this favoured minority were smaller farmers whose cultivated acreages varied a good deal between one and another. Apropos of this, commentators who have tried to estimate, or guess, the diarist's own income have gone astray because they calculated his total receipts from tithe as being the amounts he collected at each of the tithe audits. In fact only the bigger farmers, an average of about 20, were invited to his "Frolick", but everyone who occupied farm land paid tithe, and the diary frequently shows the receipt of much smaller sums from those whose contributions would have been surpassed by the cost of the food and all the alcohol they would have consumed; so having them at the tithe dinners would have been anything but a sound economic proposition.

These lesser farmers went all the way from an acreage, and an income, not far below those of the big cultivators, to smallholders who were mainly dependent upon following a trade but at the same time kept some livestock, even if it were no more than the traditional backyard pig, or a cow to supply the household with milk and butter.Then, below them, and near the bottom of the social pyramid, were the farm labourers, dependent upon the wages paid by those of the farmers who could afford to employ them.

On the day of the first national census return the figures collected for Woodforde by "Young Stephen Andrews" shows the total population of Weston Longville as numbering 365 persons. It seems to be generally accepted that the population of England and

Wales practically doubled between about 1750 and 1800, even though some of this is to be ascribed not to natural growth but to immigration, mostly from Ireland, into the towns; so it would not be unreasonable to suggest that when the diarist arrived in 1776, exactly half way between those dates, it would have been somewhere between 180 and 230. It is possible, however, that the numbers tended to fluctuate from year to year. Social mobility, as it is now called, was greater at Weston than the history books are always willing to concede for a village of this kind in the 18th century; and this was not due only to the proximity of Norwich. Studies of certain families, based on the diary and parish records, reveal in some cases a considerable movement between Weston and other nearby villages.

So it was a small place, probably scattered even then, the houses not grouped together as in some types of English village. The diary often gives an impression of an intense remoteness and quiet, particularly in winter, when at the Parsonage Woodforde and his niece were often glad of even the diversion caused by a travelling pedlar, or someone showing off a freak. In bad weather, and there was much of that in late 18th century Norfolk, the village leaves us with an impression of being virtually cut off from the outside world. When Sister Clarke was staying there, in the course of her only visit, she had much to complain of about the bad roads. No turnpikes here, like the one that ran past the Parson's birthplace at Ansford. Even the parish roads were neglected. Only once in all his time at Weston does Woodforde record sending his man out to fulfil the householder's road-mending obligation under the Highways Act, and then for only a single afternoon.

And as we read we can understand why both William and Nancy were upon occasion oppressed by the solitude and what they must have seen as the dreariness of the village, expressed most forcefully by the young man: "does not like my House at all, he says, it's a very melancholy Place and would not be obliged to live there for three times the value of the Living", and by Nancy's near-despair when she heard that the Custances were going away to live in Bath. But Woodforde, always an adaptable man, soon got used to the place and even, I suspect, began to like it, once he had arranged things to his liking.

CHAPTER 14

LIFE AT WESTON PARSONAGE

The Parsonage at Weston Longville, which incidentally James Woodforde never called by that name, there being to his mind only one "Parsonage", his birthplace back at Ansford, was a building of indeterminate age, added to and partially rebuilt by his immediate predecessor, Dr. Ridley. A clergyman named "J. Pilgrim", "whose preferment is in the Isle of Barbadoes", as Woodforde wrote dismissively, as though a benefice there was not worth having, attempted to intervene in the dispute over "Dilapidations" between the diarist and Ridley's widow. His aim was to show that the rebuilding had done wonders to the house, and before it had been done "I myself remember it the vilest Thatched Hovel I ever saw"[1]. The thatch remained, and nearly 30 years later was counted by Woodforde as one of the amenities of the house - "...our comfortable, quiet, happy, thatched Dwelling".

New College has no drawings or plans of the house, but among the Woodforde papers there is a terrier, possibly part of a larger map, drawn up in 1822 at the time the manor was enclosed by the younger Custance. It shows the fields of the Rectory glebe, some land owned directly by the college and other land in the occupation of Squire Custance, and a field area most immediately adjacent to the Parsonage, which itself is marked on the map. If the rough sketch of a building has any resemblance to what it actually was like, and is not simply a fanciful pictogram placed there to mark its position on the map, it consisted of three parts, a long central section and two flanking wings which were level with the central portion in the front but some distance shorter in the rear.

It is said, but I do not know upon what authority, to have been SW of the existing Old Rectory; something less than half a mile from the church, along the road or lane which in Woodforde's time was called Church Street. The very large garden is mentioned in the diary with great frequency, together with what appears to have been a series of quite extensive ponds. Two entries show that the garden must have come down to the road or, at least, that a part of it must have been clearly visible from the garden. There was a gravel walk up to the house and, probably one on each side, two "stunted" larch trees on two "hillocks", until 23 May 1791, when the diarist had them felled. Two door scrapers, one on either side of the front door, were purchased from "The Norwich Iron Foundery" in 1794.

If we stand, in imagination, in front of this central doorway we can visualise a house of a fair size, with two main storeys and a third, attic storey just below the roof eaves, a layout which survived, or at least did until a few years ago, in a house of similar dimensions, Hockering Rectory, the home of Woodforde's clerical friend, Mr. Howes. On the ground floor at Weston, left was the parlour, right was the study; on either side of the central hall. At the rear of this hall a staircase - a "pair of stairs", as such a flight was then termed - led up to the next floor. The back of the house was occupied by the kitchen, pantry and back kitchen; possibly also by the brewhouse and dairy, although these could have been separate buildings. There were two main bedrooms. The parlour chamber was built over the parlour as the study chamber over the study. On this floor also were two smaller rooms in which the male servants slept. From this floor another flight of steps - at Hockering it was no more than a fixed ladder - led to the attics, or garrets, where the two maidservants slept. We shall examine these rooms more closely when we come to discuss the role of the servants in the household.

If we are trying, as it were to refurnish this long-vanished house, to restore the sounds and colour and movement it once had, we have two quite essential pieces of evidence to aid us, without which it would be impossible even to make a beginning. The first is, of course, the manuscript diary. The second is the detailed inventory prepared for the sale of the late Parson's goods on 19, 20 and 21 April 1803. They are completely different one from the other. The diary is a record of life as it was actually lived, while the inventory is no more than a dead listing of material objects; but we need both. We can use our knowledge of one to complete and fill out the other. With their help and some use of the imagination, a picture of the living house and its belongings does begin to emerge, and we have before us a Georgian interior of the middle or professional class, in all its detailed complexity. It has much to tell us, even though the right interpretation of some of the evidence is by no means easy to hit on, and there are many pitfalls and short cuts to error.

The parlour was the larger of the two reception rooms, as we can tell by comparing the size of the carpets in this room and the study. It was the main room for meals, and contained a large dining table with "circular ends" that could be joined on to extend it. There was another table, and a card table also, round which "After Dinner we got to Cards", as Woodforde so often wrote. The Rotation dinners, to be described later, and all the other formal parties were held here, and Woodforde's famous "Tithe Audits", or "Frolicks", although only the most important and respectable of the farmers were invited to be "Parlour Guests", the others being unceremoniously relegated to the kitchen. "Genteel" visitors who came for tea-drinking and social chat were ushered into the parlour. The rector's niece Nancy, writing on 3 September 1790 to her aunt Melleora, Brother John's wife, lists with great pride not only the squire and his lady but also the Townshends of Honingham Hall and Mr. Townshend's sister Lady Cornwallis, the widow of the late Archbishop of Canterbury. She adds: "I wish you could have seen us all seated in the Parlour".[2]

It is plain that the parlour was a sort of hybrid of dining-room and drawing-room. On rising from the dinner-table the guests did not go into another room as they, or at least the ladies of the party, would have done in larger and more fashionable houses. The card-playing, or singing, or whatever amusement was put on, evidently took place here, once the food and crockery and cutlery had been taken away.

In the light of this use of the parlour, it is tempting to consider it as the room used for public and formal occasions, as distinct from the study, the private room. But the facts will not let us accept any such easy simplifications. Sometimes the Parson and his niece were unable to use the study as a living-room and were then obliged to fall back on the parlour for that purpose. The Parsonage must have been in some respects an uncomfortable house to live in. Both parlour and study chimneys smoked badly when the wind happened to be in certain directions. The diary is full of complaints about this, and the problem was never solved in Woodforde's lifetime. Of the two rooms, the study had the worse smoke problem. On 27 April 1789 the diarist wrote: "My Study smoked amazingly this morning was obliged to have a fire in the Parlour and let the other be taken away". He was, however, reluctant to take this step, and had literally to be smoked out of his favourite study before he would leave it. On 19 December 1797: "We have been almost a Week in the great Parlour as the Study being subject to smoak all the time - It is much more unpleasant to us than the Study". But even without the smoke, he sometimes went over to the parlour. On 5 November 1792: "Mrs. Jeans and my Niece in very bad Colds - Fires every Day and all Day, in the study Great Parlour and Chamber over the Parlour. The great Parlour our constant keeping room now". As Mrs. Jeans' two children were also staying in the house, the parlour was evidently preferred for its bigger size.

But, granted that the study was the private sitting-room in all normal times, there is evidence that it was occasionally used for meals. When some of the farmers occupied the parlour for their

"Frolick", Nancy and any female guest who happened to be staying in the house at the time had dinner in the study. In 1788, after the dinner, five of the tithe-payers "drank a Dish of Tea about 7. o'clock with my Niece, Betsy Davy and me in my Study". There was no dining-table in this room at the time of the sale, probably indicating that it was not used regularly for meals. Among the articles in the study were a" Mohogony tea chest and canister" and "Three tea canisters and spice boxes", reminding us that a prudent housewife did not allow servants free access to expensive tea and spices but kept these fragrant luxuries safely under lock and key.

With regard to the furnishing of this room, it may appear strange that the inventory has no form of "easy chair", either here or anywhere else in the house. In fact, chairs with padded backs and arms seem not to have been much in evidence between the end of the 17th century and the Regency period. But we do not know what may have been removed before the sale took place, and if Uncle James had possessed a favourite armchair, the legatees, niece and nephew, may have wanted to take it for a keepsake. In the same way, we know from the diary that he owned several prints and pictures, a few by his nephew Samuel, the painter. But there is no trace of them among the effects in the inventory.

On the other hand, comfort was certainly the keynote in Woodforde's own bedroom, the "study chamber". He slept in a four poster bed with "moreen" hangings.[3] The "bed furniture", as it was called, could be pulled round to exclude the light, as also the draughts that plagued all 18th century houses. There was a fireplace in the room, but it was a point of honour with the diarist not to have a fire lighted there, or even to have his bed heated by a "warming pan" full of hot coals thrust between the bedclothes. The bed was equipped with a "mattress", a "goose feather bed", a bolster and two pillows - there is no mention of sheets - and a cotton counterpane. There was a "Scotch carpet" by the bed. He had a "Mohogany dressing chest with drawers". His "Mohogany wardrobe, fine wood, 7ft. 1 inch high, 5 ft. wide", brought in the unusually high price for a single lot of £13. In the bedroom stood the "Mahogany writing desk neatly fitted up", at which we cannot help speculating that he may have sat to post up his diary before he went to bed. There was, however, a "stained writing desk" downstairs in the study, at least at the time of the sale. If this was there while the Parson was alive, it would have been more comfortable, in cold weather, to use it.

The kitchen must have been a large one, because this was in many respects the working heart of the house, so much being made or prepared there which our age does not attempt to produce at home. Woodforde often mentions the kitchen and occasionally the back kitchen, but the inventory does not recognise the latter as a separate room. We take it, therefore, that the two together consisted of a single, extensive, undivided space, taking up perhaps a third of the ground floor area. There was a back door which opened directly on to the yard, and visitors are once or twice seen approaching the house from this direction. Both the kitchen and back kitchen had a chimney and fireplace, as we see from the diary entry for 12 August 1797, when both chimneys were swept. In November of that year part of the wall of the back kitchen was found to be on the point of collapse.

The inventory shows the kitchen to have been well appointed, and its contents made up 51 separate lots, many of them consisting of more than one item. Here were the "Servants' Table, Form and Bench", at which Ben and Betty, Sally and Briton, and their predecessors gathered at mealtimes, and the village ancients sat at their charity dinner on Christmas afternoons. Most of the lots were of implements and household utensils. There were plenty of pots and pans, and some weird-sounding tools. What was a "flesh fork" and a "sausage knife"? What were "Sugar clippers"? But the cooking arrangements were fairly primitive, at least by modern standards. Woodforde's very popular "rost" meat was cooked by means of a "spit", a metal spike driven through the joint, and a "jack", a weight-driven mechanism to make it revolve. As the fat dropped into the pan, it was ladled back over the meat. Otherwise it was boiled, and roasted and boiled meat dishes often appeared in the same meal, however odd this may sound to us. A third way of cooking meat was to bake it in the oven, but this proved less satisfactory and sometimes the dish came to the table imperfectly heated through. The diary was little interested in culinary processes for their own sake, and usually mentions them only when things had gone badly wrong in the kitchen. Woodforde was clearly a man who expected his meals to arrive, properly cooked and appetising, on the table at the right times; and the only cook he ever went out of his way to praise was not one of his own servants but Bridget Dunnell, whose husband was the sub-tenant of Weston Parsonage when he arrived on his inspection visit in 1775:

Had as fine a Leg of Mutton boiled & Caper Sauce
for Dinner, as one would ever desire to sit down to
and dressed as well as could possibly be done
I made a very hearty Dinner tho' by myself on it - 4

The qualification may be noted here; Woodforde saw meals as essentially a social experience and in normal circumstances never ate alone. This is perhaps the best place to mention the diarist's attitude to food, the aspect of his life most clouded with misconception and error. Briefly, his largely undeserved reputation as a glutton derives in the first place from the way Beresford edited the diary, giving a totally unbalanced prominence to entries dealing with food and altogether blurring the distinction between very elaborate and even luxurious spreads, such as the banquet of his own choosing which he partook of at New College on Christmas Day 1773, already cited, and the much simpler fare of everyday. But food of any kind is hardly mentioned in the early diary of his life at home, and not featured much more in that of the Oxford years, in spite of the University being renowned for good living. No doubt he became more fond of his food as he grew older, in common with many people, and would have agreed with Johnson when he said: "I mind my belly very carefully, for I think that a man who does not mind his belly will hardly mind anything else".[5] At the same time, as has been pointed out in our Introduction, Woodforde did not begin to list each daily dinner until 1791, when he had been writing the diary for 32 years. Dinner was the one hot and especially prepared meal of the day, the most that could be expected from a household such as his, and with the cooking facilities then available. Dinner was usually served around 2 o'clock, and if we are tempted to generalise by remarking that a large quantity of food was always consumed at a Georgian dinner by all those who could possibly afford it, on the other hand people of that time were not always nibbling as we tend to do, and the space between breakfast and dinner was a long one. In any case, breakfast like supper was a scratch meal consisting usually of left-overs from the dinners of previous days. So little account was taken of this meal, that even smart London hotels did not provide breakfast for those of their patrons who were about to take early morning stage-coaches. In 1793 Woodforde and Nancy boarded the Bath coach out of London at 4 a.m., and got nothing to eat until it arrived at Maidenhead.

This chapter might conveniently end with an attempt to reconstruct a typical, ordinary Woodfordean day in the early Norfolk period of his life. He is in his early 40's, active and in quite good health. It has been suggested, indeed, that his health improved after he left Oxford; he was leading a busy enough though essentially peaceful life and was drinking a good deal less,[6] while the circulatory and other troubles of his later and more sedentary years had not yet arrived to plague him.

Early rising was customary, and those who found it difficult to acquire the habit were always ready, like Samuel Johnson, to upbraid themselves over long lying in bed; and Woodforde himself was mildly scandalised when, calling on his early friends the Rooke sisters, he found the young ladies still in bed at 11 in the morning.[7] On 30 January 1780 he wrote:

> Nancy and myself get up every morning before 7. o'clock
> under the penalty of forfeiting sixpence each Day -
> Sundays only excepting -

Much was done in the early morning that we prefer to leave until fortified by some breakfast. The Parson might do a little sick visiting. Having had and recovered from smallpox at Winchester, and believing as he did that this conferred lifelong immunity from the disease, he never displayed the least reluctance to being in the same room as a smallpox patient, although generally so nervous about his health. He might walk over to Weston House to pay a call on the Custances, superintend the killing of a pig, or do a little coursing with his greyhounds. More in line with the duties of his profession, he might conduct a wedding or baptise a baby, especially if the child seemed not likely to thrive - otherwise a private baptism for village people was a mark of special favour. All these activities are shown in the diary as being carried out in the morning. The afternoons receive less detailed attention in the diary. Woodforde very often writes just: "Dined and spent the Afternoon ...", without specifying what he and his friends or dinner guests may have done. The afternoon was typically the time of rest after the big meal of the day; although Woodforde never, so far as I am aware, mentions sleeping in the daytime. In the evening he and Nancy often played cards, cribbage being a special favourite; and occasionally he read to her, out of the *History of England* he had bought on the instalment plan when he was an undergraduate at Oxford. Late hours are associated with entertaining or visits to friends, and mentioned whenever they occur; so after a quiet day spent at home the Parson was usually in bed by 10 o'clock. As he always notes down whenever his sleep was troubled, or he had disturbing dreams, the inference is that at all other times he slept soundly, free from care.

Anna Maria(Nancy) Woodforde, 1757 - 1830
(by Samuel Woodforde, R. A.)

CHAPTER 15

Uncle and Niece

Anna Maria Woodforde, the eldest child of Heighes, the Parson's brother, and his wife Anne Dorville, was born on 8 March 1757 at her mother's ancestral home in Alhampton in the parish of Ditcheat, Somerset, a house which, much altered, still stands. The date is only six weeks after her parents had gone through a second marriage ceremony, the first, the result of an elopement, having been at the Savoy Chapel in London in 1754, and already illegal following the passing of Lord Hardwicke's Marriage Act the year before.[1]

Anne's father, Ralph Dorville, who appears to have died a few months after her marriage at Ditcheat, had been a notable pillar of the community, serving in turn as Churchwarden, Surveyor of the Highways or Waywarden, and Overseer of the Poor. There is evidence from the Ditcheat parish records that for some years Heighes tried to follow in his footsteps. Just as his father-in-law had done before him, Heighes signed the Highways accounts for three years, in 1757, 1759 and 1760. In 1758 he also became a Churchwarden and served a three year stint. Heighes made out these parish accounts in a very careful hand, quite like that of his brother the Parson. In 1758 he also took in a parish apprentice, "to be instructed in Husbandry", a sign that he was firmly domiciled at Alhampton. But from 1761 his name disappears from the parish records.[2]

As for his relations with Anne, Woodforde has a number of entries showing them together in apparent marital harmony. William, the "Nephew Bill" of the diary, was born a year after his elder sister. There is no record of his baptism at Ditcheat, but the Woodforde *Family Book* says that he was born on 4 May 1758. Then followed Juliana (1760) and Samuel (1763), the painter and R.A. It was not until 1 November 1764 that the diarist wrote: "There have been sad Quarrels between Brother and his Wife". Shortly after this we hear that Heighes had moved to Castle Cary. It is impossible even to speculate on what their relationship was in these years, for other entries appear to show them as still together. However, by 5 May 1769 they were definitely living apart. On that day Woodforde tried unavailingly to bring them together:

> I took a Walk this Afternoon with Dr Clarke to All-
> hampton, if possible to reconcile Brother Heighes with
> his Wife, and she would not by any means -

Heighes then moved into the Lower House, and that period began, very unhappy for the diarist, when all three brothers were living there together. As though to signalise the break, Heighes had his bed moved out of his wife's home. It was his ill-judged attempt to change the situation and return to Anne that precipitated the final explosive climax and the end of the marriage, eighteen months later. Woodforde recorded this in two successive entries, 23 and 24 December 1770:

> Brother Heighes went to Allhampton this morning, had
> his Bed carried down there by Mark Gristock, and
> was there all Day and all Night - but how it is I know not
> between him and his Wife, I imagine she is not pleased.

> Terrible works all last night at Allhampton - Brothers
> Wife sent his Bed back to our House this morning.

As a sort of gentle reminder to Heighes that his presence was not desired in Anne's house, then or ever, this seems to have worked, for the couple never had anything to do with one another again. In 1776 the first of two formal deeds of separation were drawn up, by which Heighes accepted full legal responsibility for the maintenance and education of three of the children: Nancy, Bill and Sam. Juliana, and the three youngest sons: Ralph Dorville born in 1767, Francis in 1769 and James (surely not named after the Parson!) in 1771, were handed over to the care of their mother. But this could have been no more than a legal fiction. Heighes had no resources beyond the £56 a year rental from the "Sussex Estate" left to him by his father. In 1770, recording the inoculation of the four eldest children by Dr. Clarke, Woodforde noted that they were glad to be away from her, and that she "behaves quite unnatural to them". His is no impartial testimony on such a point; but in fact all four escaped from her, in one way or another, as soon as they possibly could, while the youngest sons, who had been repudiated in the most solemn and emphatic way by Heighes as "not mine",[3] appear to have been on the best of terms with their mother and are seen living with her after they had grown up.

Nancy was apprenticed to a "mantua maker" at 12 or 13, but no more than a bare mention is ever made of this. Perhaps the Woodforde family objected to one of theirs being put to so menial an occupation. At 14 she became a pupil at Mrs. Austin's boarding school at Castle Cary. Woodforde was not greatly interested in children, and in any case his favourite niece was not Nancy but the pathetically unfortunate Jenny White, "a good Little Maid", until she died of diphtheria at the age of 10 in 1771. He began to take notice of Nancy only as a teenager, saying that she was greatly improved since she had been at the school. But even here Heighes ran true to form and failed to pay the fees. Associated with the school in some way was a Jenny Robin - a lovely name, so sweetly redolent of Thomas Hardy's rural world. She called on Woodforde and asked him to pay the debt for his brother. When he refused, the very polite creditor said "she hoped I would not be affronted if she employed an Attorney to get it". If, as seems likely, Nancy left then, such formal education as she ever received ended at this point.

After his return to Oxford, of course he saw Nancy only on the occasions when he went home for a break. On 22 May 1774 he gave her "a Pair of Silver Buckles", which cost 12/6d, bought in Oxford from Mr. Locke, the "Silversmith" in the High Street, but not yet paid for. He did not mention Nancy again for over a year. Then on 21 July 1775 he noted down:

> Poor Nancy Woodforde looks very bad & thin, she
> has an ugly Complaint in one of her Legs -

In the early spring of 1776, when he was living for the last time at Ansford Parsonage and making preparations for the journey to Norfolk, there is nothing mentioned about the state of her health and no word about his decision to take Nancy with him. Whatever discussions there may have been, the diary is absolutely silent about them. In fact, we do not hear that such a plan had ever been mooted until 20 March, when it appeared to have fallen through. Heighes turned up, the bearer of bad news. He said that "Nancy Woodforde would not be able to go with me to Norfolk", as "her Disorder is the King's Evil". A Dr. Buckland had diagnosed it and said he "could cure her in a twelvemonth".

We are here in one of those areas, often met with in the 18th century, when the "Age of Reason" collides with the world of fairytale and folklore. The disease "Scrofula", which is not to be found today in medical textbooks, was more often called the King's Evil by Woodforde's contemporaries, since it had for centuries been thought, a belief not long abandoned, that the touch of the reigning sovereign could produce a cure for the ailment. It was a disease of tubercular origin, mainly characterised by swelling and suppuration of the lymph glands in the neck. In the earlier part of this century it was common to see people whose necks bore ugly scars, where the tumours had been surgically removed. There is, by the way, no allusion anywhere to this symptom being present at any time in

Nancy's case, and it is always possible that the diagnosis was entirely mistaken, hardly a rare occurrence in 18th century medicine. We have seen that it first affected her leg; later it was her "elbow and hand", and finally the disease shifted to one of her knees, causing the lameness often commented upon in the diary.

Something of the magical nature of this malady and the atmosphere of legend and mystery that enveloped it becomes clear when we are told of the healer's qualifications. Although styled "Doctor", he was in fact " a seventh son & is a grazier and Farmer". The next day Woodforde's friend Dr. Donne came and confirmed the diagnosis. He recommended in place of Buckland another strange candidate; "he knew a Person who was perfectly cured of such Disorder by a Man near Axbridge, a Gentleman Farmer but he had forgot his Name but that he would recollect & send me his name". He added handsomely that the patient had been cured in nine months and "has been well five years", although she was previously in his, Dr. Donne's care, and in that of another famous surgeon; "but they could do nothing for her". Perhaps when he was leaving, as an afterthought, the doctor remarked that "Alford Well Water had done great things in Complaints of the Kings Evil, & very good for such Disorders".

But Nancy's ailment, and the long course of treatment thought necessary to effect a cure, had put paid to her chances of going to Norfolk with her uncle. We know nothing about her reaction, but might guess that she was bitterly disappointed. At 19, such blows of fate are hard to bear. As for Woodforde, on 20 April, and some ten days before he was due to leave the West Country for good, he selected Nancy's brother Bill to accompany him, a choice he was later to regret. One is permitted to wonder why Juliana, 16 in this year, did not take the place of her sister; perhaps because she was thought to be still too young, or because Heighes, whose favourite she appears to have been, was unwilling to let her go away so far.

And with that the Parson and his nephew, and the young servant Will Coleman riding the "Portmanteau Horse" Woodforde had just bought, rode away and vanished from their old haunts, and Nancy of course disappears from sight altogether. On 16 March 1777 Bill had a letter from his father which said that "his Sister Nancy was in a bad Way". Later on that year the exiles were back in the West on holiday. On 10 July Woodforde saw his niece at Sister Clarke's and reported that she was "very bad indeed still", although she was apparently well enough to be present at one or two of the parties and social occasions in his honour.

Once more we lose sight of Nancy. Meanwhile Bill wore out his welcome at Weston Parsonage, and his uncle thankfully got rid of him. Then in 1779 the Parson and his servant Will Coleman made the long journey across country. Nancy now appears more frequently in the accounts he gives in the diary of various family activities, and was clearly quite active. Nothing is said about her health. Perhaps Buckland, or the man from the neighbourhood of Axbridge, or even liberal potations of Alford Well water, had done the trick. It is far more likely, however, that the disease had gone into one of its phases of remission and the symptoms temporarily disappeared.

The diarist did not take his niece with him when he and Coleman started back for Norfolk on 8 September. This was because he had no wheeled vehicle suitable for a lady to travel in. The previous evening he had called on his brother Jack to say good-bye, only to find him unfriendly, for "he talked as usual very disagreeable". Nancy had been living with him and his wife, and maybe the Parson's brother begrudged the loss of a servant. As Nancy would never have been expected, or permitted, to make so long a journey by herself, it must have been arranged that Sister Clarke and her eccentric son Sam should accompany her as companions and chaperones. Back at Weston, the Parson heard on 9 October that the travellers had already left Ansford and that "Two Boxes with their Cloaths were already sent". After staying three or four days in London, they finally arrived in Norwich on the evening of 12 October, so tired after their journey by stage-coach that they "drank some Tea immediately and soon decamped to bed" at the *King's Head*. After a long and fairly inharmonious stay mother and son returned to Ansford, but Nancy remained.

Weston Parsonage was to be her home for nearly a quarter of a century, and she would stay there for the rest of her uncle's lifetime. But Woodforde was a cautious man. If we look again at the famous opening lines of the diary each day, it may be seen that in his Norfolk period he always writes that he breakfasted etc. "at home", while the same form of words applied to Nancy ends with "here". It was some years before he recognised and, as it were admitted, that Weston Parsonage was her home too.

When Nancy Woodforde arrived in Norfolk, she was just short of 23 years old. Two portraits of her exist, both by her brother Samuel. One, a chalk drawing delicately outlined, shows her as a young girl and was certainly done while she was still living at Ansford. She was not a beauty, having a rather plump and puddingy face which lacks the character seen in her mother's picture. Nancy's best feature, at least on the evidence of this portrait, was her very abundant, even luxurious hair, which sweeps round her face like a veritable cascade. The other portrait, a full-length in oils,

135

presents her in early middle age, reclining on a garden seat. She looks demonstrably overweight, the heavy protein meals of the Weston cuisine having done their worst to her figure. Perhaps with her, eating became a form of compensation for other pleasures of which she was deprived. Although Woodforde, while detailing many succulent meals in his diary, very seldom indeed tells us how much he actually consumed, he was less discreet where Nancy was concerned, and some of her gastronomic feats are quite awe-inspiring, guaranteed to make William George Bunter, the fat boy of Greyfriars School, seem like an ascetic by comparison. On 24 September 1790 she "eat for Dinner some boiled Beef, rather fat and salty, a good deal of a nice roast Duck, and plenty of boiled Damson Pudding. After Dinner by way of Desert she eat some greengage Plums, some Figs and raspberries and Cream". It is no wonder that some hours later she had such a jumbo attack of indigestion that she seemed to be "blown up as if poisoned". Her uncle's remedy was nothing short of heroic: "A good half Pint Glass of warm Rum and water", after which she was soon "a little better". Nancy's dietary splurges did her no lasting harm since she lived to be 73.

The impression of people we read of in a diary must of course be that which the diarist has of them and transmits to us, not necessarily anything like and perhaps in many cases very unlike the view they have of themselves. With Nancy we are rather fortunate, in that she has left us something of her own, and we can hear her speaking with her own voice, free from the interposition of her uncle's personality. The Bodleian Library owns a MS book containing autographed letters to members of her family, copies made before she sealed up and posted the originals; together with a single one which did actually go through the post. Nancy did not bother to date the copies, but all except one are to be identified as belonging to her first two years in Norfolk. She sounds happy, eagerly retailing gossip about clothes and parties, the charm and bright sophistication of her new Norfolk friends, the kindness of the squire's wife. She went to the Norwich Music Festival of 1790, where Signora Storace sang 'Angels Ever Bright and Fair' - "most divinely".[4] Miss Donne of Norwich came to Weston on a one-night stay. Nancy slept with her and they "laughed and talked till near 4 o'clock in the morning".[4] She emerges from all this as a generous, friendly girl. To her brother Bill, knowing the circumstances in which he had left Weston, she wrote: "<u>Don't</u>" and she underlined the word - "be afraid of my uncle's being angry with you for I will say as much as I can for you". When she heard that her cousins Robert White and Sophia Clarke had eloped, she wrote to Melleora

Woodforde: "I can't imagine why her friends" - by which term she of course meant the Clarke family - "should be so averse to the match and it is by no means beneath herself. Pray tell them, if they are married, that I wish them all the joy and happiness in the world". As we should expect, she was lavish in her praise of the Parson whose bounty had given her this new and exciting life. To her sister Juliana she wrote: "I like my uncle exceedingly; he is a very worthy and good kind of a man and I hope heaven will reward him for his goodness. We have not been a week this summer without company or going out." 5

There were, it is true, some unpleasantnesses to be borne. Heighes, who at Ansford had employed her as a go-between when he was trying to beg small loans from his brother, still embroiled her in his murky schemes. He applied to Nancy asking her to prevail on the Parson to act as guarantor for a loan he was trying to raise. Her embarrassment at having to reject the proposal is obvious in what she writes. On the debit side also was the question of her illness. Firmly located in her knee it remained to come and go. Whenever there was a flare-up of the condition, it made her so lame that she was unable to walk "without holding". In the intervals of remission the lameness disappeared, so that we find her rather naively bragging to Juliana: "I suppose you will be astonished to hear that I have rode nearly a hundred miles this summer. I have often rode twelve miles in a day and many times six miles before breakfast. All these miles on horseback, remember!". But in a previous letter written about a year before, she had told her sister: "I use a great deal more exercise here than I did in Somerset in hopes of getting better of my lameness, but I am afraid I never shall be able to walk without the assistance of a stick". In later times, when her uncle gave her little opportunity of getting about and she herself had grown older, she would be reduced to walking round and round the garden whenever she was in a condition that made this possible, and clocking up the mileage, a pursuit that might almost stand for a symbol of her life.

The early period at Weston was a golden time for her. She had never been, or would be again, so happy, so carefree, her life so varied and exciting. Yet, however much she may have enjoyed her environment, and cherished her escape from the atmosphere of penny-pinching and squalor surrounding Heighes, she was still a poor relation, without independence. For the happiness she experienced in her best years depended upon the whims of another person; and if his ideas of what constituted pleasure were to change, hers must perforce change too. We shall see how this happened.

From Woodforde's own point of view Nancy's coming into his

household was a considerable benefit. He was a gregarious man and had felt desolate at the imminent departure in 1777 of even the unsatisfactory Bill, writing pathetically in his diary: "When Bill goes I shall have no one to converse with - quite without a Friend". Nancy was far more docile and amenable to his will than any young man could have been. Their temperaments were rather alike, both on the phlegmatic side. He appreciated her sense of humour, and when she had been away on a visit to neighbouring friends, liked to hear the rather acid comments she occasionally passed on some of them - she had "never seen so poor a Honey" as Mrs. Jeans' brother. Nancy was his link with the past and with his own youth. They had common topics and mutual remembrances which he could discuss with no-one else. Even her voice, the accent so different from that of the Norfolk people, must in its way have been a comfort to him. They got on so well together, their "design for living" as we in our time might call it, worked so smoothly that he can never really have wanted to change it, even in his last cantankerous years when he found her more and more "pert" and "saucy", and was calling her "Miss Woodforde" in the diary.

If in their happier and more active days when she was young and he no more than healthily middle-aged, he had been told that the dismal late times could almost be predicted, and that he was preparing for poor Nancy an inevitable existence of barren celibacy that would stretch for years beyond his own lifetime, he would without any doubt at all have most indignantly denied the mere suggestion of it. Was he not doing his duty by his niece? He had rescued her from poverty, he fed and clothed her, took her about whenever it suited him, and gave her a pig, or its cash equivalent, every Christmas. What more could she really expect? And was not the society in which they lived full of old maids, very many of them much worse off than Nancy?

But she must have seen the situation in a very different light, and more strikingly as she grew older. In the beginning, she can scarcely have helped nursing a few very agreeable daydreams of some handsome young bachelor clergyman riding up to the front door of Weston Parsonage to ask for her hand. But the years passed. Her uncle's clerical neighbours were either married or elderly like his close friend Mr. du Quesne, impossible to think of as suitors.

Feelings of this kind were to surface and play their part in the crisis which at least temporarily interrupted the harmonious relationship of the Parson and his niece. We shall look at that in its right place.

CHAPTER 16

FRIENDS AND ROTATIONS

Regional differences and variations were, of course, very much more marked in Georgian times than they are today - now, when the same shops, the same restaurants, the same official uniformity greet the traveller in these islands, irrespective of the area we visit, they can scarcely be said to exist at all. A move from Somerset to East Anglia, having as its object a life residence in the latter place, must have been looked upon as an adventure, especially to a stay-at-home man like Woodforde, whose movements hitherto had been restricted to a smallish round consisting of his own part of Somerset, and the district about Oxford, with a few short stay visits to Bath and London. Dr. Hargreaves-Mawdsley, in the introduction to his *Woodforde at Oxford*, says that he took Weston Longville on an impulse, "without really liking the idea", simply because a year had gone by since his return to New College and this was the first living to turn up. The editor continues: "Ironically enough a West Country living became vacant soon after". I doubt whether there is anything that the diarist wrote which supports the notion that he accepted his benefice on an impulse and the last cited comment is wrong on two counts: first, the living in question was that of Paulerspury in Northants, a long way from the West Country, and second, it was taken by William Master who previously turned down Weston and who had the first choice of both; so Woodforde could never have become the incumbent of that living.

Until he actually visited Weston, the diarist's only contact was George Howes, "my Curate", as he calls him. But no-one ever hurried in the 18th century without a very good reason, and the much admired figure of the modern whizz-kid, endlessly flailing around in a void of his own making, would not then have received the adulation we are so eager to bestow upon him. Woodforde, as we saw, was appointed to the living on 15 December 1774, but it was not until 26 March in the next year that he wrote to Howes, and his letter was simply to inform the curate of his forthcoming inspection visit. On 4 April he wrote again, saying that his trip would have to be deferred, "Webber being bad in the Gout" and all the duties of the Junior Proctor having fallen on him and his friend Washbourne Cooke, whom he had no doubt already chosen to be his companion on the coming journey: "I promised to frank him all the way to

Norfolk as he goes to oblige me". But when, after a stopover in London for the purpose of being instituted by the Bishop of Norwich, Dr. Horne, "a short fat Man" who "behaved exceedingly handsome and free", Woodforde arrived at Weston Longville "by 2 o'clock in the Afternoon of 15 April", Howes was not long in coming to him. Howes had alerted the sub-tenant at Weston Parsonage, Barnard Dunnell, so that "Beds &c. all in readiness for us when we came", although on the blotting paper opposite this day's entry he noted down:

> Nothing but Bacon & Eggs to Day for
> Dinner at Weston -

Next day was Easter Sunday. Cooke "read Prayers and Preached", while Woodforde administered the sacrament to "near 40. Communicants". Howes came back and brought his wife and her niece, "Mrs. Davy", as the diarist nearly always spells the name. Howes insisted that the newcomers should get into his chaise and drive to his house, Hockering Rectory, where they dined and spent the afternoon. In this way Woodforde's introduction to his new parish was eased, and he met three new friends. It is true that later two of these relationships were to crash; but if taxed with this I am sure that he would have replied that it was not his fault if they did. We shall be able later to see who, if anyone, was to blame.

George Howes was born at Morningthorpe, Norfolk, in 1709. A graduate of Clare College, Cambridge, he was to some extent a protégé of the powerful Townshend family, who provided him with most of his church preferment. The head of one branch, Charles Townshend (1718-1810), created the 1st. Baron Foxley in 1797, lived nearby at Honingham Hall. Howes had been in 1750 made rector of Honingham and was incumbent of the consolidated living of Mattishall Burgh. He was officially licensed as curate of Weston in 1760, but his signature appears in the church registers from 1756. Mrs. Howes was born Catherine Roupe or Roope, his third wife. By his two previous wives, Howes had three daughters, of whom two were married, and at least one son; other children had died in infancy.[1]

Mrs. Howes' brother, Dr. Charles Roupe, a physician of Pulham Market, had ten children by his two wives. Elizabeth was the fourth child, born in 1749, and so aged 27 at the time Woodforde met her. When he called her "a very young Widow", he evidently meant either that he took her for younger than her real age, at a time when women aged more quickly than they do now, or that she was young to be widowed. She had married Lancelot Davie, "Surgeon", of

Southwold, who died in 1773, leaving her with two small children: another Elizabeth, or "Betsy", born in 1770, and Nunn, born in 1771. A third child, named Thomas, had died in the same year as his father.

Elizabeth Davie was undoubtedly a very attractive woman, and many people in the diary testify to her charm, including Woodforde's nephew Sam, a smart young man with sophisticated London tastes. She was intelligent, businesslike, a born manager; but with her everything was subordinated, as we shall see, to her obsessive search for a meal-ticket for herself and her two children. In this she appears to have badly overplayed her hand. A long liver, she may be traced so late as 1832, but at that date she was still Mrs. Davie, and none of her prospects succumbed to the blandishments she had proffered.

The Mrs. Priest whom Woodforde also met during his inspection visit, who was staying with the Howes, was Mary, the second wife of Robert Priest, wine merchant of St. Giles Broad Street, Norwich, and also a partner in a pharmaceutical business, carried on from the same address. His brother Richard was Rector of St. Mary, Reepham, and curate of the adjoining church of Hackford. The reader of the diary learns a good deal about "Mr. Priest of Reepham" and "Mr. Priest of Norwich", and their respective families. But Woodforde did not meet the brothers until the following year, after he had gone into residence at Weston.

The letters exchanged between Woodforde and Mr. Howes for the rest of the year 1775 were all on the vexed subject of "dilapidations", the amount which an incoming rector or vicar could claim from the estate of his predecessor, in respect of repairs and maintenance not carried out, and which the new man had a right to be compensated for. The two sides hardly ever agreed on this, and settlement usually came only at the end of long and tortuous negotiations. Passing through London on his way back to Oxford, Woodforde went out to Greenwich to see Dr. Ridley's widow (he found Mrs. Howes staying there with her) and to make it clear that his estimate of the sum he was owed was many times larger than hers. "My Curate Mr Howes very much for Mrs Ridley", he noted down in November, after receiving a letter from him stating that "a Clergyman the Revd. Mr. Du Quesne", together with a carpenter at Hockering, "did not bring it to more than 26: 9: 0". It is plain that he was suspicious of both Howes and du Quesne, both being friends of Mrs. Ridley, and it was not until he had his claim met practically in full that he felt able to relax and let the friendship develop, although by that time he had already been invited to see du Quesne's "sweet pretty House & Garden" at Honingham, Berry Hall, received a famous present of strawberries and stood in for him twice when Mr. du Quesne was absent from his parish. This was the man who was to be the closest of Woodforde's Norfolk friends and the only one ever invited to make the journey into Somerset and meet his family.

Thomas Roger du Quesne was born in 1719. His great-grandfather was a distinguished admiral in the French navy, and ennobled as the first Marquis du Quesne. But the family was Huguenot, and in 1685, when the Edict of Nantes was revoked, left France. Our Mr. du Quesne's father was miserably poor, yet made a marriage which was to be exceptionally advantageous for the son. He married a widow, Mrs. Job Yates, the daughter of Sir Roger Bradshaigh, second baronet, of Haigh in Lancashire, who was related to the Townshends. They took good care of Mr. du Quesne, who indeed became a conspicuous example of the value of patronage. Educated at Eton and King's College, Cambridge, he became vicar of Honingham with East Tuddenham, 1753, displacing Mr. Howes who was given Hockering in exchange, and of Scole alias Osmundeston, 1756. He was a prebendary of Lichfield, 1765; Chancellor Canon of St. David's, 1776; and prebendary of Ely, 1783, this last being "worth £300 a year", as Woodforde wrote. He was unmarried, and well looked after by servants whom he treated as his friends and to whom he was exceptionally generous. He loved music and delighted in playing the violin. Mr. du Quesne appears to us as an excellent type of cultivated, civilized 18th century cleric, although the system which enriched him kept others, some of whom were his neighbours, in a state of grinding poverty. [2]

It was entirely through the good offices of du Quesne and Howes that the diarist was so soon accepted by the clerical society around him. A measure of that acceptance was their inviting him to join the "Rotation Club", consisting of themselves and Castres Donne. He was a much younger man and quite a few years the junior of Woodforde, still in minor orders and curate of Mattishall for an absentee vicar, Dr. Goodall. Castres, an amiable man who wrote bright, amusing letters, was the son of the late Rev. Roger Donne of Catfield, whose sister had married a clergyman named Cowper and became the mother of William Cowper the poet.[3]

Woodforde was invited to become the fourth member of the club on 13 January 1777. It had a set of very simple rules, meeting on Monday, the clergyman's "day off", in turn at each other's house. A leg of mutton was most often the chief dish on the menu, and after Woodforde joined, they very often played quadrille, specifically a game for four persons. It is rather difficult to keep track of the Rotations in the diary, since the meetings, at first strictly kept to the same day of the week, later on were held irregularly on other days, and sometimes extra guests were present. In 1779 Castres Donne obtained a living of his own, and after a round of farewell parties, including two Rotations in one week, he left the neighbourhood. His place was taken by Thomas Bodham, who married Castres Donne's sister two years later. Bodham was a wealthy man, made even richer by the death of his father and brother. He was a graduate of Caius, Cambridge, but owing to some unexplained nervous disorder never advanced in the Church beyond minor orders.

The Bodhams lived at South Green House, in the parish of Mattishall. In the year of their marriage, the non-resident Goodall died and John Smith became vicar, instituted by Caius, the patrons of the living. Ironically in view of what was later to happen, Woodforde described him at their first meeting as "a very good kind of a Man about 50. Years of Age". In reality he was several years younger. Coming from a place on the borders of Norfolk and Suffolk, John Smith had a distinguished career at Caius, where he was at different times Greek Lecturer and Hebrew Lecturer. His movements from place to place in the Church sound rather like those of Woodforde in reverse, since in 1780 he was given the living of Bratton Fleming in North Devon, on the western edge of Exmoor; but he had been there only a few months when Mattishall fell vacant and Smith thankfully moved back to East Anglia. He was an expert in practical farming and greatly increased the tithe value of the benefice to the college. [4]

Smith was the last man to join the Rotations Club, which lasted for some years but broke up at last through strife between the members, as we shall see. But this group made up the tally of Woodforde's intimate friends in Norfolk, and with no others there were his relations to be so close. Other clerical friends and neighbours are seen often enough in the diary, as occasional guests at Weston Parsonage, or acting as hosts in their own homes, or met with at clerical functions such as confirmations or episcopal visitations. We might call at least some of them friends rather than acquaintances; but the degree of mutual amity is of a rather casual nature.

We might instance here the two Wilsons, father and son, both named John. The older man was vicar of Elsing, and one very early day in the diarist's residence came riding over with a bundle of asparagus in his coat pocket. But no real friendship developed, possibly because Woodforde disapproved of the way that Wilson treated his son. If people in this society, like our own, may be divided into winners and losers, Mr. Wilson junior was a full-time loser. Having married without his father's consent and approval, he had been disinherited by his unrelenting parent. He had as a result no home, and when he learned early in 1775 that Woodforde had become the rector of Weston Longville, he wrote asking to be allowed to stay at the Parsonage until such time as the diarist went into residence. Wilson lived a hunted existence, afraid to go out except on Sundays as the bailiffs were after him. For most of the ten years when Woodforde's Winchester and New College friend Henry Bathurst was vicar of Great and Little Witchingham, Wilson was his curate and ran the parishes. Where he and his family lived is a mystery. It could not have been the Parsonage House at Witchingham, which was uninhabitable, the roof having fallen in. Wilson was constantly pestering the diarist for advances on his salary. Somehow he managed to survive, and kept going by a series of clerical odd jobs. He outlived Woodforde and is found concluding a wedding at Weston in the Spring of 1803. This occasion affords our last glimpse of him.

Other clerical friends who appear from time to time in the diary are Mr. Atthill (called "Attle" by Woodforde) of Sparham and Foxley, and his successor Mr. Stoughton, remembered for his once turning up in hunting dress with presents of game: Mr. Shelford of North and West Tuddenham and his sons: in later years Mr. du Quesne's successor Mr. Mellish, a young man with flaxen hair and a lisp, whose loss of his mother stirred Woodforde into an expression of grief for his own mother, who had died more than 30 years before. Yet others, such as Mr. Fayerman of Loddon - it was his living that Castres Donne succeeded to - and Mr. Nelson of Strumpshaw, were clearly no more than casual acquaintances seen once or twice for their appearances to be recorded in the diary. One or two, whose names can be picked up from the contemporary list of Norfolk benefices and who lived no farther off than a few miles away from the diarist, are never mentioned at all.

CHAPTER 17

DISSENSION
THE FOURTH MRS. HOWES

One of James Woodforde's favourite terms of expression, used when he wanted particularly to praise someone, was "good natured". He even applied it once to a horse, Jack, the original "Portmanteau Horse" of his journey to Norfolk in 1776, and was upset when the beast died. If he had been asked whether it fitted his own character and could be applied rightly to himself, I am sure he would have answered that it did and could. And, in a broad sense, he would have been right to make that claim. Unlike his brothers, he was never quarrelsome, noisy or violent. The calm, even tone of the diary is the product of a placid temperament.

At the same time, he had about him an obduracy, a peculiarly unforgiving streak that shows up plainly in many passages in the diary. If he really felt himself offended, he would walk away rather than make a row about it; but he would remember the slight, resent it and, if he found the opportunity, pay it back. This shows itself even in very minor and inconsiderable violations of what he would have looked upon as an obligatory code of good manners.

There was a rigid protocol in matters dealing with hospitality, in obeying which most educated and cultivated people would have been at one with him. Yet, just as in his time as Sub Warden and Pro Proctor at Oxford he had shown a particular zeal for carrying out the disciplinary part of his duties, so now his interpretation of the rules was, I think, weighted on the side of punctiliousness. To avoid a solecism, to his way of thinking, you did not issue an invitation to a friend to visit you unless you were prepared to go to his house, on an even basis. If you were prevented from keeping the appointment, you had to send a note excusing yourself, to arrive in good time before the other guests sat down to their dinner. And if you were circumstanced as Nancy and her uncle were, you must "send the Carriage" for the lady, to save her from having her elaborately piled hair blown about by driving in the Parson's open "Market Cart". Failure to observe such civilized niceties was always commented on disapprovingly.

The Rev. James Baldwin, the incumbent of Lyng, a parish that borders Weston, was a married man with two daughters, Virtue and Nancy, who both died young and whose wall tablet may be seen on the east wall of the chancel in the parish church. One morning in

Woodforde - The Fourth Mrs. Howes

Woodforde's first weeks at Weston Longville, he walked up to his church by appointment to meet Baldwin, who was to conduct some sort of "Visitation" there, possibly the archdeacon's visitation which had not been carried out at the right time because Woodforde was not yet in the parish then. But Baldwin failed to keep the appointment, " so I marched off ". Later, the diarist met him at Mr. du Quesne's house, and gradually a round of reciprocal party-giving developed between the two men, at its height in 1778 and early 1779. On 20 April of the latter year, Woodforde was host to the Baldwin family and several other people, and at that meeting two further outings must have been arranged. On 28 April Woodforde rode to Lenwade Bridge "to meet Mr and Mrs Baldwin there, but no body came". His reaction could have been predicted. The next day he wrote:

> Sent a Note to Mr Baldwin, this
> morn', to let him know that I could
> not be of their Party to Houghton
> the ensueing Week -

After that the references to Mr. Baldwin are few indeed, and little more than incidental. By 1783 it seemed possible that relations might be getting back to something like their old footing. On 4 July Woodforde had dinner with the Baldwins, meeting there "the first Cousin to the ingenious Miss Burney", whose *Evelina* was one of the few novels he ever read. But it was too late. On 27 September: "We heard this Morning by my Butchers Lad that the Revd. Mr. Baldwin was dead - am very sorry for him". And that was all.

This may be taken as an example of Woodforde's behaviour in matters, in which he must have felt that he had been treated with insufficient courtesy by a casual acquaintance. With people he knew well, where a seemingly real tie of amity had been established and from whom he clearly expected more, his sense of grievance was much greater and he retained it much longer - in some cases for the rest of his life. As we saw, George and Catherine Howes were his first friends in Norfolk, and for several years - indeed, for so long as Mrs. Howes lived - their relations were cordial. Howes plays a prominent role in some of the best-remembered scenes in the diary. He and Catherine were present at the famous all-night pre-Christmas party, when they were given Woodforde's own bedroom (he sat up all night playing cards), only to be serenaded, the diarist's word and one which sounds much better than wakened with a start, "with our best on the Hautboy" at 6 o'clock in the morning.[1] We see the two

146

friends smoking together under the old tree in the garden at Weston. Woodforde sampled the yellow fish called "cruzers" from the pond at Hockering Rectory, and pronounced them excellent, whereupon Howes gave him some to take back with him. In return, Woodforde put a large pike in the boot of Howes' chaise as a surprise present. He lent his "engine" (this is the pumping apparatus that once nearly brained the somewhat accident-prone servant Will Coleman) to clean out the pond at Hockering; and young Jack Warton helped when the chaise broke down in Norwich on the occasion of "Bishop Blaize's Festival".

Nancy Woodforde also liked Mr. Howes. In a letter to her mother, written on 10 October 1780, obviously intended to impress with the knowledge that she, Nancy, was having the time of her life, she wrote "last week I dined at Mr. Howes's who sent his Chaise for me there I'm a great favourite of the old Gentleman".

But, as they appear in the diary, both husband and wife were notably eccentric personalities. He stayed behind at the *Cock* inn in the village although he had guests waiting at the Rectory. Another time he abruptly cancelled his wife's dinner invitation and asked his friends to tea instead, "which made all the Company stare".

If Howes was odd, then perhaps he and Catherine were well-matched, for much of what the diarist has to say of her sounds decidedly strange. In a good mood, she was surely a jolly sort of woman. It was she who gave Woodforde and his nephew bits of "plumb" cake to put under their pillows, so that they would dream of the girls they were to marry. She took in good part being "sent to Coventry", and did not spoil the joke. Although in her 60s, she looked handsome in a new lilac silk "sack". But she could also be a considerable nuisance. The hospitable diarist could hardly have been pleased when, as a dinner guest in his home, she "found great Fault with many things, especially about stewing the Fish - she could not eat a bit with such Sauce &c,". Even more strange was her indiscreet willingness to reveal marital disharmony at the Rectory not only to Woodforde but also to young Bill, and this when she could hardly be said to have known them long:

> ... Mr Howes went to bury a Corpse for M^r Du Quesne, &
> when he was gone Mrs Howes told us that she lived
> very unhappy with her Husband, as he wants her
> to make her will & give every thing to his Family -
> I advised her to the contrary, & to give to her own - 2

Typical Woodfordean advice, that, from someone who always believed that charity begins at home! However, between two and three years later he was very embarrassed when Mrs. Howes took the offensive and set about her husband in public, at his own Rotation:

> ...Just as the Company was gone Mrs Howes attacked
> Mr Howes about putting down the Chaise and she
> talked very roughly to him & strutted about the Room
> It was rather too much in her - I did not stay long to
> hear it, but soon decamped & was at home before 10. [3]

Not long after this her health weakened. A number of entries mention her being ill and she died, rather unexpectedly at the last, early in January 1782.[4] Woodforde lavished a good deal of praise on the efficient organisation of the funeral, which he attributed entirely to Elizabeth Davie. For the remainder of the year, and some time beyond, things appeared to go along without change. Mr. Howes continued to attend the Rotations, sometimes accompanied by Elizabeth Davie who was acting as his housekeeper, as she had probably been doing unofficially for some time before her aunt's death.

In November there was one of those petty imbroglios, turning on a point of etiquette, which the people of Woodforde's time took so seriously. Mr. Howes and his niece turned up for dinner at Weston Parsonage, and on leaving wanted Nancy to return with them to Hockering and stay overnight, as they were going to Robert Priest's in Norwich next day. Woodforde refused permission for a long time, and finally relented and gave it only with the greatest reluctance: "Poor Mr Howes and Mrs Davie had set their Hearts so much on it, that they almost cried and said they would never be friendly with me if I did not admit of it - Mr Howes said he would never enter my Doors more". Woodforde's objection was that Nancy had not been specifically invited by the wine merchant; therefore "I did not approve or ever could that my Niece should make so free at Mr Priest's". After his visitors had gone, taking Nancy with them, he still felt "uneasy ... as I cannot by any means approve of it on any Account neither should I at last, unless to make old Mr Howes easy".

The impression one receives from all this is that Woodforde thought it advisable to humour the poor old widower, apparently lapsing into senility. There is certainly no hint, here or anywhere else, that quite soon the ancient man would be remarrying. Whether or not he was surprised when he heard the news there is no knowing, but on 10 April 1783 he recorded it in the very tersest of possible terms: "Mr. Howes was this Day married to his 4. Wife, a Mrs. Brown". He was either not invited, or declined to attend the wedding, but Thomas Bodham, another of the friends and a fellow-member of the Rotation club, signed the register as a witness.

Five days later Woodforde rode to Hockering, Nancy being there already on a visit, to dine and meet the new Mrs. Howes. His report on the lady sounds the reverse of enthusiastic: "... his new Wife an agreeable Woman enough". The next day he and Nancy received some "bride-cake" from Hockering, sent with a note by Mrs. Davie, who was now about to lose her place and resume her peripatetic life and search for a second husband. For a time the Rotations continued as before, although they were now being held at less regular intervals. But by 15 July, it being the day of Smith's Rotation, the diarist was complaining:

> M^r and Mrs Howes not there which I think very rude.
> as they promised, and their going this Day to Shipdam -
> but I apprehend they intend dropping the Rotations -
> which for my Part I am not sorry for, as Mrs Davie is
> soon going to board at Mattishall in the Parsonage House -

I suppose the inference is that Woodforde, with no foreknowledge of the way that the widow was to sink in his esteem, meant that she was the only one of the Howes set he still wanted to see. And when on 25 July the Howes couple failed to turn up to his own Rotation, that was really the last straw. He would treat them as he had once treated the Baldwins, and serve them right:

> We invited M^r and Mrs Howes, but
> they would not come themselves nor let Miss Howes.
> I have therefore done with them entirely.

The final showdown came on 29 July, the occasion being Bodham's Rotation:

> .... As we were coming away Mrs Howes came to me and
> asked me to her House it being their Rotation next, but
> I entirely refused to go, as they had not only kept away from
> mine very lately, but would not let Miss Howes come
> who was very desirous of coming to Weston - I gave it to her -
> and most of the Company seemed pleased with my behaviour -

The ultimate casualty of this open disagreement turned out to be the Rotations, which were dealt a heavy blow they never quite recovered from. They were in abeyance until October, were then restarted and went on until August 1784, then rather self-consciously taken up again and continued at irregular intervals until they became embroiled in another quarrel, which finished them off entirely.

As for the Howes, they never held or attended another Rotation, and they vanish altogether from the diary. Many a woman takes a dislike to the male friends of her husband whom he had known before marriage. If Judith Howes had consciously striven to detach her husband from his old friends, she certainly succeeded.

On 30 June 1785 Mr. du Quesne, paying a social call at Weston Parsonage but not dismounting from his horse, told the diarist that "he buried poor Mrs Howes last night - she died on Sunday last - her Disorder was the Dropsy". But once having "done with" people entirely, Woodforde was not to be moved. He made no attempt to get in touch with Mr. Howes, not even to the extent of sending a servant round to express his condolences. Howes survived his last wife by only seven months. He died on 27 January 1786. Woodforde did not register his death in the diary, as he does almost as a matter of course in the case of many people he had known far less well, and his one mention of Howes shows how completely he had blotted this old friend out of his mind. The passage is dated 14 May 1786 and runs:

> ... A Sale this Day at Hockering Parsonage House of
> all the Furniture &c. late Mr Howes'

Perhaps he had quite forgotten that it was in that "Parsonage House", he had taken his first meal with friends in Norfolk. Or he may have remembered, but the memory stirred no chord of feeling in him.

CHAPTER 18

MRS. DAVIE AND MR. SMITH

I do not believe that James Woodforde was ever within measuring distance of proposing marriage to Elizabeth Davie. The abortive romance of Betsy White had revealed his ingrained caution, his tendency always to draw back before committing himself. And, if he cannot precisely be said to have been afraid of women, a person like Mrs. Davie, with her efficiency, her way of managing things, would seem almost calculated to arouse his mistrust. After their estrangement, he had much to say about her "boldness", her "impudence". In an age when women were praised for submissiveness, he must have come to see her as someone who, if given half a chance, would have dominated him and turned his life upside-down, laying to waste all its most cherished routines.

Yet there can be no doubt at all that he was, even if it was for rather a short time, greatly attracted to her, and I should say attracted in a directly physical way. For a graphic illustration of this, we have to go back to June 1777. Elizabeth was then living in lodgings in St. Stephen's parish. On the 10th Woodforde had to attend the Bishop's Visitation at the Cathedral. In the evening he went round and "drank Tea ... with Mrs Davie in St. Stephens Parish with Mrs Roupe her Mother-in-Law and a very pretty young Lady from the Boarding School - ". The entry ends like this:

> made a very late Evening of it being out after
> Supper & so engaged in Company that I could not
> leave them till near 2. in the Morning -

This is Woodforde at his most non-committal. Even in a private diary he is plainly not willing to be too informative about the way he spent some of his time. But the other people he mentions being with were present much earlier in the day, at "the Maids Head Inn not far from the Cathedral". It is unlikely, I think, that either the stepmother ("Mother-in-Law") or the girl from the boarding school would have stayed up so late, and I think the diarist is giving us a cryptic account of a tête-à-tête with Elizabeth, prolonged to a very late hour.

Two events came together to make the relations between Woodforde and Elizabeth Davie more intimate. She and her two children moved in with the Howes at Hockering, considerably nearer to Weston than Norwich.[1] And Nancy Woodforde came to live with her uncle. That made it possible for her to stay overnight at Weston Parsonage.

At first, though, it was her daughter Betsy who was the more frequent visitor. She was born in 1770 and therefore between 10 and 11 at the time that Woodforde was most friendly with her mother. Woodforde no doubt never stopped to consider the unsuitability of a child of that age to be the friend and companion of a young adult woman, for Nancy was 23. But Betsy was no ordinary teenager. She was highly precocious, "talks like a Woman", as Woodforde said, and could hold her own in adult company. She was also neurotic, a bed-wetter and, as the diarist believed, in very poor health; possibly bullied by her mother, who seems not to have known quite what to do with her, since Betsy alternated between tagging along with her from one temporary home to another, and being dumped in various schools, where she was very unhappy.

The high point of the relationship lasted for only a very short time. It began on 15 December 1780:

> Mrs Davie called here this Aft: in Mr Howes's Chaise
> with her Daughter Betsy, who is just returned from
> School and is to spend a few Days with Nancy -
> therefore Mrs Davie left her with us ....

Five days later Mrs. Davie, who seems to have gone about by herself much more than would have been thought proper for a lady at the time, arrived "on foot", stayed until the evening and then went back behind Mr. Howes' servant who had come for her. Betsy stayed on through Christmas and on New Years Day her mother arrived with the Howes and stayed three nights. On 13 January the little girl was "very ill". Woodforde gave her some "Rhubarb", his inevitable remedy for almost everything, and hoped for the best. But three days later the child appeared to be worse than ever:

> Betsy Davy very bad indeed to Day, was obliged to be
> brought down Stairs about noon, but could not sit up
> long being in such violent Pain in her right Knee &
> left foot, something like the Gout - The Pain was so
> great that she cried incessantly

The maid Betty was put to sitting up with her, while Nancy and her uncle stayed up all night playing cribbage. A message was hurriedly sent to Mrs. Davie at Hockering, and to Dr. Thorne the local physician who was also a social companion and friend. Elizabeth stayed on for over a week and did not leave until 26 January 1781. On 30 January she returned and now stayed until 13 February, when both she and Betsy went back to Hockering. It was during this time that there took place the extraordinary round of fun and games, culminating in the incident of Mrs. Davie's garter, which has contributed so much to the popular notion of Parson Woodforde as a comic, even a buffoonish figure. It may have begun, in all probability did begin, in the most innocent way, as a series of joking actions designed to cheer Betsy up, when she was just starting to feel better. But I think there can be no doubt that Woodforde enjoyed being made the willing victim in what the Victorians would have called "romps", the first of which occurred on 24 January:

> I was sadly used this Evening by Mrs Davie, Nancy and
> Betsy, had my Money picked out of my Pocket of - 0 : 11 : 6

And its sequel two days later:

> The 11/6 that was taken out of my Pocket the other Night
> Mrs Davie is to lay out on an Apron for Nancy by my Consent

On 3 February he had another trick played on him:

> Had but an indifferent Night of Sleep, Mrs Davie and
> Nancy made me up an Apple Pye Bed last Night -

Four days later there comes the notorious entry, in which may be detected the fatuous tone which men so often assume when they imagine they are proving a success with women:

> We did not get to bed till after 12. this night the
> Wind being still very high - we were as merry as we
> could be I took of Mrs Davie's Garter to night & kept it -
> I gave her my Pair of Garters & I am to have her other to Morr'

It may be remarked here that garters were worn by women below the knee, as the only possible way to keep stockings up. But even when every allowance was made it was by 18th century standards an indecorous scene enough.[2] And he never did get the other garter, for on the very next day Mr. Howes sent his chaise over, and the three females got in, while Woodforde took his horse and rode after them, to what was evidently a pre-arranged party. It was "Mrs. Howes's Birth-Day", although she was "very poorly", and perhaps in the excitement of the tussle over the garter he had forgotten all about it.

He was to go on seeing Elizabeth Davie for some years to come, but as time went on he thought less and less of her. So early as June of this year he was recording:

> Nancy being with Mrs Davie has learnt some of her
> extravagant Notions and talked very high all Day -
> I talked with her against such foolish Notions,
> which made her almost angry with me, but when we went
> to bed we were very good friends and she convinced - [3]

The reaction against succumbing to Elizabeth's charm had already set in. If she had once dreamed of being the mistress of Weston Parsonage and counted the loss of a garter not much to attain that desirable end, Elizabeth must have come to see that the dream was never going to turn into reality. After the death of her aunt and the remarriage of the widower, she moved out of Hockering Rectory and went to lodge with an "exciseman" named Matthews at Mattishall. In one entry Woodforde calls the house in which she boarded "the Parsonage House". The incumbent, John Smith, who was briefly introduced in the last chapter but is soon to emerge as a major participant in Mrs. Davie's story, was instituted in 1781 but for some time appears to have had no house of his own.[4] When he moved in, Woodforde wrote fairly dismissively that "Mr. Smith's House is small but Furniture handsome", which does not sound much like the description of a Georgian Parsonage. It is possible that the exciseman and Mrs. Davie lived in the Parsonage house in Mattishall Burgh, not required by Mr. Howes, the vicar of that parish, since he was domiciled permanently at Hockering. Woodforde, rightly or wrongly, locates her there, in an entry dated 10/6/1785.

Elizabeth still came over to Weston, but the usual arrangement was that she simply dropped Betsy off there, "to spend a few Days with Nancy".

The originally all-male Rotations had been amended and expanded to include ladies also. We see Elizabeth at Mr. Bodham's Rotation on 4 November 1783, "it being quite a Summers Day".

She was to be the indirect cause of their coming to a definitive end - but we must not anticipate. She accompanied Woodforde and Nancy on a trip to Norwich through heavy snow: - "in some Places almost up to the Horses Shoulders" - when he went to preach in the Cathedral.

Mrs. Davie may have given Woodforde up as a matrimonial prospect, but she had by no means lost sight of her main purpose in life. In the middle of news about dining out and receiving guests, the social interchange that occupies so much of the diary, we come across this:

> We were to have had Betsy Davie and Mary Roupe
> over from Mattishall to have spent this Day with us
> but Mrs Davie's going to Pulham on a Love Affair
> with a Mr Rand who went with her & came back with her
> but Matters however could not be settled then -
> Mr Rand is a Man of very good Fortune, keeps a Carriage
> and is an apothecary & has great business - a very
> sensible Man, a Bachelor about 50. Years of Age
> and lives at Snettisham near Burnham -5

He sounds perfectly unconcerned, and on the blotting paper opposite the entry, coolly added another scrap of news:

> To a Man this morning that brought a very pretty
> kind of a Monkey to shew - gave - 1 : 0
> He called it the Mongooz from Madagascar -

One of the ways in which Mrs. Davie may have been seen to transgress against the feminine ideal of decorum and passivity was that she showed a direct interest in men and pleasure in their company. Woodforde might well have observed to himself that at their very first meeting, back in 1776, Elizabeth had appeared "to be fond of" his then travelling companion Washbourne Cooke. And now Mr. Rand was in the toils.

But this was far from being all. Mr. Smith of Mattishall, who had been on formal dining-out and pleasure party-going terms with Elizabeth Davie for the past four years, now suddenly fell in love with her - or, conversely, had nourished a passion for her all this time without ever betraying it to the observant eye of the diarist. Now it all came out into the open:

I breakfasted, dined, supped & slept again at home -
At 4. this Afternoon I mounted my Mare and rode to
Mattishall where I drank Tea and stayed till 9, in
the Evening at Mrs Davy's with her, M^r and Mrs Bodham
Miss Donne, M^r Du Quesne and Nancy Woodforde - Mr Smith
was to have been there also - but went for London this
Morning very suddenly and much discomposed -
The Cause of it is this, Mrs Davy had a Letter this morning
from Mr Rand who is distracted after her, the Contents
of which were communicated to Mr Smith, which made
him almost frantic, he immediately made Mrs Davy an
Offer to marry her after his Mothers Decease, what answer
was returned I know not, but he marched from Mattishall directly.
Mrs Davy was extremely low and uneasy about it - 6

We may take the diarist's word for that last statement, although it is difficult not to suspect that the lady was in her element. With one man distracted about her, another frantic, she must surely have thought that her worries were at an end, and that all she had to do was to choose the right man for her husband.

But it did not work out like that at all. Mr. Smith's offer of marriage presumably cut Rand right out, and he disappears from sight. Elizabeth now makes only flying visits to Weston Parsonage. On 12 January 1785 she and Dr. Thorne "came galloping up to our House and they stayed and took a Family Dinner with us and then returned home again". Two days later she turned up again, she "came after Nancy in Mr Thorne's one Horse Chaise to carry her to Mattishall to spend a few Days with her there - About 1. they set of from hence, not pleased with me for not going with them". Smith was rumoured to be officially engaged to her, and seen about with her children. On 27 March Woodforde took the church service at Mattishall for Smith, as he was supposed to be ill, but "found him much better than I expected". Then on 29 May Mr. Dade the Mattishall weaver, father of Betty Dade, and of Molly who had recently died, the Parsonage maids, came over to "let me know that Mr. Smith did not come home last night". Woodforde stood in for him again, remarking that "the Service this morning" was "very long being the 29. of May", the anniversary of the Restoration. He himself had ceased to take any of these anniversary services, once he had a benefice of his own.

The catastrophe, in the theatrical sense of that term, was not long in coming. On 8 June Woodforde noted down:

Woodforde - Mrs. Davie & Mr. Smith

> ... I dreamt very much last night of M[r] Smith and M[rs] Davy
> and that connection entirely broke off - I told Nancy
> of it at breakfast - Just as we were going to sit
> down to Dinner, M[r] Matthews brought a Note to
> my Niece from M[rs] Davy - to let her know that she
> was in great distress, having rec[d] a Letter this morn'
> from M[r] Smith to break of any farther connection with
> her - his Friends being so very adverse to the Match -
> and that he was going to leave England directly -

Although he no longer consciously desired her himself, perhaps Woodforde was jealous of his fellow-cleric's apparent success, and had experienced a wish-fulfilment dream which he could not have been sorry to see so quickly translated into reality. As for Smith, if he really intended to leave England "directly" at the time he wrote his letter breaking with Elizabeth, he soon had second thoughts and stayed were he was. And, just as the 50-year old man had recently displayed all the unbridled passion of a love-lorn adolescent, so now he swung abruptly into its opposite, and set about slandering the widow most vindictively.

Elizabeth was, for the moment, crushed. She had to leave Mattishall, "on Account of the Affair being broke of between her and M[r] Smith". On 26 September 1785, she tried to borrow £20 from Woodforde, through Nancy, but "it is not in my Power", his favourite form of words for rejecting a plea of that kind. On 21 December he heard that she had been "taken exceedingly ill about the late disagreeable Affair with M[r] Smith -M[r] Ashill says that it has made her distracted, she is very unhappy". Only a week later:

> Had a very long Letter from M[r] Smith this morning con=
> =cerning M[rs] Davy and himself, wherein he lays the
> whole blame on her in a late Affair - accusing her
> for her great familiarity to one Clarkson - [7]

But even that was not enough. In February the next year Smith returned to the attack and proposed the meeting in Weston churchyard that is now well remembered:

> I stayed with him an Hour, talking over
> the Affair between him & M[rs] Davy - by which
> he made out that M[rs] Davy was as artful and

bad as any Woman could be -
It surprised me astonishingly indeed - 8

Although he wrote that down, many of his own comments on Elizabeth had been so carping and slighting, that it is difficult to believe he was so surprised as he made out. But this was the 18th century in which even quarrels had to move at the leisurely pace of the time and Woodforde was not yet ready to break off relations with the widow. In March she stayed at Weston Parsonage for several days and nights. Woodforde recorded: "Mrs Davy took on a good deal to Day, and soon after Tea this Evening she took it in her head to go to bed - I had been persuading her not to go to Mattishall", where, perhaps, she wanted to have it out with Smith. When the widow finally left: "Our Parting was rather cool than otherwise". The time of wine and roses, or of apple pie beds and garters, had gone for ever.

On 13 March 1787, after Woodforde had seen little of her in the intervening time, Elizabeth turned up again, "with a Servant with her", while he and Nancy were having breakfast. She had some tea and stayed half an hour but, the diarist added pointedly: "I did not ask her to stay & dine with us"; nor, when she talked of coming again on her way back from Dr. Thorne's, did he ask her to call. Later he added to the diary this low opinion of her:

Mrs Davy behaved as free as if nothing had been
said respecting her Character by Mr Smith -
She is grown much fatter than she was -
I never knew a Woman of greater Effrontery -

The friendship was clearly at an end. But so also were the cordial relations he had once enjoyed with Smith. His believing in the truth of what Smith had told him about Mrs. Davie did not make him like Smith any the more. For whatever reason, whether it was disgust at the way Smith had gone out of his way to attack a woman he had so recently been in love with, or whether he resented Smith's attempt to embroil him in the widow's affairs, just when he was congratulating himself on having escaped from them, he wanted no more to do with the Mattishall parson. In September 1786, travelling to Norwich, "about a mile from it I met Mr Smith of Mattishall coming from Norwich - we just spoke to each other and that was all".

The Rotations, already weakened by the defection of Mr. Howes, now ceased altogether. The friends knew that the two mutually hostile clerics could not be invited to the same party. Besides, they were all older now, less inclined to turn out and dine in each other's houses.

Woodforde and Smith continued to be enemies. Just once, in the autumn of 1795, Smith tentatively held out an olive branch. Woodforde and Nancy had just returned from what was to be the last of the Somerset holidays. Smith sent a servant to enquire after them. The diarist remarked coolly that it was strange he should do this after so long, and returned no answer.

Smith died in April 1803, less than four months after Woodforde.

CHAPTER 19

THE WALKER SCANDAL

Woodforde's avuncular affection for young Betsy Davie survived his gradual disillusionment with her mother. In the mid-1780s she was growing up, reaching an age when she would have more in common with her friend Nancy then had been possible while she was a child, however precocious. His own relationship with his niece had possibly deteriorated to some extent in the last few years. Nancy must have become more and more aware, as the years passed, that she was unlikely ever to have the chance of marrying. The remote somnolence, indeed the dullness of Weston, which had once so oppressed her brother, may have been harder for her to bear with equanimity. The innumerable games of cribbage, which she usually lost, no doubt struck her as a less and less entertaining pastime: "At Cribbage this Evening with Nancy won 0: 2: 0" - she was very sulky and sullen at loosing it, tho' not paid. She did not open her Mouth all the Even' after". The next evening: "Left off playing Cards with Nancy, she owes me 0: 4: 6". He may well have thought that the company of a young girl like Betsy was good for his niece, to give her companionship and keep her in a happy frame of mind.

We have already seen that Betsy was a frequent visitor to Weston Parsonage, noting her stay from December 1782 to February 1783. In the ensuing summer he met her at Mr. Howes', and found that "She was grown a very smart healthy young Lady", having outgrown her childish disabilities. In 1784 she came again, from 6 January to 1 March, and in the following year from 29 July to 26 August. For part of the time her mother was with her, and her brother Nunn who, following the medical tradition of the Roupes and Davies, was now apprenticed to a physician. On the day she left Woodforde wrote in his diary: "I was sorry to part with my dear Girl Betsy Davy", which sounds just like the kind of loving comment he had made about another Betsy, years ago. She was now between 15 and 16.[1]

However, although he as yet knew nothing about it, the cuckoo in the nest had already hatched. On 13 July Woodforde had recorded a particularly elaborate party in his home, for which he gave the full menu including fish and chicken which his "Farming Man" Ben Leggett was sent into Norwich to get. The guests were Thorne, his wife and daughter and a "Miss Pinching and M[r]

Thorne's Nephew an Attorney about 18 Years of Age", together with "Captain Thorne", the doctor's son, and the three Davies. Woodforde's summing up of the proceedings was that "Upon the whole we spent a very agreeable, merry and cheerful Day, and every thing conducted and done extremely well by my Servants". There was only one temporary hitch. Just as "the Ladies and Gentleman were going to drink Coffee and Tea in the Garden", the host was "sent for" to Weston House to "name" Mr. Custance's second daughter, who was born at 2 o'clock that afternoon, ten weeks premature: "the smallest Infant I think I ever had in my Arms". But after his return the guests danced and sang until supper. After a rest, dancing recommenced, and the party did not come to an end until 2 in the morning, Betsy staying behind with the Woodfordes when the other guests went away.

Thorne's nephew, Robert George Walker, to give him his full name, was the star turn of the occasion and the diarist singled him out for special praise:

.... We had many droll
Songs from Mr Walker who sings with great good humour
and very well - He is a mighty lively and agreeable
young Man indeed -

In the next few months he met Walker again, in the company of Betsy, a few times. Then, on 18 March 1787, he set down on the blotting paper:

Nancy told me this Evening
that Mrs Davy had had an
offer of Marriage made her but
not said whom - also that her
Daughter Betsy had had an Offer
also from young Walker who
was lately at Mr Thornes -
The above are very great Secrets -

The widow's latest suitor, like Mr. Rand and Mr. Smith, and even "one Clarkson", never materialised into a husband, but Walker and Betsy were now accepted as an engaged couple, and this gave him the entry to Woodforde's home that Betsy had been enjoying for years. Woodforde soon began to complain to his diary about it. After a day plagued by casual visitors and the intrusion of a stranger that Walker brought back with him, he expostulated: "My

House was more like an inn this Evening than any thing else". We wonder if he had been reminded of the play of *She Stoops to Conquer*, and cast Robert Walker in the role of its hero. It is true that he brought presents: walnuts, oysters, gin and once "a[n] old fashioned Tobacco Stopper, an Indian smoaking". But these were neutralized by his habit of going off, day after day, having announced his intention of travelling to London, only to return with some excuse before nightfall. Then there were lots of silly jokes. Walker sent to Betsy from Thetford "a Parcel in which there was nothing but a Fox's Brush or Tail". There can be few things more intensely irritating than to be constantly reminded of a joke which one did not think in the least funny the first time round; and this was still causing uproarious merriment on New Years Day 1789, six weeks later. The diarist growled disgustedly: "N.B. Fox's Brush &c made me quite sick & tired".

But much worse, to a man like Woodforde, a stickler for the conventions of civilised conduct, and who took it for granted that he would be treated with the respect owing to the dignity of his position, was young Walker's off-hand insolence:

> ... On his taking leave he went up to Nancy and
> wished her well shaking her by her hand, and
> then went to Betsy and did the same, but to
> me (altho' in the Room at the same time) he
> never said one word or took the least notice
> of me (tho' I also helped him on with his great
> Coat) after he was mounted and just going
> out of the great Gates then he said good Morning
> and that was all - very slight return for my Civilities
> towards him of late and which I did not expect.
> It hurt me very much indeed -   (9/11/1788)

Perhaps Walker encouraged his fiancée to behave in the same way. Woodforde's attitude to Betsy becomes markedly less cordial and affectionate. A censorious note appears: "She looks very poorly and is very bad again in her old Complaint the palpitation of the heart and Cramp in her head. Too much raking about has been I think the cause of her being so ill again, much beyond her Strength".

Worst of all, when the Parson looked to Nancy for sympathy, he did not get it from her. It is easy to understand, and to some extent, even to sympathise with her. By the standards of the time she was already bordering on middle age and she had, through the circumstances of Woodforde's life, been much in the company of people older than herself. There must have been something very delightful to her in the friendship of the young betrothed couple, in whose company she could imagine she was still young herself. Nancy had long forgotten how happy she had been just to live in her uncle's house, and how gratefully she had praised his generosity. He must now have represented for her little but dull tedium, endured for years, but for which she was now getting her own back. The new life she was leading was just what she wanted. It must have appeared wonderfully bold, adventurous and daring when Walker ordered dinner for three at the *Kings Head* on Christmas Day, and a chaise to take them there and back. "Very wild, unsteady and thoughtless Work", the diarist called it. But the young people took no notice of him at all.

He was being reduced to a cipher in his own household, and was far from enjoying the experience; but without altogether violating the laws of hospitality, upon which all civilized people of his time set so high a value, there was nothing he could immediately do about it. If he had been Nancy's father, he could no doubt have invoked the traditional rights of a parent, and forbidden her friends the house. But he had no such rights where Nancy was concerned, and perhaps she had even reminded him of that, at least implicitly. By 3 May 1789 his patience was wearing out. Having received a note from Nancy, who was staying with the Bodhams, that she was going on to Dr. Thorne's to meet Betsy and Walker, without asking his permission, he wrote "I am almost continually vexed and tormented by her Connection with the Davy's &c. They have almost alienated my regard for my Niece". Very ominous words, when it is recollected how completely her well-being lay in his hands, if he chose to exercize his real power, and deal with her in the drastic manner in which he had once rid himself of her brother William.

But deliverance was at hand. Either because the Parson had finally succeeded in making him feel less than popular at Weston Parsonage or, more likely, that Walker had more on his mind than just being rude to him in his own home, there now ensued a prolonged hiatus, from 20 May 1789 to 8 January 1790, in which he was not seen there.

In the diary of the last year, there had been numerous scattered references to Walker's state of health. "He looked ill indeed and Country Air advised for him" - "Mr. Walker looked very unwell ..." - "Saw Mr. Walker this morning at Norwich he looked poorly ..." - "... Looked very bad indeed and made us low". That last reference marks Walker's final appearance in the house, where "he dined, supped and spent the Evening with us", but was not invited to stay overnight. In other entries we hear that Walker had "a Cough"; and after one long coursing expedition with Woodforde it was not the Parson, approaching 50, who was "knocked up" but the young man of 21.

Robert George Walker had in fact tuberculosis, and possibly his headlong career of deception and debt was in part owing to a sense that he had not much time left. Three weeks after his last appearance at Weston Parsonage, on 28 January, the scandal broke. At a dinner party in Mr. du Quesne's house Woodforde met Mr. Custance, who showed him a letter:

> from Mr Walkers uncle of Woodstock to a Mr
> Barker, Wine Merchant, at Norwich, informing
> him that Walker was a profligate, abandoned
> young Man, and to guard Barker from trusting
> him with any more Money or any one else .....

The wine merchant had already given him £300. He had even borrowed from "among others Hylett, Hostler at the Kings Head". Woodforde learned with enraged astonishment that the young man had used his name and those of Mr. Custance and Sir Thomas Beauchamp, Mrs. Custance's brother (to whose wife there had once been some talk of Walker's being related) in attempts to borrow money. The diarist himself had been passed off as Betsy's guardian, ready to pay over her "fortune" as soon as she was married.

Although Elizabeth Davie seems not to have been implicated in any of this, it is very clear that the Parson used the Walker scandal as a pretext for putting an end to any sort of friendly relations between them. The lady also weighed in with a letter to Nancy - the first, Woodforde said, for "the last twelvemonth" - "relating almost the same bad Actions that Walker had been guilty of &c.". She asked Nancy to look out for "a house to board at in her Neighbourhood as she intends leaving Foulsham very soon". This was the last thing he wanted, and his annoyance fuelled the composition of a long diary entry making his intentions unmistakably clear: "I wish now to break of every Connection with Mrs Davy and her long train of Acquaintance". Then comes an ultimatum delivered at Nancy, with its implied threat: "I desired Nancy to drop her Acquaintance by all means - which if she does not (as their Characters are so well known) she will disoblige me as much as she possibly can do - and so &c.". Her "character" (by which of course he meant her reputation) was "not talked of so well". Then, having worked himself up into a mood ready for vigorous denunciation, he let fly:

Betsys Character is entirely ruined by her indiscreet
ways, many times out by themselves, suffered
herself to go for his Wife at public Places &c. -
Walker even boasts (as people say) of his behaviour
to Betsy & says the worst of things of her -
he now proves to be one of the most profligate,
wicked, artful, ungrateful and deceiving
Wretches I ever heard of - I never liked him -
I believe both Mother Davy & Daughter also to be very
cunning, close and not without much Art
I never wish to meet them again at my House none of the 3. (2)

And, indeed, two of the three he never did meet again. As for
Robert George Walker, his course was run. On 27 April his uncle
Dr. Thorne, who also, with all his family found himself banished
until Woodforde's last years, when the Parson's increasing anxiety
about the state of his health led to something of a reconciliation,
wrote to say that Walker had died and asking for the burial to take
place two days later. Flamboyant to the last, he arrived in "a Hearse
with 4. Horses", but "there was not the least Description on the
Coffin or any kind of Ornament, quite plain uncoloured".3

The diarist never saw Mrs. Davie again. Nothing is heard of
Betsy, apart from an unfounded rumour that she was to marry the
brewer's son at Reepham, until 1800, when she turned up
accompanied by her husband Joseph Shrimpton and little boy.
Woodforde said he was "hurried" at her sudden appearance, but it
was a complaint he often made, at this late stage of his life. The
husband was "a Dissenter, I believe a Presbyterian, he is rather plain
and I should take him to be about 35. Years old". Betsy looked
"remarkably well & of good Spirits". It is interesting that Betsy was
in the district to see Dr. Thorne, who had been Walker's relation, not
hers.

Nancy submitted at once, as indeed she had no option but to do.
The overriding factor in her case was that she was a poor relation,
and her uncle represented her only prospect of a life spent in
reasonable comfort. In the only one of her letters written in this
period to have survived, addressed to her aunt Melleora, John
Woodforde's wife, she wrote sadly: "We were lately invited to dine at
Dr. Thorne's but uncle would not go or let me. He does not like
them on account of the Davies. This is between you and I. I never
hear anything of Davies". Many of the Woodforde family wrote
private diaries, but Nancy limited her efforts in this direction to odd
jottings in the annual pocket diaries of the "Lady's Pocket

Companion" type, except in one year, 1792, when she procured a large notebook in which she kept a real diary, challenging comparison with that of her uncle.

The two references in it to Mrs. Davie and her daughter show that Nancy was quite a resilient sort of girl, able to repair the strained but by no means broken relationship with the Parson. The tone of both is so unlike that of the passage just quoted that they may be taken either as showing that she had quite spontaneously come round to her uncle's point of view or, at least, that she was anxious not to put herself in the wrong by annoying him again. The first was written on 7 January: "Mr. Thorne called yesterday to invite me to meet Betsy Davie but that I shall not do. I have had trouble enough about her and her mother too". The second and last is part of a long entry dated 12 April: "Mr. and Mrs. Thorne called whilst I was at Weston House but did not come in. They came to invite me to spend a few days with them. Betsy Davie being there my uncle made some excuse for my not going. I wish they would never invite me to meet the Davies for I have had trouble enough about them".

Her small rebellion was over.

CHAPTER 20

MR. & MRS. JEANS
A CHEQUERED FRIENDSHIP

As we have seen, Woodforde's early friends in Norfolk were all people whose hospitality drew the diarist into their circle and made him a part of it. Thomas Jeans and his wife Mary, on the other hand, were newcomers, who arrived only after Woodforde had been established in the district for almost a decade. As friends and neighbours, they started off with much in common: both men of the West country, Wykehamists and ex Fellows of New College, but it must be said that Mr. Jeans never became really integrated with the clerical society around him. This may be because Woodforde did not try so hard as he might have done to welcome him, or because Jeans was less adaptable than his fellow-cleric, one possible explanation not excluding the other.

Thomas Jeans was born at Christchurch, Hampshire, and admitted to Winchester in 1763. A very bright pupil, he reached the top Sixth class by 1766. After taking the Winchester Election for the second time in 1767, the year in which he was "Prefect of Hall" and chosen to deliver the famous oration "Ad Portas", which greeted the Examiners from Oxford, he was given 13th place on the "Roll ad Oxon" and a few weeks later provisionally matriculated from Merton. At the Election of the following year he romped home in third place, directly after the two "Founders Kin" candidates, which made his acceptance by New College virtually assured. He became a Scholar on 15 April 1769, was B.A. 1773, M.A. 1776 and, many years later, was made Bachelor and Doctor of Divinity on the same day in 1817.[1]

Woodforde and Jeans knew each other as fellow-collegians before they met in Norfolk, but not very well. Jeans was at one time the sub-tenant of the rooms retained by the diarist during his 10-year absence from college, at the rate of £5 a year. But this would have been arranged for them by others without there being any occasion for them to meet, and a year's rent paid on 22 December 1773, after Woodforde had gone back into residence, was collected by a go-between. Two days before, he had been made Sub-Warden, and it was in this capacity, on 11 May 1774, that he "proposed two Testimoniums in the "Anti-Chapel"; one of which was for Jeans, who was taking Priest's Orders. On 8 June Woodforde invited him to breakfast in his rooms - but after that he disappears from the diary, and no more is heard of him for ten years.

The incumbents of the 36 tied livings of New College were life-tenants who, once appointed, were very little troubled by the college, as indeed Woodforde's diary abundantly proves. The only supervision ever exercised, and at long intervals, was through the tour of inspection, or "Progress", as it was called. In 1784 it was the turn of the benefices in Norfolk. Woodforde should have been at Weston to receive the four man party, but it was the last day of the County Parliamentary Election, and he was in Norwich for it. Instead of going back to let his parish be inspected, he took the New College people on a sightseeing trip round the city and then left them without ceremony in the evening to join some friends of his own at the theatre, where they were playing *The School for Scandal*. Next day the college party left. Accompanying the Warden and Steward were two "outriders". One of them on this occasion was Thomas Jeans.[2]

Not far from Weston Longville, the two consolidated parishes of Great and Little Witchingham, tied livings held by New College, were in the hands of Woodforde's aristocratic friend Henry Bathurst. He was a total absentee, and in the 10 years during which he held the livings is positively known to have been in the county only twice, and at neither time was it for the purpose of visiting his parish. The impoverished curate Wilson carried out the ordinary parochial obligations, although even he did not live there. Bathurst's tithes were collected for him by Mr. Francis, an attorney who looked after the legal business concerned with New College properties in Norfolk; but when he found that he was being charged 1/6d. in the £ for this, he asked Woodforde to do it instead for nothing. The diarist not only agreed, but also attended all the tithe audit dinners, something he by no means looked forward to even in his own parish. He then went to Norwich with his bag of coins, exchanged them for negotiable bank bills at Kerrison's bank, and sent the proceeds to Oxford, where Bathurst was living the comfortable and undemanding life of a canon of Christ Church. [3]

In 1785 Bathurst, having snapped up a rich prebend in the diocese of Durham and resumed a sinecure in his own part of the country, gave up the Norfolk cures, the Witchinghams and St. John Maddermarket in Norwich. The New College records show that Thomas Jeans was presented to the livings on 22 December. Early in the next year - 4 February 1786 - the diarist received a letter from him "informing me that he had accepted the Witchinghams".

Mr. Jeans was one of a minority of newly beneficed priests who did not avail himself of the "Year of Grace" allowed by the college.

A *North East Prospect of the New THEATRE in Norwich.*

T.R. delin 1758.

North-East prospect of Norwich Theatre, 1758. The theatre as Woodforde would have known it, before it was rebuilt in the early years of the nineteenth century

The reason was that he wanted to marry; and he lost no time in taking the step.

"Jeanes was only married last Thursday in London, she is very young it is said". In fact, the new Mrs. Jeans was a girl of 19, and we know, again from Woodforde, her exact age; she was born on 23/6/1767. Her maiden name was Springer, and she came from Lyndhurst in the New Forest. Her Christian name was Mary.

Woodforde did what he probably thought was expected of him to make the newlyweds feel at home. He invited them, together with Mrs. Jeans' aunt, "a Miss Short ab^t 30. Years of Age", who had travelled to Norfolk with them as the custom then was, to Weston Parsonage (25 April), and met them in Norwich, where they were introduced to the Custances and Mr. du Quesne. Having done all this, however, he and Nancy went off on one of their Somerset holidays and did not return until October. He found the Jeans still putting up at the inn at Lenwade Bridge where he had left them.

Parishes where the nominal incumbent was an absentee, and in which parochial affairs were in the hands of an ill-paid curate, were seldom in good shape. The roof of the Parsonage House at Great Witchingham had fallen in and the tenant disappeared. It might be thought that the cost of repairing the house and possibly the erection of new outbuildings would have been met by New College, the landlord and "lay rector". This was far from being the case. The incumbent, not the college, had the legal responsibility of keeping the premises in good repair.

On 7 October Jeans took out a mortgage, through Mr. Francis, by the terms of which he borrowed the large sum of £400 from New College, for the repayment of which he pledged the "temporalities" of his cure. These mortgages were authorised by the 'Clergy Residences Repair Act' 17 Geo. III, cap. 53, the first clause of which is headed: "Incumbent of any ecclesiastical living where is no proper house, etc. may borrow money to build one, etc.". The transaction required the intermediary of a third person who was far more than a mere guarantor of repayment. The snarled-up legal terminology of this Act is far from easy to decipher, but it appears to say that this nominated third person received the loan on behalf of the borrower, and it was he who had to see that the work was properly carried out. If the borrower defaulted on the loan, the third person was liable to pay double the sum borrowed.

There is no difficulty about identifying the person who guaranteed repayment of the Jeans mortgage, for we know that it was James Woodforde. The mortgage itself has survived, and is among the archives of New College. It bears an endorsement in the following terms:

Received this Day and year first within
written on the within named Warden and
Scholars the within mentioned Sum of
Four Hundred pounds being the   ) £400
consideration Money within specified to
be paid by them to me pursuant to the
Directions of the within mentioned Act

Witness my Hand Js. Woodforde
Witnesses
A. M. Woodforde
Brett Scurll

This would seem a plain enough record of a transaction; but in reality it is highly mysterious when compared with the following entry in the diary, dated 27 October:

I took a ride & called on M^r & Mrs Jeanes
this morn at Witchingham, saw their new
building, only Offices, which I think are
too many & too great for only a private
Clergyman, especially for the Dairy -

I think this shows that Woodforde had not previously seen the work being done at Witchingham and in particular could have had no hand in supervision of that work. There is at least a partial confirmation of the passage in the form of a pencilled ground plan of Witchingham Vicarage, also at New College. The neatly drawn sketch reveals that only part of the house was rebuilt, when a second parlour, with a bow window and "parlour chamber" above, were broken out. The outbuildings shown are certainly numerous, take up a lot of space and are mostly marked as new.

But when did Woodforde receive this money? The date on the mortgage is 7 October 1786, presumably the day on which the document was signed by Mr. Jeans, who affixed to it a very magnificent impression of his seal in red wax, still as fresh and unbroken as though it had been put on no more than a few hours ago. That day Woodforde spent in London, on his way back from the West Country. The fact that the servant as well as Nancy witnessed his signing of the endorsement goes a long way towards proving that it must have been done at Weston Parsonage. Possibly

Robert Francis the lawyer or someone authorised by him appeared there with the document and the money. But there is no trace in the diary of anyone from Norwich calling about that time. And when did the diarist, if indeed he took receipt of the money, hand it over to Jeans? The day after Mrs. Jeans had stayed at Weston overnight, that is, on 19 October, her husband arrived to pick her up. That would seem as good a time as any. But Woodforde makes no mention in his entry for that day, of any financial matters, although he gives what they had for dinner, and a number of trivial details. Indeed, and this is the most bafflingly mysterious thing about the entire affair, from first to last he makes no mention of the Jeans mortgage, in which the other evidence appears to show him as so intimately concerned. The only unmistakable fact, in the final outcome, is that it was with this cash that Jeans embarked on his over-ambitious building programme, and thereby very likely sowed the seeds of his later financial trouble, which was at the last to drive him and his family out of Norfolk altogether.[4]

On 3 November, the diarist wrote:

> ... Sent M[r] and M[rs] Jeans a large sack of
> Apples (Beefans) a couple of Pigeons and
> a very fine fat Duck ready for the Spit
> to them at their Parsonage at Witchingham,
> they being very lately got in there with
> almost every inconvenience, they were highly
> pleased with the above -

When next month Mr. and Mrs. Jeans spent a night at Weston, Woodforde thought that "M[rs] Jeanes did not look so well as she did. Has been much worried by Change of Servants, &c.". Also - a characteristic Woodforde aside - "M[r] Jeanes's Servant Lad G. England seems fonder of Kitchen Fire than any work". In January 1787, as Nancy reported to her uncle after a visit to Witchingham, Mrs. Jeans looked pale, but then she was now "far advanced with Child". He was prepared in these early days to make every allowance for the social deficiencies of the couple. Even a very poor dinner at Witchingham on 9 February was not criticised with the acerbity he usually reserved for his friends' culinary failures. "I cannot say that I made a very good dinner but met with a very friendly and warm Reception", was his mild comment.

However, he very soon realised that Jeans was hardly the man to give anything for nothing. Four days later he sent over a present of "a small salt Fish and some Oysters" (not then the expensive luxury they have become in our time), with a note to say that he and his wife had to go to London "on some important Family Matters where he is to meet his Wife's Mother and will be absent 2. or 3. Sundays". Woodforde was asked to take the church services for him until his return.

On 4 March the diarist rode over for the third successive time to take the service at Great Witchingham. It was a terrible day, with a huge blustering gale. When he arrived, he felt no more at his ease than when he had been out on the open road.

> ... Very cold and uncomfortable in Mr Jeanes's
> House - nothing but a cold Kitchen to set in
> & little Fire - The Stable where my Horses
> stood unroofed, and as the Wind was high,
> was afraid that the high Ends of it would
> be blown down on the Horses -

But what, we ask ourselves at this point in the narrative, had become of the famous "Offices", which quite recently Woodforde had declared too luxurious for Jeans' station in life? Had Mr. Jeans perhaps applied some of the £400 from New College to other purposes of his own, and left the building programme suspended in the air?

Worse still, Jeans' servant Jeremiah Allden had received a letter from him, which the diarist was given to read. "Not a word about his returning or Comp^ts after anyone". A fortnight later and Woodforde, much against his will, was carrying on at Witchingham. Jeans, he now learned, had sent for "his Stallion", and Jeremiah had gone off riding the beast. It was 30 March before the couple returned. They called in at Weston Parsonage on the way home, stayed an hour and "refreshed themselves with some cold roast Beef & Porter &c.". They had "a close Carriage and a pair of black Horses to go in the same". Mr. Jeans was riding his stallion, because he had been unable to get the price asked for the animal in London.

Woodforde was now, perhaps, beginning to "see through" Jeans; but they remained on quite friendly terms. On 17 April the Jeans couple had been invited to the diarist's Rotation dinner. But if this were a move designed to have Jeans accepted as a member of the Club himself, it failed since none of the others followed Woodforde's lead. About this time the diarist sent over many presents to Witchingham, mainly of garden vegetables and fruit.

On 9 July Mrs. Jeans was "brought to bed of a Daughter", early in the morning, and her husband came over to Weston with the news. The first-born child was named Mary, after her mother. When on 14 July Woodforde and his niece called: "We did not see Mrs Jeanes at Witchingham (she being in the Straw) or her Mother - only Mr Jeanes". The saying is found in *The Oxford Book of English Proverbs*. The diarist wrote of Mrs. Jeans' mother Mrs. Springer, that "she has been a fine Woman".

The following year, 1788, saw the high water mark of the friendship between the two parsons. That summer the Jeans must have decided that the time had come for them to show that they had settled in at Witchingham. They invited all their nearest relatives on both sides to stay with them. Mrs. Jeans' brother Charles was pronounced at first, "a very modest young Man about 17. or 18. yrs. in some branch of Trade belonging to the India House" - which probably means that he was employed in the London Head Office of the great East India Company, in Leadenhall Street. Later he was to lose favour, and it was of him that Nancy made her now famous remark that she "had never seen so poor a Honey". Mr. Jeans' father, from Christchurch, made an instantaneous good impression, being called "a mighty cheerful good natured plain downright Man" (11/6/1788), and "all life and good nature" (21/6/1788), while his wife is described less glowingly as "a meek kind of a Woman, rather coarse". Since Mrs. Springer had been in Norfolk for the birth of her granddaughter the previous year, she had married again, Her new husband was "a Man of Fortune in Hampshire and keeps Horses". He became the subject of one of the diarist's most lively vignette portraits: "Mr Locke a very neat well looking old Gentleman, and Country Esq. fond of hunting, keeps 16. fox Hounds, talks plain Hampshire and delights also in farming".

All these people, together with Parson Woodforde, Nancy and Betsy Davie, Mr. du Quesne and the Reepham Priest with his wife and daughter, assembled for the great housewarming party on 11 June 1788. It is no wonder that the diarist complained about it: "We were much crowded at Table, rather unpleasant". When a friend of Jeans named Major, later Colonel Lloyd, of the Norfolk militia, and his two eldest daughters joined the party for tea, it "made the whole Company consist of 18. in Number". For once he enjoyed a meal served up in that house, calling it "a most excellent Dinner", and "Miss Kitty Lloyd sang delightfully indeed". But his final comment was non-committal: "Upon the whole we spent a very agreeable Day".

The two clerics were never again to be so friendly. Indeed, the elements of dissolution were already there. The more Woodforde saw of the Jeans couple, the more he found to dislike, complain of and criticize about their ways. In brief, the Jeans "showed off". Yet, in spite of their pretentious ways they were seriously deficient in the politeness and good breeding so prized in that society. Their vulgarity was expressed in extravagances of dress and behaviour upon which the diarist never failed to comment disapprovingly. "Mr Jeanes was in a very frenchyfied black silk Coat, Waistcoat and Breeches with a Chappeau de brache under his left Arm" (22/8/1787): "M^r & Mrs Jeanes were at M^r Du Quesnes and dressed in high Style indeed" (27/11/1787): "Mrs Jeanes behaved with very much Affectation, talked exceeding high" (17/2/1790) - the last two reported by Nancy: "Mrs Jeans very affected, & talked very consequential" (4/6/1793). And, possibly because Woodforde himself, an outsider in Norfolk, had become very touchy and tended to stand on his dignity, little storms in teacups were always liable to blow up. On 20 November 1789 the Jeans couple, asked to stay to dinner at Weston, refused: "I asked them also to dine with us on Tuesday next to meet Mr du Quesne, but Mrs Jeans said it was inconvenient, tho' she had the assurance to invite us on the Wednesday following without once offering to send their Carriage for the Ladies. We declined accepting the Invitation immediately".

On 29 November the diarist wrote: "Immediately on my return home found a Note from Mr Jeans to invite us to Dinner on Tuesday next without offering his Chaise. I sent a verbal Message by his Servant that we could not wait on him, it being my Tithe Audit Day, which very likely they knew". This was precisely the kind of behaviour that had led him to " give it to" the last Mrs. Howes and caused a total breach between the two households. And he had already met with much "Affectation" from Mrs. Davie.

But the Jeans pair also on occasion displayed some ungenerous behaviour. Like many people given to ostentation and personal display, they could be mean about the payment of trifling sums:

Mr Jeans's Cousin William called on us
this morning, and stayed about half an hour
here - His chief business I find was to in=
= quire about the price of washing things, our
Neighbour Downing having washed some things
for some French people now at Mr Jeans's
Mrs Jeans thinking that she charged too much -
but as we wash all our things at home, could
not say any thing about it. The whole was
but a trifle and not worth making words
about, especially as the poor Woman

had a Walk of 6. Miles to carry the things
home after washing them - The Woman wanted
her money for them when she carried them
back, but she was not then paid and has
not from thence to this time - 5

The "French people" in this entry must have been emigrés, a
reminder of the changes brought about by the Revolution. They
were presumably lodgers at the house of Mr Jeans, a sign of his
comparative penury. He also at different times took and boarded
pupils; the cousin William was there "to learn Norfolk farming". A
young woman, the sister of the Kitty Lloyd we heard singing at the
party, was also there for a time. Her position in the household seems
to have been a fairly ambiguous one, since she told Nancy that she
"could not endure being there, as she is treated by them like almost
unto a Servant, and ordered about so". This revelation was made
while Nancy was staying at Witchingham Parsonage for the usual
"few days". When the Parson's niece returned home, "she gave me a
worse description than ever of the bad management in Mr Jeans's
House and dirtier than ever."

After Mary, born as we saw in July 1787, Mrs. Jeans gave birth
to two more daughters in Norfolk, Charlotte and Caroline. The
diarist was no longer on such terms with the Jeans that he was
moved to record the birth of their children, but the Great
Witchingham register states that "Charlotte Daughter of Thomas
Jeans vicar and Mary his Wife (late Springer, Spinster) was born and
privately baptised 31st Dec 1789". On 9 July Woodforde sent to Mrs
Jeans "for her little puny Daughter who is now weaning, a spring
Chicken by Briton". The child died, aged two years, on 11 January
1792 (burial notice dated 14 January), and the diarist wrote: "It is I
doubt not a happy Change for her, as she never was well from her
birth ... Mrs Jeans paid the greatest Attention and acted the part of
the kindest of Mothers to her always". This sounds like the most
generous remark he ever made about Mary Jeans; but when we
recollect his constant charge that she was "affected", the seemingly
innocent comment might conceivably have a hidden sting.

The third daughter, Caroline, was born on 7 April of the same
year. She was still a baby when that series of happenings took place
which forms one of the most vivid, and at the same time most
amusing episodes in the diary. Jeans asked another favour. He
proposed to leave his whole family at Weston Parsonage while he
went to London "for a few days". Unaccountably Woodforde
consented.

Woodforde - Mr. & Mrs. Jeans: A chequered friendship

On 1 November 1792 Jeans, losing no time, was knocking on the door before the diarist was up, although he invariably rose early and this morning was downstairs before 8 a.m. Then "Mr Priests Chariot from Reepham with Miss Mary Priest in it, and with her Mrs Jeans and her two Daughters Mary and Caroline with their Nurse Susan Harrison" all made their appearance. They had breakfast upon "Tea and Toast", a rare illusion in the diary to the composition of that little noticed meal. If this were all that was taken until dinner around 2 o'clock in the afternoon, it is easy to understand why the Parson used to enjoy his dinner with the best. Just now, he was laid up with the "Gout". As he wrote next day: "My right Foot much worse this Morning, can scarce walk at all on it".

The children were a nuisance from the first. On the first night the baby "was ill about ten o'clock at Night, vomited a great deal, after that had a very small dose of Rhubarb and went to sleep". One can imagine the exhausted peace that fell upon the household when all was quiet at last. Then Nancy and Mrs. Jeans both came down with heavy colds. "Fires every day and all day, in the Study, great Parlour and Chamber over the Parlour", the Parson wrote gloomily, thinking of his coal bills. On 9 November he entered in the diary:

> ... Dinner to Day hash-mutton and Suet
> Pudding - Mutton Stakes and a roast Goose
> &c. - no tidings of Mr Jeans as yet, how
> long they stay with us cannot tell he
> only begged to be taken in for 3. or 4.
> Days and now it is more than a week - the
> Children particularly the smallest very
> great trouble, continually fire above
> Stairs, washing &c. -

Next day the wanderer returned, but his behaviour offended Woodforde so much, that in the diary his heartfelt relief at being rid of the Jeans family is relegated to the end of a long passage:

> As my Servant Lad, Billy Downing, was
> going to Lenwade Bridge after some flour
> for the House - he saw Mr Jeans with a
> young Lady in a Post Chaise, going to
> Witchingham, and the Chaise went thro' our
> Parish - Mr Jeans asked him if his Wife
> were gone home, to which the Boy answered

no - however, they went on for Witchingham
Parsonage, and about 3. o'clock or rather
after a Note came for Mrs Jeans from Mr.
Jeans with a Servant Boy and a little
Cart, to convey Mrs Jeans and the Children
home - accordingly as soon as they had all
dined, Mrs Jeans with her two Children got
into the Cart, and went for Witchingham -
the nurse, Susannah Harrison was sent for
afterwards by the same Convenience - tho'
rather dark when she went - I cannot say
but it was by no means genteel in Mr Jeans
to go thro' the Parish and not call - That
they are gone neither myself or Niece much
lament, as the Children gave much un=
=necessary Trouble, and Mrs Jeans too affected -

One must make allowance here for the testiness of the lifelong
bachelor who sees his cherished routines upset, and the spinster
whose maternal feelings never had a chance to develop. But neither
the Jeans children nor any others ever stayed at Weston Parsonage
overnight again, in the Parson's lifetime.

The incident with the children served to mark a further stage in
the slow cooling of friendship between the two clerics. The round of
mutual hospitality continued as before, but at longer intervals. On 5
March 1793 Woodforde and Nancy drove in the "little Curricle" to
pay a morning visit on the Jeans at Witchingham, where they found
Mrs. Jeans and "her Cousin, a Miss Mist out of the West Country ...
about 17, very delicate and pleasing". Two months later, on 6 July,
returning home from church where he had been to conduct a
wedding, he found the Jeans couple and Miss Mist again: "they
came to take a Family Dinner with us, but we were engaged out".
Woodforde always used this term to denote an occasion when guests
called uninvited, to take "pot luck", as we should say. This is
evidence that the two parsons were on at least intermittently good
terms   so late as 1793, although Woodforde sometimes felt that his
neighbours' hospitality was forced on him:

After Breakfast I drove Nancy over to
Witchingham being fine Morn' to Mrs Jeans's
and spent the remaining part of the Morn'
with him and his Wife. We met Mr Jeans in

our Parish coming to us. Mrs Jeans is far
advanced in Pregnancy. We stayed there till
almost 2. o'clock, they pressed us much to
dine with them, but there being no Moon and
likewise some Rain falling we could not, but
borrowed an Umbrella and Mr Jeans's french
Cloke for Nancy & returned home by three
o'clock. It rained tho' very gently all the
way. Dinner to Day Knuckle of Veal boiled
& Pigs face and neck of Pork roasted with
apple sauce.
Mrs Jeans was pressing for us
to dine with them more than was agreeable.
It was rather beyond the line of being
pleasing - 6

A return morning visit soon after had Mrs. Jeans bringing along
the two children and the nursemaid. It was now Mrs. Jeans's turn to
refuse dinner, because there was no moon. Her first son arrived on 6
December. There is again no mention of this event in Woodforde's
diary. Another hiatus intervenes, until on 24 March 1794
Woodforde was trying out a new horse in his "curricle", in place of
Rodney who had gone blind. He drove with Nancy to Witchingham,
where Mr. and Mrs. Jeans were at home and "very glad to see us".
But after that they did not meet again until 26 May, when uncle and
niece made a "Family Dinner" at Witchingham upon "a comical
gooseberry Pudding, some very indifferent Mutton Stakes, the best
part of a Rump of Beef and plenty of Garden Stuff". There is no
further mention of the Jeans until 25 August, when Woodforde and
Nancy ate "a very genteel Dinner" at Hungate Lodge, home of his
rich curate Mr. Corbould. "M^r^ and Mrs Jeans drove furiously by
our House" - I suppose to avoid picking up the Woodfordes. During
the meal "Mrs Jeans took Miss Woodforde up pretty sharply, but
Nancy silenced her very soon". One would give much for a record
of this lost repartee.

On 7 October this year there was a confirmation service at
Reepham, which was presided over by the young and recently
appointed bishop, Charles Manners-Sutton. But first there was
breakfast at Mr. Jeans's home, to which Woodforde and Nancy were
invited. It was an elaborate as one would expect from an occasion
of the kind and people so ambitious socially as the Jeans couple.
"We had for breakfast, Chocolate, green & brown Tea, hot Rolls,
dried Toast, Bread & Butter, Tongue and ham grated very small".

This meeting appears to have led to a temporary revival of social relations between the two parsons. On another church occasion, the archdeacon's Visitation held at Reepham, on 13 October, Woodforde left Nancy to spend the day with Mrs. Jeans before driving on there. Twice, in October and November, Nancy stayed a night at Witchingham. On the first occasion, Mrs. Jeans had taken her to St. Faith's Fair in Norwich. On 23 December the diarist for the last time served Great Witchingham, Mr. Jeans having gone to London. "Mrs Jeans was very civil and obliged to me. It was a cold, damp, disagreeable Day, but no rain".

Next year, however, although various comments were made about the Jeans couple, no meetings are recorded for the first four months. On 1 May 1795 Mrs. Jeans was in trouble with the diarist, when he called on her husband and she failed to put in an appearance, "which I think is very ungenteel indeed". Perhaps Mrs. Jeans, that showy, exhibitionistic woman, whom he had so often criticised for pushing herself into notice, was invisible because of something the Woodfordes had done, or omitted to do. On 25 May he noted without comment that Jeans, by himself, had been among his guests at a fairly large party held that day.

And now a very long silence intervenes, which suggests that relations between the two households had wholly broken down, although there is no mention of a quarrel in the diary. The Witchingham register tells us that on 1 August Mrs. Jeans had her second son and fifth child, the last of her children to be born in Norfolk. He was named John Locke, after his step-grandfather, the foxhunting man of Hampshire.

On 14 June 1796 Woodforde set down this terse remark:

> ... it is reported that M^r and Mrs Jeans
> are going to leave Witchingham for 3. Years
> or so - We have not seen M^r or Mrs Jeans for
> 12. months past -

There is a number of explanations to account for Jeans's decision to leave Norfolk. In the first place, he was quite evidently no countryman. His preference was for the town, as we can see by his later residence in places in Surrey and Middlesex, within easy reach of the capital.

But it is clear that he was also pressed for money. He was probably in debt, and perhaps in actual danger of arrest, like the unfortunate Mr. Wilson.

A third reason was that he was not a tactful man, and had no doubt made enemies locally. One such example we know of, which demands a brief explanation. Woodforde had in his parish a holding of what he called "College Land", for which he paid £16 a year (later £17) as sub-tenant from the Le Neve family, who themselves held it from New College together with a much larger amount of land, with a high rental value, in Witchingham parish. The last Le Neve in the male line died in the 1760's, and left the tenancies to his two daughters, who sold them in 1790 to their illegitimate half-brother, Peter Foster the miller of Lenwade. On Jeans' first coming to the parish, he and Foster were on friendly terms. In 1786 Foster's wife had borne twin daughters, one of whom was christened "Mary Jeans". But for whatever reason (and we have insufficient evidence to be able to speculate about it) Jeans quarrelled with the miller, who then told Woodforde about it:

> ... M^r and Mrs Foster of Lenwade Bridge
> called on us this morning. They came to
> talk with us about the behaviour they have
> received from Mr Jeanes since M^r
> Forster has purchased the College Estate
> at Witchingham of the Le Neve's.
> That Mr Jeanes behaved very strangely to him and
> his Wife on Sunday last at Church and after
> Mr Jeanes in such a violent Passion with
> Mr Foster ... 7

It was probably unwise of Jeans to have antagonised Foster. He was an outsider, a "foreigner", while the miller, whose paternity was acknowledged and who was also known as "Peter Le Neve", was no doubt looked upon by the Witchingham folk as one of their own. In 1794 Foster was shocked at the amount of the "fine" for the renewal of his lease imposed by the college, and in this the diarist plainly saw the hand of Jeans, who was "so inveterate against him, that he has been the chief Actor in it". In one of the letters written to Warden Gauntlett (Oglander's successor) years later, Jeans was to say that his devotion to the interests of the college had made him unpopular at Witchingham and enforced his departure. One way and another, there can be no doubt that Jeans had made the place too hot to hold him.

Between June and October 1796 Woodforde saw Mary Jeanes just twice. He missed one opportunity, when she staged a tea party "at John Bakers near Weston House ... the Design is to see Weston House and Mrs Jeans to give Coffee and Tea afterwards ... Mrs Jeans very coolly last Saturday invited us but as they have behaved very so, so, to us, did not go. Mr. Corbould said that it was all Hurry & bustle &c. in a small Room, bricked Floor - with a Carpet". The entry for the previous Saturday, on the blotting paper as though put down by an afterthought, merely says that "Mr Jeans called at the outer Gate this morning but would come no further".

On 31 August the Parson dined with the Corboulds at Hungate Lodge. Mrs. Jeans was there. She was, he commented sourly, more affected than ever. "We have not been in Company with her for near Eighteen Months". He was also scathing about her travelling arrangements: "We all returned to our respective Houses, all in two wheel Carriages - five in all. Mrs Jeans had three in hers, and a little grey Horse in it, about the size of a Calf". The "little shabby Cart and poor little grey Horse" also appear in an account, nearly a week later, of the last time he actually met Mary Jeans. It seems a far cry from the two "fine black horses" to pull the Jeans carriage, and the stallion; and would have meant a great deal in an epoch to which horses had as high a status value as the varieties of motor car have in ours.

On 29 September "Mr & Mrs Jeans with young Ward drove by our Gate between two and three in the Afternoon, but did not stop to call or enquire. They had no servant". Woodforde's "young Ward" was a pupil, the son of Lord Dudley and Ward. The following day Woodforde was at Reepham to attend "the Generals", i.e. the meeting of the general council of the archdeaconry. Calling on Mr. Priest, he saw Jeans with the pupil, and added pointedly that the latter was not going to attend the meeting but would conduct his pupil round Blickling Hall instead.

And so to the final departure:

> ... Mr and Mrs Jeans and Family have left
> their house at Witchingham and gone to
> reside in London - They have let their house
> ready furnished to the Revd. M. Beevor,
> Son of Mr James Beevor of Norwich

No doubt Woodforde thought he had seen the last of Mr. Jeans. But, rather like Betsy Davie, he was to return for a fleeting visit in the diarist's last year. This came about because of Augustus Beevor, who had not only taken over Mr. Jeans's house but also assumed the role of curate and looked after the two parishes. In 1801 he got into trouble of a kind which was growing rare by that date. He fell out with an army officer named Payne and rashly challenged him to a duel. The authorities were not having this, and threw him into the

Woodforde - Mr. & Mrs. Jeans: A chequered friendship

King's Bench prison "and is to continue there some time".[8] This contretemps left the Witchinghams unprovided for, and led perforce to the temporary return to Norfolk of Mr. Jeans. Woodforde heard the news on 9 May. Jeans made no immediate effort to get in touch, but near the end of the next month, 22 September, he turned up at Weston. He "looked remarkably healthy and well", so Woodforde said, but "would take no refreshment with us".

There is a little postscript to this scene. Early next year Mr. Foster called about the annual flour bill and other matters. The diarist was now in a very bad way. "Sitting so long at one time with Mr Foster this morning and in one place made me almost at last unable to move". A sign perhaps of the change that had come over him is that he forgot to ask the miller for a receipt for the money he had paid. One piece of information, however, did arouse sufficient interest for him to remember it and note it down afterwards in the diary:

> ... Mr Foster told me that Mr Jeans of
> Witchingham was in the Kings Bench -

This was, of course, a debtor's prison as well as a place of confinement for persons awaiting trial on criminal charges. As the story was told to Woodforde, it was merely a rumour, which he could have had no means of testing for its veracity. It must also have been the sort of tale which the miller, with memories of the quarrel he had had with Jeans, where the Witchingham parson had been the aggressor, would have taken a pleasure in disseminating. In fact when I searched through the prison Committal books and Abstract of Committals for 1800 and early 1802 there was no trace of Jeans' name. Taking into account the diarist's state of health, we might even suspect that Foster had been merely talking about the Beevor case of the previous year, which had occurred in Mr. Jeans' parish, and that Woodforde had confused the two in his mind.

Woodforde was, by then, near his end; but Jeans had a very long life, and much lay before him which lies outside the confines of this book. He successfully fended off the efforts of one Bishop of Norwich to make him go back and reside in Norfolk (significantly, with the advent of the easy-going Bathurst, his former fellow-collegian at Oxford, he was left alone), and out of the 50 years in which he held the benefices, he kept them for 39 on a strictly non-resident basis. On the other hand, his repeated pleas either to be given an additional living or to be allowed to exchange those he had for more lucrative ones fell on deaf ears at New College. Most remarkable of all were his adventures as Head Master of the charity school at Egham, Surrey, where the way he rigged everything to his own satisfaction and advantage brought down on his employers, the Coopers' Company, a long law action which cost them a lot of money, but almost inconceivably allowed him to keep his job. [9]

He died on 11 February 1835, a time when his kind of career had become almost legendary.

CHAPTER 21

SERVANTS AND SERVANT PROBLEMS

In view of their vast numbers and social and economic importance, it is surprising that the servants of Georgian England have received little attention from historians. It is not too much to say that, just as our particular life-style is wholly dependent upon machines and technology, so that of Woodforde's contemporaries rested on a basis of personal service.

There were several reasons for this. One was that labour-saving devices were very primitive, where they existed at all. Another was that, at a time when the population was increasing, the inequality in the distribution of wealth meant that there was never any shortage of people who were perfectly willing to work for what must strike us, even when every allowance has been made for the discrepancy in money-values between the diarist's time and the present day, as extremely low wages. One thing that always strikes the perceptive reader in 18th century domestic history is that while the most exhausting and dangerous tasks were as a matter of course handed over to the "lower orders" (and here we cannot help thinking again of the two employees of Mr. Sudbury the "Upholsterer", not forgetting the sideboard and the "Cellaret")[1], members of the leisured classes, certainly the women, but often and to a considerable extent the men also, considered themselves much too delicately constituted for any activity involving hard physical effort, which was carried out for them by their servants.

The higher up the social scale one was, the greater number of servants likely to be employed, as is testified by such social phenomena as the 100 gardeners of Blenheim. The great landowning magnates thus were employers of labour on a grand scale, and this function was imitated for a long way down the social ladder until the opposite end of the spectrum is reached with a small tradesman who might take in a boy or girl from the local workhouse. Unemployment was a problem throughout Woodforde's time. The employment of servants was one important way of relieving it.

Finally servants, their number, the way they were dressed and their behaviour, were a mark of status, a clear sign of aggrandisement, a walking advertisement for the wealth and importance of their masters. Generations of satirists poured ridicule on the hordes of posturing flunkeys, with their gold sticks and gorgeous liveries, without doing anything to reduce their attractiveness as a symbol proclaiming the power of those who so tricked them out. It was particularly the new rich, the "nabobs", those who had come up from obscurity by making a lot of money in often decidedly dubious ways, who were most open to criticism on that score.

From the viewpoint of a young villager it might seem to have been no more than elementary common sense: if he did not want a life spent as a farm worker, in which endless heavy labour, an inadequate diet and a total lack of any protective clothing were only too likely to turn him into a rheumatic wreck by the time he was 40, the smart thing to do was to be taken on as a domestic servant, in a household where the standards of food and accommodation were likely to be greatly superior to anything he might have been used to in his own home. But as a matter of fact servants were very seldom recruited from the labouring class. The majority appear to have hailed from the class above, at least in rural districts: that of the small farmer and petty tradesman.

Among 18th century diarists, I should be inclined to call Woodforde in a class by himself as a chronicler of servants' lives. He was not a strikingly good employer, and the wages he paid were on the low side for the time. He never took the trouble to train any of them, so that they had to be already experienced, and anyone who failed that test was quickly sent about his or her business.[2] He was very unlike his friend Mr. du Quesne, who treated his servants very well and who went out of his way to write an exceptionally generous Will, by the terms of which his housekeeper was well provided for, for the rest of her life. By contrast Woodforde's last quartette, all tried and trusted people who had been with him for years, were not left a penny.

Yet Woodforde saw his servants as human beings and they interested him, just as the people he met in other walks of life secured his interest. Most assuredly he never troubled his head about literary style, and perhaps had little or no knowledge of what that term meant. Yet the very artlessness of his delineation of the various servants makes them "come alive". Also from the incidental remarks he put down from time to time about his own servants, we can gain insight into the lives of servants in general.

These characteristics are less in evidence in the diary of his early life in Somerset. He was only intermittently at home, and there the servants who looked after him were his father's. Even after he began "housekeeping", as he called it, and employed Mary Crich (or Creech), whom he had brought with him when he left Babcary, and her daughter Betty, eventually housekeeper at Ansford Parsonage, his references to them are usually limited to a bare mention. The only servant who stands out is William Corp.

He was the long-serving, trusted family servant, whom James inherited from his father. He did all sorts of jobs but was perhaps "accident prone" (to use the modern expression), for the diary records a number of times he injured himself at work. Perhaps all this aged him, for Woodforde often calls him "Old William". He was 45 when he died suddenly. Long engagements were quite customary among servants of his kind, for very obvious reasons - we shall come across another such case in the much later diary. On 12 May 1774 Corp was married to his "old Sweetheart" Christian Speed in Ansford Church. A few hours later he fell dead in the street at Castle Cary. Upon learning this through a letter from Sister Jenny, Woodforde drew one of his ominous pointing hands in the margin opposite the entry.

Corp is remembered only through the dramatic nature of his end. The servants of Woodforde's Norfolk period, with hardly an exception, are seen in much sharper focus. Whether or not the people living in it realised, there is something claustrophobic about Weston Parsonage. Although less than 10 miles from Norwich, it does give a reader of the diary an impression of great remoteness, particularly in winter, when sometimes a day, or a succession of days, must have gone by without the sight of an unfamiliar face. As Woodforde grew older and became less energetic, he spent far more time at home. He had always been one to concentrate on the prospect immediately before his eyes, to the exclusion of more distant things and people; a characteristic, I think, of those whose power of imagination is limited. The abundance of detail about the Norfolk servants derives from the simple fact that in his later years he saw more of them and so had them, as it were, in the forefront of his conscious mind.

From the time he went to reside at Weston in 1776 to his death over 26 years later Woodforde always had five living-in servants; two adult men, two women and a boy, known variously as a "Yard Boy" or "Skip Jack". One of the men, Ben Leggett (Leggatt, Legate), might have been called a farm servant rather than a domestic: indeed Woodforde called him "my Farming Man". He looked after the Rectory glebe of some 46 acres, together with various other parcels of land tenanted by Woodforde. He was a skilled man who could be trusted to sell the Rector's crops in Norwich without supervision. Yet we find him doing a great variety of jobs, some of which he would have been unlikely to take on if he had worked for a farmer. He was undoubtedly the Founder Member of the servants' circle, since he arrived with his father to apply for the job during Woodforde's first year in Norfolk and was taken on at a wage of £10, still unchanged in 1802.

Ben, utterly honest and dependable, is one of the most attractive people in the diary. His habit of returning home drunk after being sent round the parish to tell each of the farmers the date of the coming Tithe Audit, seems to have derived from his weak head for alcohol rather than the amounts he actually drank. Once he did not even return, for he fell off the Parson's horse in "Peachmans Lane", the animal leaving him lying there.

The other man might be called a footman. His chief task was to wait at table, not only at home but also when his master dined out with friends. There were only two of these: Will Coleman to 1785, and then Brettingham Scurl, or "Briton".

Coleman was one of the small minority of domestic servants who came from the lowest labouring stratum of a village, and the only person among Woodforde's Norfolk servants to come like himself from the West Country. His family was associated with that of the diarist in the typical paternalistic way that has no parallel in the later diary. Will's grandmother, old Alice Stacy, used to trot about Ansford and Cary doing jobs for the Woodfordes. He himself first appears in the diary as an infant. When he was 15 Woodforde took him on at 6d. a week. Riding the "Portmanteau Horse", he was with Woodforde and Bill on the 1776 journey into Norfolk. His first adult wage was 4 guineas a year. Briton, his successor, was receiving £8 before his service with Woodforde ended.

The turnover among the female servants was much faster. Between 1776 and 1794 there were fifteen. Of these two left to get married. Two left for what one might call the opposite reason; they became pregnant while unmarried, and a further two were overtaken by the same fate after they had left Woodforde's employ. Two again left through illness, one of these dying a few weeks later. Two were dismissed. The rest went of their own accord, in two cases because the maid in question could not get on with the other girl.

One of the two maids was the cook. The meals prepared were fairly simple as the master had no taste for what he called the "Frenchified" dishes he was offered in grander houses than his own. The other girl would clean and sweep the rooms and make the beds, one of the least pleasurable parts of her duties being that of emptying the chamber pots which stood under the bed in every house of the time. Woodforde once uses the term "House Maid" but more often "Under Maid", as distinct from the cook, who was his "Head Maid". She was originally the higher paid of the two until Woodforde abolished the distinction and stabilised both girls' wages at five guineas. Also Betty Dade, who came in as an Under Maid and a replacement for her ailing sister, rose to become virtually an unofficial housekeeper and superior in status to any of the cooks.

Of course, there were no "conditions of service" in Woodforde's day, no trade unions to define and limit the boundaries of liability to do a particular job and no more. Weston Parsonage was much nearer to being self-supporting than any modern household. At the time of his death Woodforde had three milch cows; and one of the girls must have done the milking. Bread, butter, cheese, jams were made at home. Sally Gunton, the last Under Maid, could hive the bees that kept Weston Parsonage in honey.

And then on very special occasions, all the servants would turn out to help. Harvest was the most important of these; but there were others, such as "Washing Week" (actually two days every fifth week), and the annual Tithe Audit, or "Frolick", at which upwards of twenty farmers sat down to dinner, or any of the big parties that Woodforde held. At one of these, because the host and some of the guests stayed up all night, the servants did so too.

The improvised way in which some of the work-load was shared comes through most clearly in relation to the "Yard Boys". It is likely enough that they had no prescribed duties at all, but simply helped the other servants as and when directed. They are seen working at the harvest. One of the boys was riding on top of a load of barley being transported from the field to the rector's barn, when it slipped and he fell off. The boys, like the other servants on occasion, had the chance to pick up a tip here and there, but they had to behave themselves. After the tithe dinner of 1788: "I used to give my Boy a Shilling, but he made himself so beastly drunk that Day, that I gave him nothing".[3] The boys, doubtless to their own satisfaction, sometimes accompanied their master on his coursing and fishing expeditions.

They were usually taken on at about age 10, were employed for two years and then dismissed as having reached the top age for a "Skip-Jack". The exception to this general rule is found in the career of the first and most satisfactory among them. He was the boy mentioned as being, along with Will Coleman, the only one of Woodforde's domestic servants to come from a poor labouring family. In the official records the family always appears as "Wharton", and the diarist's use of another spelling may have been due to an unconscious reminiscence of Joseph Warton, the "Hostiarius" in his time at Winchester. The agreement by which the boy, who was between 10 and 11 years old, came into his employ is in the diary:

> George Warton's little Boy John came to live with me
> last thursday and I am to give him his Victuals and
> some Cloaths when he wants the same - He does not
> sleep at my House as he has not had the small-Pox -

Some time later he entered a strong protest against having to pay the Male Servants' Tax for Jack, as he was employing the boy "out of Charity". He was, however improbable it may sound, a Tax Commissioner himself, although he appears to have attended only two meetings of that body. After that he quietly assessed himself as having only one taxable male servant - Ben being exempt as a "Farming Man" - and got away with it. Jack quickly made himself a place among the servants, and little more than a fortnight after his arrival his employer was handing him a sixpenny tip. On the first occasion when he paid all the servants together at the beginning of the year, a practice he continued for the rest of his life, he added:

> Gave my Servant Boy, Jack Warton, as he has no
> Wages, and which I intend giving him annually - 0:10:6 (4)

For the next two years the same payment was made, Woodforde throwing in an extra 2/6d "as a free gift" in 1783. That year also, on the day he paid Jack and the other servants for their years work, he wrote down an entry in the book he was using to record his accounts with the household staff:

> Mem: Janry 13 - 1783 - I promised then to
> Jack Warton, to give him the ensueing Year
> 1. Guinea for Wages -

Jack stayed at Weston Parsonage for two more years. By the autumn of 1784 he had been there for just over eight years and must have been between 18 and 19. Only the mutual liking and respect of master and man could have kept him there so long, and in such a capacity, since from the age of 18 he would have been

entitled to seek a place which would give him a full man's wage.
Woodforde wrote on 7 October 1784:

> ... Jack told me this morning that he is advised
> to get another Place being too old for a Skip-Jack
> any longer - He wants to be a plow Boy to some Farmer
> to learn the farming business as he likes that best.
> I told him that he was very right to try to better
> himself, and at Lady Day next he is to leave my
> house for that Purpose - He has been a very good Lad
> Ever since he has been here -

In the introduction to the 2nd volume of *The Diary of a
Country Parson*, Mr. Beresford has a typically sentimental aperçu,
the remark of a commentator to whom the past is never quite real:
"He (the reader) will rejoice that Jack Warton wanted to be a
ploughboy, and not worsen himself in the city ...". In writing this he
missed the important point, which was that if Jack had gone to work
on a farm some years ago he would by now have learned the duties
well enough to be employable as a ploughman; whereas, after
spending so much time in Woodforde's household, he would still be
a learner at any farm he might go to. Hence his determination to
waste no more time.

After Jack, the Yard Boys all had wages from the time their
employment began. Like him, they received a guinea a year, until in
1788 Woodforde took on a boy named John Dalliday or Dalady, at
two guineas, "but no Cloaths whatever". It would be interesting to
know if this change reflected an increase in the price of clothing, as
employers had always to balance the actual value of cash wages
against payments in kind. All the later Skip Jacks had two guineas.

One or other of the boys feature in some of the best
remembered episodes of the diary: Billy Downing who held an
umbrella over his master's head at a funeral in Great Witchingham
churchyard: Tim Tooley who ran off and volunteered for service in
the "thirty-third Regiment of Foot", having with another boy been
offered 10 guineas, a huge augmentation of the traditional "King's
shilling" - but this was wartime and the Government anxious to
increase the numbers of its armed forces; and Tim's brother Tom,
taken on in his place but soon sent away, "as he would do nothing at
all".

These later boys met with little approval. Only one of them,
Barnabas Woodcock, lasted so long as three years. The others were

either dismissed as soon as their two year stint was up, or fired out before reaching that time. They may have been an unsatisfactory lot. On the other hand Woodforde, as he aged, grew perhaps more crotchety and harder to please. John Brand was magisterially presented with the order of the boot and sent on his way, having inspired this thumbs-down report:

> My Boy, John Brand, left my Service to Day, as
> he had proper Notice so to do, being the most saucy
> swearing lad that ever we had, and am afraid
> that if he does not soon do better, he will bring his
> poor Mother with sorrow to her Grave -
> He can do his Work well if he pleases, but cannot
> be trusted out of Sight, but the worst is, he is profligate - [5]

The last charge probably means that he had been caught making a pass at one of the maids. Fallacious hopes were raised by the "open honest Countenance" of Henry Daines; but appearances were delusive and Henry turned out a total disaster. The same kind of epithets were expended over him and his departure that had been lavished on Brand:

> We breakfasted, dined, &c. at home -
> This being Old Michaelmas Day, I paid
> my Servant Boy, Henry Daines, three
> quarters of a Years Wages due this Day
> at two Guineas per Annum - 1:11: 6
> and dismissed him from my Service
> not behaving in the manner that I expected
> from him, as he could not be trusted to
> do anything if not overlooked, and also
> a very saucy, foul-mouthed lad - [6]

Nor was Robert Case much better. The diarist recorded mournfully, more in sorrow than in anger:

> ... My Yard Boy, Robt Case hath behaved of
> late I hear but indifferently - He has
> been guilty of many bad Actions of late -
> A bad return for the Waistcoat I lately gave him -
> It vexed me a good deal to hear it - [7]

This was the boy who later fell off the cart. Woodforde might have been still more vexed if he had lived in our times, and in danger of being sued for negligence by his employee, in not having made sure that the load could not slip!

With Robert Case we are nearing the end of the diary; and one of the very last entries written by Woodforde is about the arrival of another Yard Boy, his successor. Less than a week later, he was attacked by the seizure that ended the diary and, after ten more weeks, the life of the diarist.

To read about the daily concerns of life at Weston Parsonage is to savour the strange mixture of the easy-going and the harsh that prevailed there. It would be only too easy to present a view slanted in either direction. The servants could if invited go to visit their counterparts at Weston House, or have their friends in for dinner in their own kitchen. Woodforde did not mind their staying out all night, so long as they asked his permission first, although he got very annoyed if they neglected to do this. Woodforde was a kind man, but his generosity had precise limits. In 1789, when the cook of the time, Nanny Kaye, lost her father; "therefore she desired to go to the Funeral to Morrow at Foulsham. And as it is supposed that she and her sisters must be at the expense of burying their Father, I gave her towards defraying the same the sum of 1: 0: 0:" [8] But Foulsham was 10 miles off, and Nanny had to walk the whole distance, there and back, as it clearly never occurred to the Parson to provide transport for her.

In some circumstances it was clearly felt that kindness need not be shown; indeed, that it was wrong to show it. Mary Woods was suspected of being pregnant by everyone around, even the "two Washerwomen" who came in as occasional workers. She persisted for a long time in her denials, and when at last she threw in her hand and confessed, Woodforde's reaction might have been predicted: "... it is necessary for me to part with her as soon as possible - To Morrow therefore I intend at present [sic] to dismiss her". [9] And on the very next day Mary, seven months pregnant and laden with a bundle of her own things, walked away from Weston Parsonage and a long walk she had, into another parish, like a character in one of the gloomier scenes of a novel by Thomas Hardy.

In any dispute between servants and their employers, it was the latter who for obvious reasons held all the trump cards. They imposed the conditions and made the rules, and the servant's only choice was between acceptance and dismissal. At the same time we do come across examples of considerable independence. There was the girl interviewed by the diarist who turned down an offer of a place (although it was later accepted) because "she did not chuse to wash Dishes". There were also the cases of servants who, as though unconscious of the essential weakness of their position, brought down on their heads their own ruin. The word is used advisedly, for in the matter of servants the employing class stuck together, so that in the absence of a "Character", or as we should say a reference, a man or woman became unemployable.

Will Coleman is a case in point. He was no doubt an exceptionally foolish man, with a number of bad habits: unreliable, fond of drink, and noisy and abusive when drunk, his behaviour often an embarrassment in an age when inability to control one's servants was looked upon as a sign of weakness. Yet, banking both on the old association of his family with the Woodfordes and the diarist's notorious aversion from any sort of confrontation, Coleman acted as though his security were impregnable, and continued to misbehave, ignoring the repeated warnings Woodforde fired at him. When at last the master nerved himself for the ordeal by getting up early in the morning, and finally dismissed him, the servant after an initial display of bluster quickly grew frightened. Woodforde, who did not want to see harm come to him and no doubt thought that, left to himself, Will would sink into vagrancy or crime, like many discharged servants, helped him to get back to Somerset. At the age of 40 he got married and fathered a large brood of children, who must have been supported out of parish relief and a few odd jobs tossed to him by one or other of the Woodfordes. He died in 1832.

His successor, Brettingham Scurl or Scurll, was the eldest son of a baker living at Hackford near Reepham. He is best remembered by the name "Briton", usually taken to be a nickname bestowed upon him by Woodforde, but probably the way in which Brettingham pronounced his name.[10] His family was well schooled in the habits of thrift and had the habit of buying up small items of property. Woodforde once advanced his wages, giving them to him before they were due, so that his father could buy a house.

He was more intelligent than Will Coleman, and much better balanced. As a good example of the disorganised and slapdash way in which quite important decisions could be made in this society, it may be mentioned that Briton turned up at the Parsonage in 1785, just at dinner time and was immediately ordered into the parlour to wait at table. Having triumphantly passed that test, he was taken on and stayed at the Parsonage for the rest of Woodforde's life. In general, he did well. He soon became an established and trusted member of the household. He was considered reliable enough to escort Nancy on various short journeys; could be sent off alone to

Norwich and other places, entrusted with commissions of one sort or another, and accompanied Woodforde and Nephew Bill on a tour of coastal Norfolk. Travelling in Somerset with his master and Nancy, his quick thinking averted what might have been a serious coach accident. It is true that Woodforde and his manservant occasionally fell out. Reprimanded for going out without permission to visit the Bidewell family and staying out late, Briton fired up and, two hours after he had been told off, "he gave me notice that he had rather leave my Service at Michaelmas". After the young man had gone off to bed, Woodforde growled to his diary:

........Such is the gratitude of Servants-
he has been with me nine years the 21. of April last-
Which I find is much too long for any Norfolk Servant
for they will then get pert, saucy & do as they please-

Next day he told the servant that he would "by no means keep him after Michaelmas"; to which Briton retorted that "he did not care for he could get a Place he did not doubt, if not, he had a home to go to, his Fathers -" After which, working in the garden, one of his duties, he began to sing "very loud, which was very impudent -".

But when tempers had cooled, both men probably realized that they were both likely to lose rather than gain by parting. No more was said, and Briton stayed on, although next year he was in trouble with his employed again when, having gone with Woodforde to the Archdeacon's Visitation at Reepham, " being in Liquor", he was "very saucy in his return home with me - he is treading fast the steps that poor Will Coleman did before he was obliged to be sent away - ". But again there was no sequel to this misbehaviour, and Briton, even when "tipsy", even when relieving his feelings by " singing in a loud and bold and impudent manner", seems quite adequately to have summed up his master's character, knew how much he could safely get away with, and never went past the point of no return.

In his later, post-Woodfordean years it is possible to keep track of Briton only by reference to the property he owned and his activities, arising out of his possession of that property, as an elector. Norwich was a so-called "freeman borough", but had also a "freeholder franchise", giving the vote to people who possessed freehold property in the city of a certain value. Briton's electoral right came from the ownership of "two Cottages or tenements with the Yards, Outhouses and Appurtenances thereto belonging" in Cockey Lane, King Street, parish of St. Julian.[11] From 1809 he owned in addition a "double tenement" at Hardley, near Loddon. Although this probably entitled him to vote also in the county elections, there is no evidence that he did so until very much later.

At the time of the 1812 General Election, he was noted down in the Poll book of that year as a servant. By 1819, on the other hand, he had become a "Gentleman" - at least that is what he must have told the poll clerk at the hustings. I think it is very unlikely that the statements of voters about their occupation were ever checked; but we can probably take it for granted that by this date he was no longer in domestic service. He had by now left Norwich and was living at Bergh Apton, outside the city, registered as a country voter, but still empowered to vote in the borough elections through his city property.

Very little else is known about him. He was the eldest of fourteen children; but in spite of that was alone in his old age, since he outlived all his siblings and was never married. He left his properties to a nephew, Brettingham Potter Scurl, who was carrying on the family trade of baker. Briton died in 1840, aged 80, and it was a neighbour who registered his death.

Although the names changed from time to time as servants came and went, there were always five people in the house, thrown together by their employer's arrangements, rather than by any desire of their own to be there in one another's company. If we enquire how, in these circumstances they managed to get along together the answer must be that for the most part they lived in mutual harmony. Of course we know of their rare disagreements. Will Coleman once actually came to blows with the maidservant Betty Caxton. We hear of one girl who left her place because she could not possibly agreed with her colleague, the favourite Sukey.

But if there was hostility at times, and some degree of mutual antagonism, could not the experience of living and working in constant proximity to each other have resulted also in affection, or at least desire, coming to life? Indeed it could. Will, again, went temporarily out of his mind and jumped into the "Great Pond", from the waters of which he was immediately extricated by Ben, because he had fallen in love with Lizzy Greaves and wanted to marry her, while she would not have him at any price.

In Woodforde's last years, Ben and Betty Dade emerge as a betrothed couple, something that often happened with senior servants in a household. She was highly efficient and capable, could run a house well and was indeed, as I have said, a housekeeper in all but name. She was also a highly neurotic woman, with a string of mysterious and probably psychosomatic ailments. The Parson, clearly impressed, reported that she was taking five different kinds of pills a day. The most outstanding of her illnesses was "her old Complain, Husteric-Wind Cholic". For this he subjected her to a formidable regime of dosing: "Port-wine and Water, Rum & Water, Lavender Drops etc": the "etc" making us wonder what else she was given, as Woodforde loved nothing better than getting people to swallow his mostly home-made remedies, and the servants made up a captive audience. He realised that Betty's ailments had an emotional basis, and was inclined to fix the blame on Ben, saying that he hoped that "he hath not been too intimate with her".[12] The engagement was in trouble, certainly, but it was Betty who was rocking the boat. Woodforde reported that she had "turned off Ben, and was now engaged to his cousin Thomas Leggett of Ringland, small farmer under Lord Bayning". No wonder Ben "abused her" when he heard this, perhaps saying: beware the fury of a patient man. Betty seemed unable to make up her mind between her two suitors, for just over a month later the diarist noted: "Betty & Tom Leggett's Connection all done with and Ben accepted again by her". But this last mention of the pair on 28 June 1801 says: "Thos Leggett & Betty again talked off(sic)"

I have in the past spent time checking the registers of various Norfolk parishes in the hope of finding the marriage of Betty Dade and Ben or, conversely, to Thomas of Ringland; but never got anywhere. Nor may this be called at all surprising since they did not marry. Only a short time ago I learned of the existence of two records. One is a gravestone in Mattishall churchyard which states that "Elizabeth Baldwin Daughter of William and Elizabeth Dade died November 23rd, 1834, in the 70th year of her age". The other is an entry in the register of the same parish, recording the burial of Elizabeth Baldwin, of Dereham, buried on 27th November 1834, aged 69. The conjunction of the full names of the parents and the dates of death and burial which fully agree with the baptismal entry in the same register makes it certain that this is the Betty Dade of Woodforde's diary. At this moment it is impossible to go further, until the Norfolk record Office is once more open and the register of Dereham may be examined. Then we may be able to find out something out about Mr Baldwin, who appears to have knocked out both the Leggatts! We know that Thomas married at Ringland, not long after the Parsonage household broke up. But Ben's later career is so far an impenetrable mystery. He is seen once, fleetingly, after the death of Woodforde, when on one of the days devoted to the auction of the effects of his late employer he bought for 17 shillings "A parcel of Thillar's harness" (a 'thillar' was the shaft horse of a team), and for 2 shillings an unidentified item, the printed list for this part of the sale having disappeared. After that Ben simply disappears without trace, and nothing more of him is known anywhere.

CHAPTER 22

TWO DESTINIES

Woodforde's first two maidservants were provided for him by Mrs. Howes. One of these was named Molly Salmon, "a very pretty Woman", who understood cookery and was skilled at "working at her needle". Although recommended by Mrs. Howes, she was unemployed, having been "turned away" by Catherine Howes herself, "for not getting up early enough". Woodforde took her on, as from Midsummer Day, at 5 guineas a year, a wage for a woman servant he never afterwards exceeded, "and tea twice a day".

For a time master and servant appeared to get along together in perfect harmony. After Molly had been at Weston Parsonage some four months, he heard that "A particular Friend" of hers was "lying very dangerously ill in Bungay", 21 miles away over the border in the next county. He not only gave her leave to go there but sent Will with her as far as Norwich.

But not long after, on 4 November, he fell seriously out with her. Dr. Thorne had just inoculated Ben and Jack, and ordered a "low diet" for them in the first few days. This included "rice milk", and he himself, for no easily discoverable reason, had "a pint of the same". Finding that Molly had put eggs into it, he was so angry that, for once he put his foot right down, and gave her notice on the spot.

Afterwards he was rather sorry he had done this. He allowed that she was "good tempered", and if she had only asked him to let her stay, he would "have been glad to have kept her". But she made no such request, and so he paid her off at the end of her six months, "being no longer a Servant of mine"; and she departed for Hockering, no doubt to tell Mrs. Howes all about it.

It is an example of the independence occasionally shown by servants of the period.

Next day, the last of the year 1776, a new girl arrived to fill the vacancy: Susan or Susanna Buxley - this appears to be the spelling of her name most often found on official documents; Woodforde called her "Boxley" and, once, "Bucksley" - was born at Taverham on 23 September 1753,[1] and was thus just over 23. Her mother, presumably widowed, lived at Weston, and was invited to dinner in Woodforde's kitchen before a month was up. By that time he had already bestowed on the girl one of the "pet-names" he always gave to his women servants, and was calling her "Sukey". Clearly she was attractive, and bright, able to act upon her own initiative. She sold "2. little Piggs" to Ben Leggett's father for 15/-, Woodforde was pleased and gave her a shilling for herself.[2] He tipped her also after the 1777 Tithe Frolic, because she and Will had had a lot of trouble and "did every thing entirely to my satisfaction". A sign that she was establishing herself as a favourite with him was that even when she did things of which he could not approve, he did nothing about it. Once she brought her sister, quite uninvited, to spend a night at Weston Parsonage, but all he did about it was to grumble: "I think it is taking too great Liberties with me to bring home a Stranger to sleep here - I do not like it at all", and to rub this in, he pointedly ignored the sister next morning".[3]

The under maid, Betty Rix, left because she could not get along with Sukey, probably a sign that the favourite had dislodged her. In her place came a very shadowy Anne Taylor, the only one of the Norfolk servants of either sex whose coming is unannounced in the diary. We can, however, piece together at least something of her story. She was one of the three daughters of James Taylor, who went off to join the army and deserted them. Anne was so entirely destitute that Woodforde had to pay Mr. Cary, the village shopkeeper, the greater part of her year's wages, which at £2 were very unusually low, for essential clothing. The advance payment was deducted from her wages when she left, a year after she had come to work for the Parson. She was to play a rather ambiguous part in the drama of Sukey's downfall.

1777 had been a good year for Sukey, and the next year began as though it would continue in the same way. On 25 February she reached the high point in her relations with her employer. He had promised to buy her a gown, a present, not something to be paid back like the money spent on Anne Taylor's clothes. Now he lent the trusty "Portmanteau Horse, or "my great Horse", who now had a name, "Jack", so she and Mrs. Hardy the builder's wife could go into Norwich for her gift.

In March Sukey was asked if she wanted to go to a puppet show; but "chose to stay at home"; and he gave her the 6d. admission fee. The other servants had been to it, two nights before; and stayed out until after 11 o'clock. So far he still appeared to be pleased with her. But on 11 May he wrote what became one of the blacked-out passages, in which a deliberate attempt was made to destroy vital evidence which someone wanted to be forgotten. The part that can be deciphered reads:

Woodforde - Two Destinies

Bill was up in the Maids Room this morning, and Sukey was
still abed - I think there is an intimacy between them -

Woodforde's nephew had now been two years at Weston, and it
was not a happy time for him. He had no role there. Sometimes
indeed his uncle's friends invited him to their houses; but mostly he
appears to have been left to his own devices. He was plainly not
encouraged to make friends of his own age among the farmers'
sons, since Woodforde was unsure of his own position and felt the
need to uphold his status as Rector. Far less adaptable than his sister
Nancy would be, the young man was bored and impatient. Many of
the references to Bill in the diary about this time have been deleted,
but enough has survived to show that relations between uncle and
nephew swiftly deteriorated. Provoked by really desperate ennui,
Bill could upon occasion resort to gross insolence: "my Nephew was
very dull this Evening - does not like my House at all, he says, it's a
very melancholy Place and would not be obliged to live there for
three times the value of the Living". Woodforde tended to react to
this kind of rudeness by telling the young man he would have to
go: "Bill made me very uneasy and very angry with him at Breakfast
by contradicting me in a very saucy manner. I therefore told him
that he should not return with me to Weston but that I should leave
him in the West" on returning from his holiday in Somerset. But
like many another, he found it easier to make threats than to carry
them out. Bill travelled back to Norfolk with him; but by the
summer of 1778 affairs were reaching a crisis. The Parson could see
that he would have eventually to get rid of Bill: on the other hand,
he seems to have dreaded the loneliness of Weston Parsonage once
he was left there by himself.

By the last week in August, 1778, everything seemed to be
going wrong. It was oppressively hot and although they were in the
middle of the harvest, people wanted to see the rain:

The Grass Ground about us instead of Green looks
quite rusty, being burnt up so long by the Sun, some
are obliged to feed their Stock with Hay now - 4

Ben, lent to the farmer Stephen Andrews to help with the
harvest, returned so helplessly drunk that the Rector, seeing a light
in his room from outside, went to investigate and found him lying
fully clothed, flat on his back on the bed with a lighted candle
flaring beside him, a hazard that would have shaken many a
stronger-nerved man: "I waked him, made him put out the Candle

and talked with him a little on it, but not much as he was not in a Capacity of answering but little". Agitation commonly had the effect on Woodforde of making him write in this ungrammatical way. The entry ends with the words: "I was very uneasy to see matters go on so badly". [5]

He was made still more uneasy next day, when Sukey came to him with a confession. She would have to leave his employ at Michaelmas, she said, because she was "with Child and half gone, & that the Father was one Humphrey, and that she was not concerned with any other Man ...".

Woodforde must have heard this with considerable relief, after what he had seen last May having reason to believe that Bill would be charged as responsible. Not that he had been blameless, for, Sukey went on, he "had come into her Room when she was in Bed and tried every way to get her to comply but she said ...". What she said has been so heavily scored out as to be indecipherable, but presumably it amounted to "No!".

To understand this it is necessary to have some knowledge of the working of the Bastardy Act of 1753. The maintenance of an illegitimate child was the liability of the parish in which the mother "had settlement", under the Settlement Laws, unless the father, or more strictly speaking the person whom the woman chose to incriminate, could be induced to accept the charge. [6] A man who refused or was unwilling to give this undertaking could be imprisoned, only until the baby was born; but I do not suppose the parish overseers would necessarily always divulge that information and many a villager, ignorant of the law, may well have thought he could be kept in jail for life, and agreed to marry the woman, in order to effect his immediate release. This was the origin of what Parson Woodforde called the "compulsatory marriage", of which there are some examples in the diary. But there was another option that could be taken by a man whom the parish was after. He could simply disappear. It is of course a myth that, before the Industrial Revolution and the era of cheap railway travel, people tended by and large to stay their lifetime in the place of their birth. Among the people in Woodforde's diary there is evidence of a quite considerable movement of families between villages, or from village to town.

Now, with these facts in mind, let us look at Humphrey. First, there is no trace of him in the official Weston records. In the diary there are two direct references to him by name. One, as seen, is in Sukey's confession. The other is part of the entry for 21 February - just three days, incidentally, before Sukey and the mason's wife had gone into Norwich on the "Great Horse" - Woodforde who had bought a "Tin Reflector", a kitchen gadget designed to direct rays of heat on to the viand to be cooked, had arranged to have it collected at Norwich and brought to him "by Stephen Andrews's Waggon". The next line reads: "Gave Humphrey, Stephen's Man - 0: 1: 0". To judge by the diarist's usual way of alluding to men of the labouring class, "Humphrey" must here be a Christian name. On 26 April "2. fine Horses" belonging to Stephen Andrews died, and were declared to have been poisoned. It was a crime of the utmost seriousness in that rural society, and was far from unknown to have been committed by the employees of a farmer who bore him a grudge. On 6 May Woodforde wrote: "Stephen Andrew's two Men were had before the Justice this morning on suspicion of their poisoning his two Horses, but it not being proved, they were dismissed - ". Andrews was a substantial farmer, but it is most unlikely that he had more than two full-time adult men in his employ, so our mysterious "Humphrey" was almost certainly one of them. Note also that the pair had by no means been cleared by the magistrate, but were released purely through lack of sufficient evidence to charge them. There could have been no possible future for such men in a village like Weston, and it is not surprising that he is never heard of again there. This made him an extremely bad choice as the putative father of Sukey's child, whom the parish might successfully pursue to get him to contribute towards its maintenance; but an excellent one for use as a smoke-screen if she wanted to hide the real father.

On 28 and again on 29 August Sukey "went before Justice Buxton ... to Swear to the Father of the Child she is big with - ". The magistrate "granted a Warrant to take up Humphrey". This was the usual procedure, and in a large proportion of cases remained totally ineffective, as here.

I think that much of the depression perceptible in many of the diary entries of this summer was due to anxiety about his own reputation, just as he had been uneasy at the thought that his brothers' scandalous behaviour at the Ansford Lower House, years ago, might rub off on him. He was still fairly young, not yet 40, and had been living in a house of which the other occupants were a youth and two girls, one of whom had now publicly declared herself pregnant. A layman would have seen no cause to worry, but the situation could be most damaging to a bachelor clergyman, especially one who, like Woodforde, was a comparative newcomer to the district.

All this summer Bill Woodforde had, in a rather hot-and-cold manner, been making plans to join the Navy, augmented as it was by the American War then in progress. His uncle encouraged him in this, less I am sure because he saw in the young man another

Admiral Rodney than because it was a first class opportunity to get rid of Bill altogether, without annoying his relations at home. He had enlisted the aid of Mr. Hammerton, the proprietor of the Lyng paper mills, who had a brother at the Admiralty, and an interview for Bill was arranged with "a Captain of a Ship". So, on 30 August, the day after Sukey had seen the J.P. for the second time, he really put himself out to ensure his nephew would keep the appointment. He gave him the sum of 5 guineas. Then "about 6 in the evening" he took Bill into Norwich, booked his seat in a stage coach for London, gave him supper at the *Angel*, where the "London Machine" started out from, and even, taking no chances, saw Bill safely into the coach before repairing to his favourite hostelry the *King's Head*, a few doors away. But the coach did not go out until midnight, and Woodforde had put his nephew through a gruelling third degree:

> I questioned Bill a great deal in the Evening at the Angel
> about his being great with my Maid Sukey, and
> he confessed something of it to me, that he had been
> great with her 3. or 4. Times - The first Time was
> Feb. 28 early in the morning in her Room -

The next few lines have been so determinedly blacked out - and surely it could only have been William himself in his respectable later days when he had been transmogrified into the squirelet of Galhampton and inherited the diary m.s., who could have done it - that not a lot of sense can be made out of what is still decipherable. But the entry then continues:

> Sukey had admitted that Humphrey was great with her
> and that the first Time was in March, and if so Bill
> certainly had Sukey first -

As in a "whodunit", the reader is presented with a number of different solutions. Sukey may have been promiscuous enough to have had two lovers more or less at the same time. Or Bill could have been indulging in the sort of sexual boasts to which young men have at all times been addicted. The remaining possibility, which is attractive because it shows Sukey in the best light, is that she was in love with Bill, a "Gentleman" and right out of her class, whom she could never have hoped to marry, and that she used the figment of "Humphrey" to protect him, and perhaps the Parson too, averting the scandal that would have reigned if his nephew had been cited; also, as Bill had no money of his own, saving the Rector the cost of paying the parish to look after her baby for many years. I must admit that the latest piece of evidence on Sukey, which has come to light very recently, has cast doubt on the reality behind that romantic speculation.

I think that Woodforde parted from Sukey with some reluctance. Certainly he was in no hurry to see her go, and in this there was a great contrast to the way he treated another peccant maidservant a few years later. As we have seen, Mary Woods, seven months pregnant, for she had refused to admit her condition for a long time, was unceremoniously fired out with her bare wages and left to trudge away into another parish, carrying a heavy bundle. It is true that he wrote in his diary: "I told Sukey this Morning my Opinion of her respecting the late Affair that has happened to her". (3/9/1778). But that was all. She did not leave the house for another six weeks. On 14 October he paid her final wages. They had gone up to £4, a sure sign that she had been giving satisfaction before her disgrace. He added a last present of 4/-. "Sukey this Evening left us but in tears most sad". Even that was not quite the last of her. She returned for a day in November to show her successor "how to make butter and to help in ironing". On 23 November he wrote on the blotting paper opposite the entry for that day:

> Privately named a base born Child
> of my late Maid Sukey Boxly by Name Thomas

This was in itself a favour, not usually granted to village people, unless the child was thought not likely to live. Thomas, by the way, was the name of Sukey's infant brother, who had died before she was born.

She came twice more to the house. The second time was early in the next year, on 10 January when she dined in the kitchen with Mr. and Mrs. Hardy, friends of happier days. Woodforde has no more to say about her, but her story has been filled out to some extent by a very recent piece of research. Examination of the church registers of Lyng, the next parish to Weston, has revealed that Humphrey Garrod and his wife Susanna, nee Buxley, had three sons: William (baptised 5/4/1785), George (16/7/1786) and Charles (30/8/1790). Details of the marriage have so far not been found, but there can surely be very little doubt that this is our authentic Humphrey cited as Thomas' father. The dates are a little disconcerting. Over six years elapsed between Sukey's last appearance in the diary and the first baptism in 1785. Of course, the couple might have had other children, before they went to live in Lyng. But at least we can be sure of one thing. Sukey was not, like many another unfortunate girl in her situation, driven on to the streets of some town in order to keep herself and her baby alive.[6]

Time moved on. It was now the summer of 1784. Nancy had taken the place of the unsatisfactory Bill and had long established herself as her uncle's companion. Sukey had been replaced by someone as unlike her as could possibly be. Elizabeth Claxton came from "Little Melton about 4. Miles from Easton", and Woodforde had greeted her arrival with a marked lack of enthusiasm: "... She is not the most engaging I must confess by the first Appearance that she makes .." She was a mature woman, exactly his own age, and had a brother who was an upper servant with Sir William Jerningham of Costessey Hall. After a stay of nearly five years she caused a major crisis by unexpectedly announcing "in these abrupt and ungracious Words "Sir, I shall leave your Service at Michaelmas next". It turned out that she was to marry Charles Cary, son of old Mr. Cary who was both the village carrier and owner of the village shop, about 15 years her junior.

Not long before, a new under maid had come to Weston Parsonage. Mary Dade, or Molly, as Woodforde at once began to call her, arrived with the very best recommendations: "her Friends [i.e. her family] bear great Characters of Industry &c,".[7] Born in 1767, she was the younger of two daughters of William Dade, a handloom weaver domiciled in Mattishall, and Parish Clerk for over 50 years. Woodforde called him on one occasion "a cunning, long-headed man". One of his sons in later years became Master of the House of Industry at Dereham.

Right from the start, Woodforde and his niece were charmed by Molly. Tall, pretty, well-mannered, gentle, quiet, honest, industrious, willing, generous, Molly seemed to have all the virtues. To the Parson, she must have been Sukey over again, without the other girl's weaknesses. It was true she had a bad cough, and though so willing that she would cheerfully do more than her fair share of work, it exhausted her. But since the Parson had been dosing her with Tar Water, a favourite nostrum of the time, "she is greatly altered for the better, as well again ..." It is this kind of pronouncement, well-intentioned and futile, that strikes us as so desperately sad when it is put against reality. For Molly Dade was not only beyond the power of Tar Water, but beyond the reach of any human aid, struck down by a disease about which nothing was yet known. She was already far gone in what is called the acute miliary form of pulmonary tuberculosis, or what contemporaries called "galloping consumption", in which the progress of the disease is reckoned in months or even weeks, rather than years. So it was with Molly. Through the summer and into the autumn of 1784 they worked side by side, a middle-aged woman who was soon to begin a new life, and a young girl who had no future in this world. Elizabeth was strong and tough. When, some time back, a bad local epidemic of malaria had broken out, called by Woodforde "Ague and Fever or intermitting Fever", and "Whirligousticon", an allusion to the dizziness that was one of its outstanding symptoms, Elizabeth was the only one of the servants not to catch it. But now she had an accident and hurt her thumb. Molly good-naturedly took on some of her work, which made the girl's cough worse. Her reward was to be told by Elizabeth that "she is in a Consumption - which made the poor Girl very unhappy". But by this time he too believed that it was so. He decided to send Molly "to stay a few days at home to see if change of Air would do her Cough good" - an idea of the time that almost everyone believed in. Her sister Betty came in her place as what was intended to be a merely temporary replacement. In the event she was to stay for the rest of the Parson's life. The entry continues:

> Poor Molly is as good a girl as ever came into a
> House, I never had a Servant that I liked better -
> Nancy also likes her very much indeed -
> I wish to God she might get the better of her illness - [8]

Meanwhile a very pressing problem had been solved when the Parson, having rejected his ratcatcher's daughter, and another woman because she came from a village which he did not approve of, full of people who were "guilty of many felonious Acts and but very few Years ago", finally took on Molly Peachman as the new cook, in spite of the fact that she was the girl who objected to washing dishes.

On 3 November Molly Dade's father called, and the account of his visit adds a poignant touch to the story: "He came after her Stays that were here, the others being too large for her - so much of late has she fallen away". No-one thought she could recover, and Dr. Thorne had given her over and said he could do no more: "Pray God Almighty comfort her - and with patience wait the Almighty's Will - as good a Girl as ever Lived".

Next day he sent Betty back home, taking with her "a Knuckle of Veal for Broth and a Jar of black Currant Jamm". This seemingly mundane remark, has a certain significance, as it illustrates the blend of rational thought and legendary belief.[9] So, Woodforde knew very well that Molly Dade was dying. At the same time, it was thought

207

that black currant jam was "good" for colds. Since in some of its phases tuberculosis produced the coughing and mucus that were superficially like symptoms of a cold, there was a prevailing notion that what was supposed to benefit one might be useful in treating the other.

We know that prayers were Woodforde's customary reaction to the serious illness and death he was always hearing about. In Molly's case there was less of a routine element, as though they did indeed come from the heart. On 17 December, Betty having returned from Mattishall with the news that her sister "gets worse and worse - cannot live long", he added: "Pray God grant her a Speedy relief from her present Situation - to Life if it be thy good pleasure, or happiness".

Molly was still alive when the year came to an end. On 6 January 1785 Woodforde took Betty on permanently, offering her five guineas, "as I designed the same to her poor Sister, if her health would have permitted to stay with us - but that is all over". He now abolished for good what we call the cash differential between the two maids; and Betty, although still called the Under Maid, would rise to being an unofficial housekeeper.

Molly died on 23 January, patient and resigned to the last. "Pray God bless her Spirit and comfort her Relations". Again we note a feeling of personal sadness although, after giving her sister two days off to attend the funeral, he never mentioned her again. Yet she is still remembered by those who read the diary:

As good a Girl as ever lived -

Norwich Cathedral, 1793
(watercolour by Edward Dayes, 1763-1804)

William Woodforde, 1758- 1844
Parson Woodforde's "Nephew Bill"

CHAPTER 23

VILLAGE FOLK AND OTHERS

At first sight, it may well seem that to analyse the social structure of Weston Longville presents no difficulty, and that it may be explained in terms of the simplistic clarities of the history text book. It was quite a small village, with a population of between 300 and 400 in Woodforde's last years. A large proportion of the cultivable land - Weston Great Field - was still unenclosed, and was to remain so until 1822. There was a resident squire, Mr. John Custance, by far the largest landowner, although others, not domiciled in Weston, also held freehold land in the parish. No professional man other than Woodforde himself lived there, and the local doctor had his home at Mattishall. Perhaps the most prosperous of the farmers was John Girling, or Galland, as the diarist at first pronounced his name. He was the squire's steward or land-agent and managed the Home Farm, while his eldest son became in the 1790s the gamekeeper on the Custance property. He had numerous servants and the list of households drawn up for the 1801 national census shows his home as containing one more person than the Great House itself - an unexplained mystery.[1] Men like him, or like the brothers Stephen and Michael Andrews, with their string of marriage alliances connecting them with other prominent families in and about Weston, were the acknowledged village notables. Their names appear and reappear from one generation to another in the records, as holders of the various offices under the vestry system.

Confusion begins to sully the hitherto clear picture only when one goes on to contemplate the smaller farmers for, as we have seen, they form a heterogeneous category all the way from those with quite substantial holdings, even if the acreages are nothing like Mr. Howlett's 400 acres, to smallholders with just enough land to support a cow or a few pigs. We see examples of men who combined farming with some other occupation, like John Pegg who was the local tax official, or "sub-collector", as he was named. When he finally left the village his brother James, also a farmer, took over the job.

Another thing we learn as we pursue these long-gone villagers in the records is that, once the humbler strata of village society are reached it is impossible to separate people into groups marked respectively "farmer" and "tradesman". Often a man whose chief occupation was to follow a trade also looked after a smallholding.

Or he might be the son of a farmer and work on the parental farm only as and when needed. The story of the Dunnell family comes in appositely here.

Barnabas and Mary Dunnell were not natives of Weston; nor were they married there. They first appear with the baptism of their seven children, born between 1740 and 1762. Henry or Harry Dunnell, born in the same year as Parson Woodforde, was a carpenter. His brother Barnard, whom we have already seen as the occupant of Weston Parsonage before the diarist went to live there, was a shoemaker. A third brother, Thomas, was also a woodworker, and made a special pair of gates for the Parson.

Less than a year after the baptism of his youngest child, Barnabas Dunnell died and was buried on 8 January 1763. Mary carried on with the farm. Although no unmarried woman would ever be granted a lease of a farm, or a licence to keep an inn, no objection was usually made to widows, who are often found presiding over both. By the time her husband died, the sons were growing up. She employed only one hired hand, an elderly man named Robin Buck, until he died in 1779 and was not replaced, which might suggest that her resources as an employer of labour were limited; but we know her sons also assisted her. It is difficult to estimate the extent of her farming operations by the size of her tithe contribution, for this was not consistent. In 1776 she paid no more than the inconsiderable sum of £4. 2. 6. But in the following year we are told that she was sub-leasing some of the "College Land", and paid £17. 1. 6. By 1781 her total obligation for tithe had risen to £20. 9. 6.

The member of the family with whom the diarist had most to do was Harry. He may not make much impression on the reader who meets him only through the selections in the O.U.P. edition of the diary. In the part of the manuscript dealing with the entries of the early Norfolk years, faithfully transcribed by the Parson Woodforde Society, his name occurs very frequently. Harry took part, as also did his brother Barnard, in the Parson's fishing expeditions. He also did an immense variety of jobs and ran all manner of errands. We find him "loading Brick" from a piece of wall bought from the owner of the recently demolished Witchingham Hall, driving his mother's horses when they were used "all Day to haul Earth to fill up the Hollow in my Garden", shearing and doing other farm jobs with Ben, fetching goods from Norwich, going for the doctor when Neighbour Downing was so ill with smallpox and, most curiously of all, bidding at an auction for "two oil Pictures" that Nephew Bill wanted. Harry was not only in regular employment about the Parson's home, but Woodforde took the step, most unusual for him, of paying him a retainer. We have the agreement for this, set down in the diary:

> This morning made a Contract with Harry Dunnett be=
> =fore my Nephew to give him 6/6 per Week and a
> Dinner each Day to work for me from this Day for one
> Year, and to which he agreed - A Dinner on Sundays - 2

The sum actually paid out was sometimes more or less, according to the amount and nature of the work done. Woodforde did not always specify what this was. In 1778 he did not renew the yearly agreement with Harry, either because he found that he no longer needed the workman's services on a regular basis, or perhaps found that it was less expensive to pay for the work that was actually done, at the time it was carried out. Woodforde continued to employ Harry on a variety of jobs, but as time went on the payments to him became less frequent.

In addition to employing them, he had other dealings with village people. He quite often bought meat and poultry from his neighbours, usually to supplement his regular supplies. In return, he is found occasionally selling off the surplus from his own farming operations. He has dealings with the parish officials, the churchwardens and overseers of the poor, although less is heard from him about these than might have been expected. He picked up scraps of village gossip. So, in one way and another he must have learned a great deal about the Weston people, although that knowledge, as relayed through his diary is scattered, fragmentary and needs to be searched for with some assiduity.

The best remembered of all Parson Woodford's actions in connection with his parishioners, ever since the appearance of the O.U.P. edition of selections from his diary in the 1920s, is the Christmas Day feast which he gave to the "poor old Men" and, finally, even an odd woman or two. This stemmed from a similar custom instituted by Woodforde's father at Ansford; but there had been a larger number of people invited, the parish clerk formally officiated as carver, and women and even children were invited - Will Coleman was once there, as a little boy. On the other hand the feast was in abeyance some years, but at Weston it was kept up without a break from 1776 to 1801. The emphasis was really on age rather than poverty; yet, as in all communities without an adequate welfare system, the two conditions were inextricably linked together.

The men who came to dinner from 1776 onwards must nearly all have been out-relief paupers, or, if they were still in work, could have been no more than odd-job men, like "Old Thos. Cushion" (or Cushing) or "Old Thos. Carr", who would come along and kill a pig for a shilling, or try to get rid of the Parson's obtrusive moles. But from 1778, and every succeeding year until 1792, quite another type of man appeared.

This was Thomas Cary, and he is particularly interesting because it is perfectly impossible to pigeon-hole him, or to turn him into the raw material of sociology. At first sight it might appear that two, or even three men of the same name were involved here; but further investigation soon makes it clear that all the references are to one and the same person. To begin with, he was a farmer, the only man invited to both the Tithe Audits and the charitable Christmas dinners; and that he did come to the former suggests that his holding was a reasonably large one, because, as we have noted, Woodforde did not accept as guests the very small tithe-payers, whose contributions would barely have covered the cost of feeding them and supplying them with drink. He was the local carrier, for years the only one, plying between the village and Norwich. Lastly, he ran the village shop, an amenity which innumerable villages the size of Weston and many much larger places had to do without. Woodforde's dealings with "Old Mr Cary" were carried out on a regular basis for many years. The carrier took letters to be posted in Norwich and collected incoming mail, and newspapers from the county town, he brought back to Weston Parsonage various kinds of shop goods, and in return sold surplus farm produce for Woodforde. He seems to have been an independent and even rather short-tempered man, and the Parson records his being "runty", or irritable, over some eggs he was asked to dispose of.[3]

The shop is often mentioned in the diary. Woodforde's main purchases there were of snuff and smoking tobacco, both of which he bought regularly. The entry for 19 November 1776 mentions buying "Snuff, garters, and Herring" - surely a very odd mixture of purchases. For the Tithe Audit of 1791 the shop supplied a pound and a half of sugar for making punch. In turn Woodforde sold to the shop excess quantities of such food items as butter. There is an interesting passage in the diary entry for 28 March 1792, which shows how the arrangement worked:

Rec^d, for one Pint of Butter this Morn
which was made last Week, but expecting M^r
and Mrs Bodham this Week we kept the above
Pint till this Morning, and they not coming
and we not wanting it sold it to Mr Cary -

The anomaly, of course, lies in his appearance at Christmas with the "poor old Men", for Mr. Cary was plainly not in need of a free meal once a year. It seems likely that, attaining the age of 60, the minimum age at which people became eligible, Cary simply added his name to the list and the parson did not object. Thomas Cary was not a native of Weston, and the first notice of him we have is the record of his marriage on 30 October 1735. His wife's name was Elizabeth; the surname is not clear enough for certainty, but may be "Moss". She died in September 1792, aged 81. There were nine children, the youngest being Charles, baptised 15/7/1753, a shoemaker by trade. In 1784, Woodforde married Charles Cary to his own former servant Elizabeth Claxton, the same who had not long before told Molly Dade that "she was in a Consumption". The Parson disapproved of this match, the bride being aged 44 and fifteen years older than the groom. But from that time he refers to the shop as "Charles Cary's", plainly a sign that his father had left the running of it to him. Eventually it became "Betty Cary's". Thomas continued to drive the carrier's cart, as a graphic entry dated on the last day of 1785 makes clear:

Poor old Mr Cary almost froze this Evening as he
came from Norwich - so very severe was the Cold -
He brought every thing safe however, he
brought me amongst other things a Hamper of
Wine from Mr Priests at Norwich - 2. Dozen -

He was still driving so late as 21 May 1792, when he was over 80. But in March 1793 it once more turned very cold, the kind of weather often fatal to elderly people with their weakened resistance. On the 28th Woodforde wrote: "Poor old Mr Cary very bad in a kind of Flux". In that context the term probably means the excessive mucus found in a severe case of bronchitis. On 4 April he reported: "Poor old Mr Cary at the point of Death". On the following day:

> Called this morning at Mr Carys, and found
> the old Gentleman almost at his last gasp-
> totally senseless and rattlings in his Throat -
> Dinner to Day boiled Beef and Rabbit roasted -
> Poor old Mr Cary died this Afternoon -

This must be one of the best-remembered passages in Woodforde, known to many people who could scarcely tell you anything else about him. It is famous because Virginia Woolf, in her essay *Two Parsons*, took it out of its context to subject it to the cool, sub-insolent Bloomsbury treatment, surrounding the quotation with her own comments, prefaced by "Life and death, mortality, jostle in his pages and make a good mixed marriage of it" and followed by "All is as it should be; life is like that". To get this effect the passage has been manipulated, the last line omitted so that it is made to end with the rabbit. In fact Woodforde made three references to Mr. Cary's death, and on 8 April 1793, after the funeral, went round and read the Will in the presence of the family. Mr. Cary's wife, the original beneficiary, having predeceased him, his belongings were to be divided between his six surviving children, "share and share alike". The total effects may have been "under £100"; all the same, his had been no pauper's life.

Real endemic poverty existed among those who, numerically by far the largest group, were at the rock bottom of the social pyramid, the labourers, often encumbered with large numbers of children, who were employed on a casual basis and were without security of any kind, totally unprotected against the contingencies of life. We meet several of these very indigent families in Woodforde; but he never describes them for us with anything like close attention to detail. It is as though, in spite of his optimistic view that the social order was divinely decreed, he was disinclined to run the risk of having his conscience pricked by the sight of so many hungry faces. In this era the term "the poor" had two quite distinctly different meanings. It could stand simply, as it does today, for poor people, those who happened to be poor. But it was also used to describe the entire labouring class, as though its existence were defined by the fact of its poverty. The term is used in this sense in such books at Eden's *The State of the Poor*.

There is one very graphic example of the sufferings which could afflict a poor workman in this society, going round from employer to employer, job to job, without regard to the dangers inherent in the work he was doing, or his manifest inability to do it at all. William Neave was epileptic, or, as Woodforde (who actually calls him "a poor labouring Man") put it, "subject to fits". Unmarried, alone, he lodged with a "Widow Hills" near the church. Threshing was one of the odd jobs by which men could keep going through the winter, the dead period of the farming year; which explains why the introduction by farmers a little later of threshing machines caused such dreadful havoc and destitution, incidentally leading to the "Swing" riots. William Neave was working for Mr. Girling on Wednesday, 11 November 1795, when he went up to the top of a barn after some barley to thresh, was seized by an epileptic fit and fell from top to bottom. When Woodforde saw him on the Sunday: "poor Fellow he appeared to me as if he could not recover - he could not speak & had no Sense at all in him - ". But his medical attendant, the inevitable Thorne, said that "no bone is broke". Woodforde left two shillings for the man, and went home. Some weeks later he parted with another shilling. But a man in the position of William Neave could not survive long without working, as for one reason or another he was clearly not eligible to receive Poor Law payments. By 5 April he was back at work, this time for Howlett, Girling's brother-in-law. This farmer was no doubt too considerate to send him up to the top of a barn, but apparently saw nothing amiss in putting him to work close to a ditch full of water. He had another fit and fell in. Woodforde supplies his only epitaph: "he was carried home but died on the Road".

But even these labourers, so long as they could manage to do their work without killing themselves over it, were not quite the worst off. However poverty-stricken and miserable their lives, they still had a recognizable though very lowly place in the community of which they formed a part. The most pitiable victims of this society were always the vagrants, people without homes or prospects, who had fallen right out of any social grouping and were alone in the fullest and deepest sense of that word.

Ironically, the English countryside in Parson Woodforde's day was more beautiful than it had ever been or would be again. But that could have brought little consolation to the unfortunate people who drifted through the lanes, without more direction or sense of purpose than fallen leaves blown on the wind. Those who have some curiosity or freak to show - a "Mongooz", or a calf with two heads - probably do best. Others are just beggars. Then, from time to time, one of them - they are usually men, although women also appear in this kind of catalogue - falls ill. He dies and is buried. Nobody knows who he is, and nobody cares. It is as though he has never lived.

CHAPTER 24

BLESS THE SQUIRE AND HIS RELATIONS

The Custance family came from the north-eastern region of Norfolk.[1] The earliest recorded ancestor was Robert, who had estates in Northwood, Winter Barningham and Bodham, "small windswept villages where the buildings are of flint". Robert's son William (b. 1533) married Frances Bacon, and his grandson, also William, married his cousin Katherine Bacon, this beginning the long alliance with the Bacon family which was still being renewed in Parson Woodforde's time. Katherine was the daughter of Clement Bacon, of Gresham, and her grandson, styled William of Gresham, married Bridget, daughter of the Rev. W. Atkins and had three sons.

The second of these was John Custance, born in 1673. The association between the rural gentry and trading and business interests had already begun in this family in the time of his father, who owned a worsted weaving concern. John Custance, however, migrated altogether to the city of Norwich and became a manufacturer of holland, a coarse linen fabric named from its country of origin. By this he became rich. He lived the life of a city magnate, residing in St. Andrew's parish, in the heart of the old city. He became Sheriff in 1712, Mayor in 1726 and again in 1750. His second wife was Sarah Hambleton, and by her he had his only two surviving children, Hambleton (b. 1713) and Sarah (b. 1715). When he died in 1752, John Custance was buried in St. Andrew's church, beneath "a handsome, urn-topped monument" erected by his son.

In the year in which he became mayor for the first time, he purchased the Weston estate for £5000, perhaps a quarter of a million today. According to a bond of 1734 it consisted of: 6 messuages, 1 dovehouse, 80 acres of meadow, 100 acres of pasture, 400 acres of land [i.e arable], 400 acres of heath, ... 10 acres of marsh, 20 acres of alder carr" ....". The estate may have been purchased as a speculation, one way of making private profits work; or to provide at some future time a place in the country where the head of the family might wish to settle. Certainly John Custance made no move towards building a country house of his own.

But the country gentlemen who had moved into the towns to make their fortune never made any move towards establishing anything like a true merchant aristocracy, such as existed in the Netherlands and Italy. The successful city merchant very often wanted no more, once he had accumulated sufficient wealth to make it possible, than to sell out and return to his origins. Land was the best of all investments, and riches derived from its possession had a far higher prestige and status value than mere money. Once they were landowners themselves, they had a fair chance of marrying their children into the nobility. The Mayors and City Sheriffs of one generation could became the Lords Lieutenant of the next.

Hambleton Custance went some way in this direction. He became a country squire after his marriage, when he bought the manor of Paston, also becoming High Sheriff of Norfolk in 1753. Hambleton was less robust and long-lived than his parents, and in 1757 he died, aged 42.

His wife, Susanna Press, was "in trade". She came from a wealthy Norwich family, which had lived for many generations in St. Saviour's parish, "their memorials cramming the dark aisles of the little church". Their tombs have the romantic coat-of-arms of a mermaid. Her father, John Press, was, like John Custance, sheriff and mayor of Norwich. She received on her marriage a dowry of £4000. Hambleton had a great friend named Thomas Nuthall, born like him in St. Andrew's parish; who also had a father who became Mayor of Norwich. A double portrait, a "conversation piece", so called, by Francis Hayman, now in the Tate Gallery, shows the two young men in sporting dress, "complete with shotgun, adoring dogs and dead game".[2] In the year Hambleton died (1757) his widow married Nuthall, but did not survive long, dying in 1761. While the portraits of Hambleton and his parents show them as rather heavy-featured people, Susanna was a beauty, and she handed her good looks down to three of her four children by Hambleton. These were John (1749), Press (1750), Susanna (1752) and Sarah (1754). Only the last was "not handsome" according to Woodforde.

The eldest was Woodforde's squire, perhaps the best remembered of all the multifarious characters in the diary, next to the Parson himself and Nancy. He was born on 18 September 1749, and, as we have seen, had lost both his parents by the time he was 12. Little or nothing is known about his early life, except that he was at Eton. His stepfather and presumably guardian, Thomas Nuthall, was a Solicitor to the Treasury, and it was no doubt through his influence that "John Custance of Ringland, Esquire", was admitted to Lincoln's Inn in 1765. He once told Woodforde about his youthful travels in Turkey, by which the great Ottoman Empire, spread equally between Asia and Europe, is meant.

Of only one thing we can be certain, that John Custance could never have wished to follow the trading interests of his grandfather. Even before his marriage, while he was still courting the young woman he was to marry, he was beginning to Plan a "new Hall". None of the Custances appear ever to have lived at Weston Old Hall, the seat of the Rookwood family. Part of it was later demolished, and its materials used in the buildings of the new mansion. The rest became a farmhouse, and survives to this day.

John Custance married at the age of 28. His bride, the "Mrs Custance" so well known through the diary, was Frances Anne, younger daughter of Sir William Beauchamp-Proctor (1st. baronet) and his wife Jane Towers of Langley Park in Norfolk. The family was descended from an Ephraim Beacham or Beauchamp, a London stonemason who is said to have worked on the construction of St. Paul's Cathedral. Langley Park came to William from his uncle, George Proctor, the son of William Proctor of Epsom, Surrey - hence the double-barrelled name. Frances was brought up in London, and married in the London church of St. Marylebone, on 29 January 1778. In that church, on the same day, her one-year older sister Anne was married to Sir Edmund Bacon, 8th, and 9th, baronet.[3]

It must have been very soon after their wedding that the Custances appeared in Norfolk. They were living at the Manor House in Ringland, familiar to John Custance from a much earlier period in his life, since as we saw, the notice of his admission to Lincoln's Inn was dated from there and his younger sister, Sarah, was actually born at Ringland. The baptismal records of the others have never been discovered, which is most unusual in that social class.

On 1 June 1778 Woodforde, happening to be in Ringland, called on Mr. Custance "to pay my Respects to him, but he was not at home". Four days later Mr. Custance courteously repaid that call. The cordial relations between the two men, which nothing was really ever to disturb, were established at the first meeting:

Mr Custance Senr of Ringland, called on us this morn'
caught me in a very great Disabelle, & long Beard -
He stayed with me above half an Hour - talked
exceedingly civil & obliging, & behaved very polite -

He first saw Mrs. Custance on 12 July, a Sunday, driving to and from Weston Church, "in a Coach & four". On 6 September, after church, both she and her husband "pressed me much to come & dine with them at Ringland any Day the ensuing week but Thursday". After an interchange of mutual courtesies the date was fixed, and Woodforde kept the appointment on the "following Tuesday".

Part of the entry for this day is very well known. The diarist was charmed and delighted by everything he saw; "I spent a most agreeable Day there and was very merry". He played backgammon with Mrs. Custance, and then she got out the "Sticcardo pastorale", a sort of miniature xylophone or glockenspiel, and knocked out tunes on the instrument: "it is very soft Music indeed". (This is one of the passages always quoted by journalists who write articles about Woodforde.) He also praised the "prettiest working Box with all sorts of things in it for the Ladies to carry about with them ... as big again as a Tea Chest". He added greatly impressed ... "It could not have cost less than five guineas".

This promising relationship was restricted at first by the absence of the squire and his family, whom the diarist did not see often, except when they turned up at his church. Woodforde exchanged the term "Mr Custance of Ringland" for "my Squire". Meanwhile the big house continued to rise, and the Parson went once or twice to look at its progress. Nancy, installed as his companion since late in 1779, was also taken by Mrs. Custance "in her Coach" to see the "New Building"; and once the young girl went up to the top floor of the mansion, although the banister rails had not yet been put in. Woodforde, with a less steady head for heights and perhaps remembering how he had once badly scared himself, scrambling about the old Town Walls of Oxford, sensibly stayed down below. At length, on 2 August 1781, the owners moved into their new house "to sleep there ..". Four days later Woodforde drank tea in the squire's new residence, while Nancy dined and spent the afternoon in it. [4]

The long and nearly always harmonious relationship of the squire and his rector was well covered in *The Diary of a Country Parson*, and this has left something of a misleading impression, as it has been taken almost as a paradigm of harmony in the pre-industrial world. I very much doubt if Custance can be taken for at all representative of the squirearchy as a whole. This was the time of agricultural change and improvements; above all, of enclosure; and enclosure, though hardly the unmitigated disaster for the labouring classes described by left wing historians, was carried out without a great deal of consideration for their interests, in most cases. It was also not so much the great landowners, among whom Mr Custance must be placed, as members of the smaller gentry and squirearchy, often in possession of encumbered estates and desperate to augment the yield of their land, who were the real pioneers of the enclosure movement. Custance himself had no time for it. He believed that it was harmful to the interests of the people, and, so long as he lived, refused to let it be done on his land. The manor was finally enclosed by his eldest son in 1822, the year of the father's death. In his dealings with his tenants and with the village people generally, he was a model of fairness and even generosity. He was a man who, honest himself, expected others to deal honestly with him. Yet, although he did not at all like to be cheated, he was far from being a vindictive man. All these things are exemplified by the story of the gardener Hylatt. Somehow Mr. Custance discovered that this gardener was robbing him and had just despatched by the Elsing carrier a small matter of the squire's finest strawberries and cucumbers, *en route* to a shop in Norwich. The indignant Custance got out a horse and chased the carrier until he caught up with it and recovered his property. He dismissed on the spot the dishonest son of the soil, but did not invoke the law against him, as he might well have done. Quite unabashed, Hylatt moved to Norwich, where he set up as a nurseryman and market gardener. It is surprising that Woodforde did not object to dealing with him, even on one occasion giving him dinner in the kitchen at Weston Parsonage. However, when the former gardener arrived, he saw Mrs. Custance's coach standing at the front door, and judged it advisable to stay out of the way until she had gone home.

For a helpmate and companion in the kind of life he wanted to lead, Mr. Custance had made a wise choice. Frances still lives for the reader as one of the most attractive characters in the diary. Allowing for the fact that for the first twelve years of her married life she was almost continually pregnant, "she had the gift of being cheerful in the most trying circumstances, and yet of feeling for the misfortunes of others". Her ethereal, beautiful face is well caught in the miniature portrait of her which has long been familiar through its reproduction in the O.U.P. edition of Woodforde.[5] Yet it is true that this apparent fragility must have been deceptive. She bore eleven children in twelve years, a frightful record which was an inevitable consequence when a married couple remained strongly attached to one another but had no available means of contraception. Three of these children died when they were still babies; Charlotte, the last born, died aged four, at the time when the family had left Weston for Bath. George, the second son, went to

India in the service of the East India Company, rose to the rank of Lieut. Colonel in its private army, and died in 1814, aged 35. All the others were long livers.

Woodforde's relations with this admirable pair were not precisely those of friendship, for they were not equals, and their respective places were bounded by the rules of social etiquette, which they were careful to observe. All the same there was a basis of mutual respect which greatly strengthened the bond between them; and even some affection. When the diarist wrote that Frances Custance and her sister, Lady Bacon, were the two best women in England, we are certainly not entitled to assume that he was being insincere, because the probability is that he really did feel in that way about them. The mercenary nexus observed in so many contemporary squires and clergy, with handouts on one side and flattery and subservience on the other, was entirely absent here. Mr. Custance was no politically influential magnate and particularly had no influence in church matters. He was never Woodforde's patron, in the sense that Mr. Townshend of Honingham was the patron of Mr. du Quesne. Although Woodforde can be seen sometimes timing his movements to suit the convenience of the Custances, they never made unreasonable demands on him, or expected him to dance attendance on them. And each time he did them a service, they paid him generously enough. When Woodforde baptized Mr. Custance's son and heir Hambleton Thomas, he was rewarded with a piece of "white Paper" containing 4 guineas. The next time he performed that service, the honorarium was upped to 5 guineas and remained at that figure. The same payment was made for the funerals of those babies who failed to survive.

The diary, as everyone who has read it must be aware, is full of the Custances: the grand parties are there, as well as the "Family Dinners" to which only the Parson and Nancy were invited. There was a constant interchange of gifts, from pearl necklaces to mackerel and apricots. Mrs. Custance lent the folk at Weston Parsonage books and her husband's copies of the *Gentleman's Magazine*, to which he was a subscriber. The children with their nursemaids, sometimes their mother, came and were given milk, cake, strawberries and cream; and were regaled with a sight of the model ship riding in the "Basin". Was this the vessel originally made by Nephew Bill, which had ingloriously capsized on its maiden voyage across the great pond, after guests had been invited to witness its launching? 6

In 1791, significantly enough just after the birth on Christmas Eve of her eleventh and last child, Frances Custance was assailed by some undefined ailment, which must surely have been brought about by so many pregnancies and the very short spaces of time between them. For five months she lay in bed, hardly able to move. When on 30 May 1792 she came downstairs for the first time since the onset of her illness, the church bells were rung and guns fired in her honour. Shortly after this, and to the dismay of the Parson, and to Nancy in particular, it was announced that the family was to leave Weston House and go to live in Bath.

CHAPTER 25

CRIME AND CRIMINALITY

The impression that one gleans from a first reading of James Woodforde's diary is of a community at peace with itself. It is true that a more detailed and searching investigation reveals traces of a latent violence, which however came into the open infrequently, and could nine out of ten times be defused without causing harm to anyone. And as the diarist, selecting like all his kind the topics he wished to write about and suppressing the rest, a process in which he was enthusiastically abetted by the first of his editors, produced what is for some part a chronicle of undisturbed rural peace, it is possible, with the aid of a little or a great deal of undisturbed skipping, for a reader to see it as depicting a totally innocuous society. Like Hazlitt's famous sundial, it could seem to be saying "Horas non numero nisi serenas" - I count only the quiet hours. It was this that made Woodforde into one of the great classics of escapist literature, and provided a very good reason for the immediate success of *The Diary of a Country Parson* only a few years after the Great War, with all its appalling horror, had come to an end.

On the other hand, if the greatest possible contrast to the gentle, placid life of Ansford and Weston Longville were sought, one could easily find it in the catalogue of bizarre murders and other crimes of gross violence with which the *Gentleman's Magazine* and other periodicals regaled their readers. We cannot explain this in terms of a simplistic differentiation between the peaceful village and the crime-ridden city. for the accounts were sent in from all parts of the country. It can only be concluded that Woodforde was lucky. His villages seem to have been almost crime-free during his lifetime. We shall note the exceptions to this generalization as we come to them.

It goes without saying that Woodforde himself was a law-abiding man. There are just two ways in which he can be seen as having broken the law. One was through his dealing with smugglers. As the passages from the diary which show him doing this have tended to be taken out of their proper context and high-lighted, it is commonly imagined that he bought smuggled goods on a much larger scale than he actually did. The other was that, after income tax had been brought in, he assessed his income at about one third below its real value. In both these evasions, most of the worthy citizens in his social class did or would have done the same, without their consciences being burdened by the realisation that in so doing they were conniving at criminal behaviour.

In the diary there are only two instances of serious crime in which he was personally involved, even to the slight extent of knowing the criminals. Both cases belong to the latter part of Woodforde's life in his native county. In 1772 Thomas Burge, "a poor ragged but bad Fellow", (who had already been compulsorily married to a woman pregnant by him, the overseers bringing him "handbolted" to the church), together with his son, also Thomas but nicknamed "Job", stole the large sum of £70 from a farmer, Edward Speed. They hid the loot in various clumsy and amateurish ways and, soon detected, were tried and both sentenced to 7 years transportation.[1] Three years later Reginald Tucker, already mentioned, murdered his wife by striking her on the head with a sledgehammer, "of the value of Twelve pence" according to the indictment, by which her skull was broken in three places. The Woodfordes were heavily involved in this case. Sister Clarke and her husband the doctor, had put the Tuckers up at "Dr. Clarke's new Hospital" until they could find a place of their own, and others of the family had been served with subpoenas by one side or the other. James himself, who had been in Oxford when the crime was committed, attended the trial at Wells as a "character witness". The judge was the elder brother of William Burland, now long dead, whose rooms Woodforde had once occupied at New College. The hearing began at 8 in the morning and took up the greater part of one day. Woodforde sat there - he says it was very hot, and no doubt, after an initial attempt to concentrate, he soon lost the thread of the legal arguments - until late afternoon; and then sneaked out to get himself something to eat. When his name was called, he was absent; but it could have made no difference to the outcome of the trial. By the time he returned, the judge was summing up. Reginald Tucker was found guilty and hanged three days later.[2]

At Weston, such law-breaking as the diarist recorded tended to be of the pettiest conceivable variety, mere peccadillos that the good-natured diarist was ready to overlook: "I caught Paul Bowden this Evening lopping an Ashen Tree of mine - gave him a Lecture and told him to take care for the future" (28/10/1788). Where it took a more serious form, the perpetrators were mainly townspeople preying upon the country dwellers:

> Mʳ Custance told me this morning that he had a few
> Days ago about 80. Turkies, geese, Ducks & Fowls   taken
> from him in one Night - many of them that were fatting -
> This is the time of the year that many idle Fellows
> from Norwich go about the Country stealing Poultry
> to send them to London to make a Penny of them -
> I never had any stolen yet, but daily expect it - [3]

The roads into and out of Norwich could upon occasion be dangerous. Mrs. Dade the farmer's wife was robbed of two guineas by a footpad, the unmounted poor relation of the highwayman, at "the 3. Mile Stone", the third milestone out of Norwich on the road to Weston Longville. This sort of crime was always freely reported in the newspapers, scaring respectable householders as much as far worse and more vicious offences do their equivalents today:

> ... Country news very bad, hearing of nothing but High=
> =waymen and breaking houses open at Norwich -
> Trade at Norwich never worse - Poor no Employment - [4]

This entry gives us another clue as to the nature of 18th century crime against property. Much, perhaps most of it, was opportunistic and non-professional, caused by want and distress and tending to fluctuate as economic conditions worsened or improved. And it must be seen in perspective. The diarist went regularly into Norwich with Dr. Bathurst's tithe receipts and his own, considerable sums of money "in Cash and Notes", to deposit them in Kerrison's bank. If he was at all worried by the possible risk of being robbed, he never confided such fears to his diary.

Is it possible, then, on the basis of the evidence, to aver that there was a kind of social dichotomy here: serious, often violent and murderous crime in the towns and those parts of the countryside nearest to the towns or linked to them by main roads, and very slight infringements of the law; hardly worth calling criminal at all, in the rural areas? The answer to that question is clearly negative. There were in fact two widespread and potentially serious crimes that were typically those of country districts, since they both grew out of the conditions of village life.

The first of these was poaching. The preservation of game had always been a perquisite of the landowning class, who by this means became assured of a supply of fresh meat all the year round. This was of immense practical benefit through the centuries when it had been difficult to keep much farm stock alive throughout the winter, owing to the lack of adequate supplies of fodder. In the 18th century, however, this traditional reason for keeping game, which was anyway becoming less important with the advances made by new or improved crop-producing and stock-breeding techniques, was supplanted by another. It became the mark of a superior status to have a game park, the larger and more liberally stocked, the better. The enclosure movement, which gave the owner the free use of land previously locked up in the communal open-field system, also tended to encourage the practice of large-scale game preserving. The temptations to steal game were more powerful, and this was countered by the growing ferocity of the Game Law, that typical reaction of a Parliament largely composed of landowners faced by a threat to their property. Between 1760 and 1816 no fewer than 33 Acts designed to curb the activities of poachers were put on to the Statute book. One of these, passed in 1760, laid down that a person convicted of poaching at night was on a first offence to be punished by six months imprisonment. Although this was replaced three years later by another Act which allowed the option of fines, these were so heavy, from £10 to £50 according to the number of previous convictions, that no man on a labourer's wage could possibly have paid them - and one who was sentenced to pay a fine could be kept in prison indefinitely, until the fine was paid. [5]

In 1800 another Act was passed, under which two or more persons found poaching together were given hard labour, and for a second offence were to be whipped, or alternatively made to serve in the army or navy. In 1803 came the notorious Ellenborough Act, by which offering armed resistance to arrest - for example, if a poacher fired a gun at a gamekeeper and missed - became a capital offence, for which men could be hanged. In 1817 even poaching by unarmed men at night was made punishable by seven years transportation. If the man returned from the penal colony before that time was expired, he was transported back again, this time for life. Further, entirely in the spirit of this one-sided class legislation, landowners were permitted to set mantraps and spring guns on their property. Some of the traps had a spring powerful enough to break a man's leg, and their long teeth could inflict a terrible wound. They were banned in 1825, not out of humanity to the poachers, but because too many keepers were getting caught in them.

Many historians, and particularly those whose sympathies tend to lie left of centre, rather idealise poachers, seeing them as poor and hungry people whose only offence was to try to eke out their children's meagre diet with an occasional hare or partridge, or something tasty out of the squire's fishpond. It may have been so, but single-handed and amateur poachers were the most likely to get caught, and the penalties prescribed by successive Game Laws must have been sufficient to deter all but the boldest of villagers. It was the professional poaching gangs which were not in the least deterred. They operated in numbers, and conducted their nefarious operations almost like military campaigns. On 30 November 1784 Woodforde wrote that "Mr Townshend went to Weston House ... to talk with Mr Custance about a Gang of Poachers, that infest his Woods". They were ready to act with the greatest brutality if challenged. Just over a year later the diarist entered:

> ... Poor Tom Twaites of Honingham who was beat by the
> Poachers at Mr Townshends the other Day, is lately dead of the
> Wounds he then recd from them - His Skull was fractured in 2.
> Places -6

He was Mr. Townshend's gamekeeper, described elsewhere as "old". The employment of an elderly man in such a position may suggest that the violence was of recent origin. The murder stayed in the diarist's mind so that when, two days later, he saw two men, strangers and "dressed meanly", walking "slowly and demurely" across one of his fields, he at once took them "to be some of the Poachers that were at Mr Townshends lately and by whom old Tom Twaites lost his life". Just over two years later one of the men involved in the murder was captured, and promptly purchased his own life by implicating eleven more people, clear proof that the murder had been the work of a large gang. 7

Apart from these references, Woodforde has little or nothing to say about poachers. He did not preserve game himself, and his participation in field sports, shooting in his early Somerset days and coursing at Weston, took place by the friendly permission of various landowners. Their employees were not always so amiable. In 1777 it was another of Townshend's gamekeepers, "Black Jack", sounding like a character in Fielding, who shot two greyhounds belonging to Woodforde. But he was invited up to Honingham Hall a week later, along with Mr. du Quesne, to drink tea. The host "handsomely apologised" for the incident, and "told me moreover that whenever I had an inclination to a Hare I was very welcome to take a course with Mr. du Quesne upon his Lands". Woodforde even made it up with the gamekeeper by sending him a shilling tip. The man responded by making him a present of a greyhound puppy.

Our other major countryside crime was the contraband trade in smuggled goods, and this is perhaps the most interesting form of 18th century lawbreaking, since it derived entirely from the particular sort of taxation favoured at the time. Smuggling was inextricably bound up with the fiscal system which had brought it into being, and upon which it preyed, rather as a parasite lives at the expense of its host.

The essential point to remember is that by far the great proportion of the national revenue came not from direct taxes, of which the Land Tax was the only important one, but from indirect or "commodity" taxation. There were five major wars in which Britain was involved in the 18th century. Each of them created its own demand for increased revenue, and while a consequence of this was a huge expansion of the National Debt, the trouble there was that such borrowing carried rates of interest which rose according to the Government's increasing need for money, and had eventually to be repaid. Anything taken in the form of tax, on the contrary, was clear gain, with no deductions beyond the cost of collection. Throughout the 18th century and beyond, the number of taxable commodities increased and the duties on those already subject to tax were pushed up higher. In 1787 there were 1425 articles liable to bear duty, many of which were taxed up to levels above their market value. A manufacture which required the material to be taken through a number of processes was taxed at each stage in its development, and a final duty imposed on the finished product. [8]

This was upon the whole an epoch of considerable though very unequally distributed prosperity, and the great expansion of industry and trade contributed to a general rise in the standard of living; most marked indeed in the higher echelons of society, but filtering down to some extent to all except the very poorest. Articles of consumption which had not long before been regarded as luxuries and available only to the wealthy came more and more to turn into necessities of civilised life, creating a redoubled demand for them. The merchant, or importer, passed the cost of the duty on to his customer, so goods naturally became more expensive as the tax on them was raised. Whether or not buyers could afford to bear the full legal charge on their purchases, there is no doubt that the public as a whole greatly begrudged the inflated prices they were expected to pay. No law, command or rule is workable if it is flouted with impunity by a large enough number of people. The only way the public had of obtaining certain kinds of goods at what was considered a reasonable price was by patronising the smuggler. Undoubtedly, to the satisfaction of saving money through the smuggler's much lower prices must have been added the pleasure of doing the Government down. Only this can explain why all over the country the most upright and respectable citizens purchased contraband as a matter of course, without in the least considering themselves as abetting criminals, and certainly without knowledge of what the smugglers were really like.[9]

Not all goods, of course, attracted the smuggler. His activities were mainly concerned with a comparatively small number of high-duty, high-profit commodities, all in the category of "Customs and Excise". The first originally meant the duties levelled on imports, the value of which was granted for life to the monarch on his or her accession, so called as being in accordance with the "custom" of the realm. Excise, new in the early years of the 18th century, had aroused such furious opposition that the first Excise Bill was withdrawn by Walpole, whose administration had introduced it. Then it was revived by the Younger Pitt, who established the Customs and Excise Board in 1784. Wines, spirits, tea and tobacco were all exciseable articles, and their illegal importation made up most of the smugglers' commerce.

Meanwhile, the dislike and mistrust which had greeted the first appearance of the excisemen, the "wretches hired by those to whom excise is paid", in the words of Johnson's famous dictionary definition, had not abated. They faced what was essentially a hostile countryside. The smugglers in their heyday enjoyed a quite extraordinary freedom of action, and were able to move about in the prosecution of their nefarious trade, almost with impunity. All over the land people who had in the ordinary way as little sympathy with crime and criminals as Parson Woodforde, knew what it meant when they heard a whistle on a dark night.

Faced by efficiently organised crime on this scale, the Government was forced to retaliate, and this led to a state of internecine war, mostly on the Channel coast but also as far away as Cornwall, a notorious smuggling centre, between the smugglers and the "Preventive men" who tried to stop them from landing their cargoes. In addition, the smugglers were in constant danger from spies and informers within their ranks, and faced heavy penalties if caught. To defend themselves they resorted to the most brutal forms of intimidation, literally terrorising the people to such an extent that even when a smuggler was brought to trial, it was often impossible to find a jury that would dare to convict him. One of the most atrocious crimes in the entire history of 18th century evildoing, in which a customs officer and an informer were murdered in the most hideously sadistic ways, came about precisely because of this kind of situation.

But a respectable buyer, like Woodforde, at the other end of the smuggling chain, would not have known about these horrors; or if they had been brought to his notice he would no doubt have answered that what the smugglers did was no responsibility of his. Many of his more intellectually inclined contemporaries would perhaps have provided a moral justification for dealing with smugglers, the argument being that the legal dues were unreasonable, even monstrously high, and that the Government was the real thief. I think it is unlikely that the Parson ever analysed the question in that way. Such mental exercises were alien to his matter-of-fact temperament. In all probability he dealt with smugglers because they saved him money, and because everyone round him was doing the same. And not only would he have been far from thinking himself tainted by the least criminality, but his suppliers, one pig-dealer, one parish clerk, one blacksmith, would also have vigorously denied any such dishonourable imputation. The dirty work, if there was any, had all been done by others, miles away, and all that was left was a perfectly innocent transaction of sale and purchase.

Woodforde's main purchases of this kind were of gin, brandy, rum and tea. He was far from relying on smugglers for any of these commodities for the diary shows perfectly legal buying-in of all these things. For example, he bought a great deal of his tea from a Mrs. Brewster, trading as Brewster and Gilman, haberdashers, in Norwich, from whom he bought a great variety of articles, including the cockades in the Tory colours for his servants to wear in their hats at the time of the general Election of 1784. But the smuggler was still always there, cheap and reliable.

In the sort of liberal atmosphere I have described, householders like Woodforde could take delivery of smuggled goods on a regular basis over many years, without having anything to fear from either public opinion or the revenue laws. There is only one recorded occasion when he was to some extent worried about the possible consequences of this. In September 1792, just after picking up a tub of rum left for him as usual outside his window, he heard what he calls "bad Reports about the Parish"; which in that context would appear to be an euphemism for rumours that the excisemen were checking up. On 17 September he wrote "I got up very early this Morning and was very busy all the Morn' on very necessary business". Mr. Beresford conjectured that this meant he was "engaged in hiding, even burying, his smuggled rum", and this is very likely to have been right. By the statute 9 Geo. III c.69 (1769), Woodforde could have been fined £10 on each purchase of contraband he was proved to have made as well as having the goods confiscated. Although this was not much of a penalty for a man in his financial position, he would surely have disliked very much the attendant scandal of a beneficed clergyman's being prosecuted for a smuggling offence.

But, by comparison with its severity in dealing with the actual smugglers the law was surprisingly lenient in this direction. The supplier, in this case, was John Buck, or "Moonshine", as he was called (it was a slang term applied both to a smuggler and the contraband goods he dealt in). He could have been fined up to £50, a very large sum for any working man to pay, even if he had been doing well out of the contraband trade. However, on 12 October Woodforde reported that "John Buck the Blacksmith, who was lately informed against for having a Tub of Gin found in his House that was smuggled, by the excise Officers, was pretty easy fined". He suspected that another villager, John Norton, had been the informer. If so, either the Parson had been left out of the denunciation or, more likely, the excise officials were not interested in prosecuting the customers. Indeed, all through the time when smuggling was most rife, it is very difficult to find cases where any action was taken against the buyers of contraband; another proof, if one is needed, of how widespread was the practice of dealing with smugglers; with so many delinquents that it would never have been possible to proceed against more than a tiny fraction of the total number.

CHAPTER 26

AILMENTS AND DOCTORS

There is a great deal about illness, and medicine, and doctors, in Parson Woodforde's diary. In a few cases we can identify the precise nature of the malady from which a given person suffered. Far more often we are left in the position of both the doctors in his pages and their patients, with faulty or non-existent diagnosis, no idea of the way to treat the illness, and descriptions of symptoms so vague as to be of little or no practical value in helping us to form an opinion. What passed for medical science was often no more than folklore attended by guesswork, the accumulated detritus of centuries of error, enlivened here and there by a few valuable discoveries, which the doctors sometimes knew how to make use of properly, and more often did not.

The Woodforde family of Ansford had upon the whole a good medical record; excellent for the times in which they lived. They started out with three great advantages, reliable weapons for fighting the battle of life. They lived in the country, and so were far less exposed to the epidemic diseases that ravaged the townsfolk. They were rich enough to be spared that malnutrition which weakened and distorted the bodies of so many. Best of all, the majority of them had the genetically acquired high resistance to disease-processes, lacking which a lifetime of anything approaching a normal length was hardly possible.

They produced some striking instances of longevity. James' eldest sister Clementina Sobieski lived to be 96. Born in the reign of George I, she lasted until six years after the battle of Waterloo. Not far behind was the much disliked Uncle Tom, who was 94 when he died. His son and her daughter, a married couple, lived into their late 80s.

But this resistance could sometimes fail, as it did with the family of Robert White, who married Woodforde's second sister Mary in 1753. When she died in 1804, only one of her children, the younger Robert, was still alive. All the others had died as children or young adults. Mary White, the eldest daughter, at 13: Jenny White, James Woodforde's favourite niece as a child, "a good little Maid", and in the midst of an epidemic of what was plainly diphtheria, aged 10: James White, the diarist's godson, who lived long enough to become the partner of his uncle, "Lawyer White", Betsy White's father; but then died, aged 27: Anna Maria White, 16, died of tuberculosis, at the Bristol Hot Well, a place renowned for the treatment of chest troubles - not that it could do anything for such afflicted patients.

The most pathetic of these untimely deaths is that of John or Jacky White, because his sufferings were so prolonged and so hopeless. He was the eldest son of Robert and Mary, and in 1771 he was 15. He is mentioned as being present at the funeral of his sister Jenny on 13 July, along with his father and two brothers - "Crape Hatbands & black Gloves ..". On 31 August Woodforde wrote: "Very sultry hot to day, poor little Jack White very bad again. The hot Weather very bad for him , he thinks he shall not recover"; and added a long and emotionally expressed prayer. It is impossible to say with any confidence what really ailed him, but he seems to have had a very large abscess, possibly tubercular, in the intercostal region. For this a really desperate expedient was decided on:

> ... little Jack Whites Side was opened this afternoon
> by Mr James Clarke, from whence issued vast quan=
> =tities of well concocted matter, which I hope by the
> blessing of God, will be the means of his Recovery -
> There now appears some hopes of his doing well - [1]

Surgical operations were for the most part confined to cutting off mangled or gangrened extremities, the cockpit of *H.M.S. Victory* being the scene that has most captured the popular imagination; the unfortunate sailor first stupefied with rum and the stump afterwards daubed with hot pitch in an attempt to stave off the almost inevitable sepsis. Among the rare possible internal operations was lithotomy, the removal of stones from the bladder, for which condition Woodforde's brother John received surgery in his boyhood. In Jack White's case, the sheer agony of such a procedure carried out without any form of anaesthesia is as horrifying to conceive as the terrible danger involved. Not surprisingly, the operation soon revealed signs that it had gone wrong:

> Sister Jane dined, supped &c. at Sister Whites, the
> little boy being very bad and in great Pain, his
> Side was closed up this morning, and therefore a
> Caustick was obliged to be put to it to open it again -
> he was better and the pain subsided. [2]

Woodforde continued to report the fluctuations of his condition. Always one to look upon the bright side, he recorded the most transient and illusory signs of apparent improvement; but is is clear that he had very little hope of his nephew's recovery. In March 1772 another medical advisor, Dr. Bragg of Sherborne, was brought in, "who probed his Side & found it to be ulcerous under his ribbs, and that opening of it would be of no Service - He thinks (I apprehend) a gone case". [3]

The most that can be said is that all this did not prove immediately fatal to poor Jacky. He lingered for some time, occasionally being able to be taken out in the chaise that Woodforde had inherited from his father, or to dine with one or other of the family. The diarist sent him veal and trout to tempt his appetite. But in the spring of 1773 he weakened, and the swelling in his side greatly increased. At the beginning of May he was so ill that Woodforde prayed for his release. The diarist's elderly Aunt Anne was also terminally ill. The two patients are often bracketed together in the diary, as in the entry for 19 May: "Poor Jack White but indifferent - Madam Anne something better". And 23 May: Poor Jack White bad - Madam Anne very bad and light" - by which last term it was evidently meant that she was delirious. There was time for only one more macabre bulletin - "He gets worse and worse poor Fellow, nothing scarce but Blood comes from his Stools & eats very little indeed" - before Jack White died on 2 July. The old woman, his great-aunt, had predeceased him by a fortnight.

In Woodforde's time much of eastern England still remained imperfectly drained. In innumerable swamps and stagnant pools the anopheles mosquito, carrier of malaria, lived and bred unchecked. The disease, always referred to by the much older term "ague", occurs frequently in the diary. Although Woodforde himself apparently never caught it, the disease was always about, and from time to time, no doubt when particular climatic conditions made the mosquitoes unusually prevalent, assumed real epidemic proportions. The outbreak that affected Weston Longville and surrounding villages in the summer of 1783 was of considerable severity, and the Parson's graphic account of the way his own household was affected is full of the detail which the readers of his diary expect of him.

The "Fever which is going about" must have made its appearance at least some days before Jack Warton, the yard boy, went down with it on 8 August, Woodforde at once gave him a dose of his favourite nostrum, "rhubarb". Next day, the "Under Maid", Lizzy (sometimes called Betty) Greaves, the immediate predecessor of Molly Dade, became ill. She was a very small girl, often called by the diarist "My little Maid", and various accounts of her suggest that she was not in robust health. Dr. Thorne was "sent for", and arrived at 11 o'clock that morning, to examine the patients, "and in the Evening they are to have some things for him to take". Woodforde then went off to deputise for Mr. du Quesne in conducting a very special funeral, that of the infant daughter of Mr. Townshend of Honingham Hall. He does not actually say that when he returned home at 8 that evening it was to find that the doctor's promised medicine had not arrived, but this is perhaps to be inferred from his next action:

> We found both of our sick Servants gone to bed & very ill
> I had them both up and to each gave a Vomit ab[t]
> 10. o'clock and then sent them back to bed after it had
> done working ... [4]

Nearly a week after this the medical man, who was being rushed off his feet, came to dine, "but was obliged to leave us immediately after Dinner, having a great many Patients to visit". He now proposed to treat Lizzy with "the Bark". This, variously known as Peruvian bark, Jesuit's bark, cinchona and, to us, quinine, was one of the few specifics in the pharmacopoeia of the time that was of actual benefit in combating a particular illness. Woodforde's interest in medical affairs is shown here in the way he copied down the doctor's course of treatment. Lizzy was to be given the "Bark every two hours" until she had taken twelve of the powders. Two of the other servants were deputed to stay up with her at night, in relays. If the medicine caused purging, she was to take laudanum, the tincture form of opium, in gradually decreasing dosages. The bark was not to be taken in the phases of very high temperature.
Ironically enough in the light of all this, after Lizzy had taken only two powders, one at 4 o'clock and another at 4 the next morning, it appeared to Woodforde that she was so much worse that he abruptly stopped the treatment. He sent a message to Dr. Thorne, who made no attempt to defend it, "and he sent her some Camphire Powders, and not take any more bark at all". Neither Woodforde nor the doctor had of course any idea of why quinine was beneficial in cases of malaria and camphor useless. But it was the diarist who was paying for the treatment, and this was a society in which the customer was always right.

At the end of August Will developed the disease; then Ben, so that four out of the five servants were ill, only the hard-boiled Elizabeth Claxton seeming to be immune. Lizzy's mother had been brought in, to help with "Washing Week" and do other jobs about the house. The epidemic was now at its height. Woodforde wrote, as we have seen, that the doctors were now calling it the "Whirligousticon", from the giddiness that was a characteristic symptom, and that it was "almost in every House in the Village". Fortunately he had a number of parties to go to: a meal with the Bodhams, who had both had the disease early on, but recovered, an exceptionally grand dinner with the bishop of Norwich when there were sixty dishes on the table, and another with Mr. and Mrs. Micklethwaite at Hungate Lodge. Each day at Weston Parsonage, if one servant could be reported better another, and on one occasion three of them together, became worse. Woodforde clearly began to feel that the situation was getting him down. On 3 October he wrote gloomily: "I had a very indifferent Night last Night, ... much oppressed with low Spirits and much hurried with startings &c. in my sleep". However, soon after this all the quartet must have got better quickly.

In the spring of the following year malaria returned. This time Nancy went down with it. When her uncle saw on 7 March that she was "very ill with Cholic Pains", he at once connected them with the epidemic of the previous summer and autumn. But her illness lasted only about a week. Dr. Thorne was called in, and at once put her on the bark. Woodforde had in the meantime completely changed his mind about that remedy, or perhaps the doctor had convinced him of its efficacy. He now wrote down in greater detail than before the doctor's "Method of treating the Ague and fever, or intermitting Fever", which included quinine, and on 18 March noted down: "Nancy brave again now by taking the Bark".

This story of the malaria epidemic, and others of its kind in the diary, can tell us something about the medical profession in Woodforde's time. It was in a state of transition, striving to slough off its ancient and traditional associations with mere blood-letting, and to gain recognition as a profession, on a par with the other professions. To a certain extent this had been achieved. The Royal College of Physicians was, on paper, an extremely powerful body. It had been granted sweeping powers of appointment and supervision, in its own court, of unlicensed practitioners. These attempts at regulation, however, were unsuccessful, because they did not have the authority, in practice, that comparable institutions possessed on the Continent, and because in an age of 'laissez-faire' such regulation was highly unpopular".5 The courts had no sympathy for the medical institutions and the public disliked this sort of medical oligarchy more than it disapproved of the unlicensed "quacks".

As a result, there were doctors of all kinds, only a minority of whom had the degree of M.D. awarded by the Royal College of Physicians. The commonest way of entering the profession was that adopted by James Clarke, who had served an apprenticeship to his father. Others, like Johnson's friend Robert Levet, had been no more than servants to some practitioner, and had managed to pick up a smattering of knowledge. No doubt at least some of these men would by long experience have acquired a considerable fund of empirical skill which came in very useful in their dealings with patients. But properly qualified doctors in the modern sense of that term they certainly were not.

The fairly low status of the ordinary village physician - Dr. Thorne was consulted by the squire's family only for trifling complaints and otherwise they preferred a more fashionable doctor in Norwich - helps us to understand why Parson Woodforde made no bones about countermanding a mode of treatment he suspected was harming the patient. It was part of a general attitude towards medicine and medical affairs that was eventually to change. From the first half of the 19th century onwards, with what became a huge advancement in medical knowledge, a gulf began to open between doctor and patient with regard to their respective ability rightly to comprehend the cause of the latter's malaise, and helped to convince the layman that blind faith in the doctor was the only possible basis for a satisfactory relationship between them

There was scarcely a trace of this passivity in Woodforde's time. A few very fashionable doctors in London and Bath became celebrated consultants who could afford to lord it over their patients. It was far more common for patients, if rich enough, to hire and fire their doctor at will, occasionally treating them with the aggressive bullying familiarity adopted by some landowners towards their domestic chaplains. A professional man like Woodforde was aware that the doctors of his time probably did not know a great deal more about their subject than he knew himself; but he was always willing to make practical use of that difference, such as it was. His usual custom was to dose himself and his servants with mainly home-made remedies, so long as the condition he was trying to cure remained lacking in danger; but once it appeared to be serious he was ready to call in the doctor.

His independence was reinforced by a feeling that the intelligent layman could safely be left to prescribe for himself, so long as he was given the facts to work on. The demand for medical literature, written in straightforward prose, neither Latin as in the past, nor the incomprehensible jargon of such productions today, was met by the booksellers, who issued every sort of medical work, from penny pamphlets to large, expensive volumes. The best-known and by far the most popular of contemporary medical books was William Buchan's *Domestic Medicine*, which first appeared in 1769 and was then reprinted for almost a century. We do not know that Woodforde had a copy, but he mentions this book twice in the diary, and it contained several Woodfordean cures, for example rhubarb, camphor, Dr. Glauber's Salts and "Turner's Cerate", all listed by the author as easily adaptable to home use. It was, of course, useless to read about medicines unless it were possible also to buy them, or at least the ingredients which could then be made up at home. But a trade in medicines had already developed. Woodforde's friend Robert Priest of Norwich, the wine-merchant, was also a pharmacist, or had a partner who looked after that side of their joint business. In 1784 a provincial newspaper, the *Coventry Mercury*, told its readers that over a hundred different medicines could be purchased from a local bookseller.[6]

Undoubtedly this must have played a part in the spread of the hypochondriac, people like Mr. Sewell, a member of the Thrales' social circle in London, who was known as a "valetudinarian", one whose sole topic of study was the contemplation of his own problematical health. Amateur physicians must often have put themselves in danger through swallowing a larger quantity of useless and semi-toxic medicaments than even their doctors would have given them. In the 17th century hypochondriasis had been classed as an organic disorder of the lower bowel, caused by having too little of the "chondria" or black bile, a notion that belonged to the old doctrine of humours. It now became a morbid mental state, characterised by anxiety about one's health, a meaning it of course still retains. It has been written, perhaps with some exaggeration, that "Georgian England was becoming a medicated society, drunk on self-drugging", many of the drugs being habit-forming and likely to lead to addiction.[7]

It is unlikely that Woodforde, at least until his last years when his health was seriously impaired, ever was a full-blown "hypochondriac", in this sense. If he tended to be nervous about his physical condition, and to use the term "very ill" when assailed by what we would dismiss as trivial ailments, he does not give us the impression of being excessively frightened.

CHAPTER 27

"WE HAVE LOST MR. WOODFORDE"

James Woodforde was for most of his life a reasonably healthy man. He lived into his 63rd year, a life-span his contemporaries would have considered long and extending into old age. He was, it is true, not one of the most robust of men. His father, as we have seen, considered him "very ill" when he conducted his baptism at three days old. As a schoolboy at Winchester, he suffered an attack of smallpox, almost certainly caused by the inoculation procedure that was intended to prevent the disease attacking him. From the age of 19, when he began to keep his diary, we have what is virtually a day-to-day record of his state of health. From this, fuller and more detailed than anything of its kind that we possess for the life of any of his contemporaries, we can see that he was fully able to enjoy an active life. As an undergraduate, he took part in the sports and games played by his fellow-collegians and other active young men. Cricket was certainly far less dangerous to life and limb than that game has become today, but it was never a pastime for invalids or weaklings. He played bowls and was quite an expert skater. Another kind of endurance is shown by his ability to stand long nights. On more than one occasion he mentions playing cards all night - and doubtless drinking hard all the time - without any seeming ill-effects.

For a long time I had the impression that he was a small, slight man, but as he several times refers to this or that acquaintance or person met by chance as "little", a term he would himself have been unlikely to use if he had been of particularly small stature himself, it is probably nearer the mark if he is visualised as a middle-sized person. Certainly he was no man of muscle, a type less admired in his day than it is in ours. He had three fist-fights during his time at University - this is not counting the time when he "threshed" the saddler's apprentice, who seems not to have offered the least resistance - and got decidedly the worst of two of them. He and John Webber, later the Junior Proctor, whom Woodforde was to assist as Pro-Proctor, quarrelled in the Bachelor's Common Room and repaired to New College garden to settle their differences, whereupon "He beat me unmercifully, being as strong again".[1] Another combat was more serious, where he got to "jawing and fighting" with an undergraduate named Russell and was so badly beaten up that he had to stay in his room for a week.[2] It is noteworthy, all the same, that these fights did not affect the continuance of his friendship with either of the men.

One of the signs that he did not have much wrong with him is his detailed descriptions of very common disorders - the boils on his "posteriors" which he had for two years running, a "Wist" or sty on his eyelid, the colds and "influenza" a word already current in his time. He recovered quickly from minor ailments, and a day or two after he had first sounded the alarm about them he was once more "brave". The one symptom at which one might have expected him to show some apprehension, the sudden fainting attacks recorded in all parts of the diary, although recurring at fairly long intervals, seem not to have worried him at all. One such attack came while he was playing draughts with Bill at Weston. He fell out of his chair, bruising his face on the floor. But it was his nephew who was "terribly frightened", just by seeing it happen.

In Woodforde's middle years, the first decade or so of his residence in Norfolk, the diary shows him in his greatest phase of activity. This is the time when the "Rotations", and all the rest of the round of social activity are near their peak. His shopping and bill paying expeditions to Norwich occur most frequently, and the pattern of his visits back to the old haunts in the West Country, on an average once every three years, are set and adhered to. He never owned the kind of horses that would have been of any use in a foxhunt and indeed apparently had no interest in hunting. On the other hand he greatly enjoyed coursing, and found it useful as well as pleasurable, since the hares his greyhounds caught either ended up on the Parsonage dinner table or were given away as presents to friends.

It was undoubtedly the brisk outdoor exercise he took that kept him healthy for so long, as it mitigated the harmful effects of the imprudence in his way of life. His diet was by modern standards quite appallingly wrong. It was an implicit belief in this society that eating meat, and as much meat as possible, was essential to maintain good health, and at the same time the infallible indicator of prosperity and well-being. This was the period when all British people believed, or affected to believe, that the French lived on "soup and roasted frogs", and would split their sides at Hogarth's engraving of "Calais Gate", with its starveling sentry, rickety and asthenic, no match for strong islanders nourished on the roast beef of old England. It is true that vegetables appeared at Woodforde's table, and that he occasionally criticised the host at dinner parties to which he was invited when "Garden Stuff", as he called it, was missing. But it is more than likely that his actual consumption of these extras was sparing, by comparison with the platefuls of meat that constituted a hearty meal.

The trouble with him, as with so many of his contemporaries, was that as he aged he grew lazy and took less exercise. It was a bad day for him when he gave up coursing, which he did in the sudden manner that marked the renunciation of so many of his discarded activities and pleasures. Less energetic, hence more sedentary, he also tended to eat more because, again in common with most of his contemporaries, he held the most untimely and unfortunate belief that, so long as he retained "a good appetite", nothing could be seriously wrong with him. This led to his eating not only more than his system needed or was good for it but, as often must have happened, more than he really wanted to consume. In spite, of the violent purges to which he was addicted, for much of the time his system was clogged with imperfectly digested food.

By the time he reached 50 he was already beginning to suffer from the circulatory troubles, such as cramp, that afterwards so plagued him. In his final decade he was often attacked by gout, or what he took for that disease. It was very painful, as he tells us but, because he believed, like everyone else in his time, in the existence of a condition known as "flying gout", which wandered through the organism until it reached a vital organ, heart or brain, and at once killed the sufferer, he was always pleased and relieved to find the arthritic state safely located in the extremities.

On Christmas Day, 1794, he was in church, had already taken part of the service, the familiar "Read Prayers and Preached" and was preparing for "the administration of the H. Sacrament", when he had another of his faints, which he called, "An Epileptic Fit".[3] What really scared him was the combination of the fainting attack and the cold. Most of the winters in the 1790s were unusually cold. It is to be remembered that mediaeval churches, their stone walls feet rather than inches thick, had no form of interior heating. Woodforde says that he had been afraid of being taken ill in church "for some Winters past". He recovered quickly and "went through the remaining part of my duty". He was touched by the kindness of the farmers in his scanty congregation, those who had braved the cold to attend. He was after all no mere William Neave, who could fall from the top of a barn, and into a ditch, without anyone taking much notice. It was indeed Neave's employer, Mr. Howlett, who "very kindly offered" to drive the Rector home "in his Cart". Woodforde refused this, and instead went into Stephen Andrews' farmhouse, where he sat by the fire until he was warm, and then walked home. But this comparatively trifling incident left an indelible mark on his mind. Less than a year later, he returned from what was to be the last of his Somerset holidays, took two more church services and then engaged Mr. Corbould as curate to do his work, at a stipend of £30 a year,[4] less than a tenth of his own income. Apparently he was never seen in the church again, and the episode marks the beginning of his slow and gradual slide into invalidism.

In the late spring of 1797 he was attacked by a serious illness, which came on suddenly on the night of 12 May. Woodforde himself never explains it clearly enough to allow a reader of the diary more than a guess at its nature. He says that he had "a fit ... and there I laid all night in a very bad State scarce sensible all the Night long". From this it appears that he did not summon assistance, so that it would have been morning when Nancy and Betty Dade put a "Blister" between his shoulders. This was another practice that went back to the old doctrine of humours, which were supposed to be drawn out of the body by the application of an irritant substance to the skin. Woodforde got up as usual, and although the inevitable Dr. Thorne, who had been "sent for", arrived and "immediately ordered" him back to bed, he did not stay there for more than a few days. He was seemingly not at all affected mentally, since he continued to write up his diary, which for some indecipherable reason he entered on loose sheets - ultimately 100 of them, identical with the paper back booklets he had used until 1776, instead of the current hard back book. Perhaps the most likely speculation is that Woodforde had sustained a minor stroke, this being strengthened by his having written on 9 June, when he was recovering: "still very weak in all my right Side", which indicates some degree of transient paralysis.

Whatever it was, there seems little doubt that this illness was the direct precursor of his death nearly six years later. It is not too much to say that, from this time onwards, he was never again really well. The diary of his last years is a long chronicle of malaise, and of the fear and depression that accompanied it. Woodforde complains repeatedly of weakness, giddiness, shortness of breath and intestinal trouble. He sleeps badly and coughs at night, probably from chronic bronchitis. He is badly affected by his old enemy, cold, and he suffers terribly in the continuing severe winters.

On 4 February 1799 he wrote "The present cold weather almost kills me", and went on to expatiate on the sheer misery of the cold: "Snow again this Evening - Frost also very sharp within Doors - Milk & Cream kept in the Kitchen"; rather than in the unheated dairy and even there it sometimes froze. A few days later: "The very severe cold Weather that have [sic] so long prevailed, is to day if any thing, more piercing. I have felt it more to day, than any yet". His nerves are so shaken that he is afraid of slipping and falling, if he dares to go outdoors. He connects this up with what he seems now convinced is epilepsy: "... having of late been very much afraid of having an Epileptic or falling fit - My Head inclining I have thought of late that way". He realises what has happened to him, and writes miserably: "Fear seems to have got great Power over me of late Days". Even at home these terrors pursue him still. One day he is so afraid of falling downstairs that he has to be helped down. And sometimes the hardest blow of all strikes him, and he loses his appetite, something that really makes him fall into the pathos of self-pity: "I did not eat a bit of Pigg for Dinner, the Gout about me, getting more and more painfull - had some Water Gruel for Supper - ". Then still striving to look on the bright side, and eager to persuade himself that his state of health was not, after all, so bad, he ends with: "Something better towards bed-time" - (20 November 1799).

The diary for 1800, 1801 and more than half of 1802 shows little variation. When Woodforde was feeling ill he wrote repetitively about the symptoms of his illnesses. But there were good days as well as bad days; ups and downs juxtaposed. He kept an eye on parish affairs, in which he no longer took any active part. There were still bills to pay and occasionally visitors to see, although the arrival of strangers, or even people he knew but had not seen for some time, made him nervous and "hurried". His relations with Nancy had long deteriorated, and he now sometimes called her "A.M.W." or even "Miss Woodforde". No longer did he play cribbage with her, or read to her out of the *History of England* that he had bought in Oxford, so many years ago. He accused her of being "pert", "saucy" and "sulky". When he suspected her of secret conversations with Betty Dade, "above Stairs", he wrote the sentence in Greek characters, presumably because he thought if she went surreptitiously searching the diary she would take it for real Greek, and be put off.

Then in July or August 1802 Woodforde went down with some kind of throat trouble. We know nothing about the progress of this illness, because three pages, covering the dates 18 July to 28 August, were ripped out of the diary, leaving only the blotting paper with its weather notes for six weeks. There can hardly by any other explanation of this vandalism except that the missing pages contained allusions to a human body now near to its dissolution which were so shocking that their immediate destruction was thought imperative. As to the type of entry which might have provoked so exaggerated a reaction, on 22 October 1800 Woodforde had an involuntary emission of seminal fluid in the night. This surely would have gone, with the rest of the page that contained it, had the censor been able to understand the contracted Latin in which it is phrased.

By the time the surviving entries for August 1802 recommence, Woodforde's throat was healing. But from then on he began to go downhill very rapidly. He could not understand why, although at least on some days he "eat very hearty", he gained no strength: "Sometimes I think, I get weaker and weaker". He was now in continuous pain from the "blind piles". He had to be helped up and downstairs. Then the characteristic œdema of "dropsy", ascites, made its appearance, an infallible sign that, as his heart weakened, his circulation was giving up. The last phase of his terminal illness was no doubt written on two further pages, 5 - 10 October, which were torn out as the others had been. The weather notes continue to supply us with odd scraps of information, that show the household continuing its usual quiet routine although, like the Parson himself, it was nearing its end. A new yard boy, "Jn. Lane", aged 13, arrived. Mr. Emeris, one of the tithe-payers, "brought us some Damson Plumbs", and "Eliz: Gray (an Infant)" was buried by Mr. Maynard, the poor clergyman often employed by Woodforde to do odd clerical jobs.

On Sunday 17 October 1802, he made his last incomplete entry in the diary over 43 years after he had started it with the great news from Oxford. For a long while now he had been accustomed to writing up the diary in two daily spells, one culminating in dinner and the other posted up just before he went to bed. Some time in the afternoon, he took his diary and wrote in it. His handwriting is the same as ever. I find myself unable to agree with others who have examined the manuscript and claim to find the latest entries to be in a shaky hand. He had a clean page to write on, p. 59 of the last hard back book, and wrote at the top, with all his accustomed clarity of expression: -

-October - We breakfasted, dined,
17th   Very weak this Morning, scarce able to put on my Clothes
-1802-   and with great difficulty, got down stairs with help-
Sunday- Mr Dade read Prayers & Preached this Morning at Weston
          Church - Nancy at Church -
          Mr & Mrs Custance & Lady Bacon at Church -
          Dinner to day, Roast Beef -

On the blotting paper opposite he wrote down the first of the daily weather reports:

Morn' - fair & fine -
Afternoon -

Then he laid down his pen for ever.

Some time in the late afternoon or evening of that day James Woodforde had a seizure, probably a massive cerebral haemorrhage, from the effects of which he died (in the sense that he ceased finally to breathe, for his life effectually ended on the last day he wrote in his diary), ten weeks later, on the first day of the new year, at "about a quarter after ten o'clock", as Nancy, who began a new pocket diary with those words, tells us.[5] She had not been keeping any kind of diary in 1802, so there is no surviving mention of her uncle's last days or hours.

His funeral took place on 5 January 1803, and he was buried inside the church, in spite of the squire's formerly expressed disapproval of such unhygienic practices, about which he and the late rector had once had some disagreement. In time there appeared on the north wall of the chancel, just above Woodforde's grave, a small, unobtrusive and rather attractive wall-tablet, owing I think much to the popular designs of Wedgwood. The diarist would certainly have applied to it one of his favourite expressions of approbation, and called it "neat". He would have been perfectly right to do so.

The inscription, below the coat-of-arms his family pinched from the Ashby Folville people, reads:

SACRED
to the Memory of the
Revd Ja^s WOODFORDE
29 Years Rector of this Parish
who died January 1, 1803
aged 63 Years.

His parishioners held him in the
highest esteem and veneration and
as a tribute to his memory
followed him to the grave.
The poor feel a severe loss as they were
the constant objects
of his bounty

This tablet is erected
by his Nephew
WILLIAM & ANNA MARIA WOODFORDE
his Niece
as a token of their sincere
regard for his many
VIRTUES

As Dr. Johnson so truly said, the maker of a lapidary inscription is not on oath. It is permissible to speculate on the feelings of the Weston villagers, as they "followed him to the grave", if indeed they did so. They had certainly seen little of him in the last few years. As for his "bounty", he left to the "poor" of the parish just £5. He had always spent a certain amount of money on mostly random and casual acts of charity, but these proofs of his benevolence, though real enough, yet amounted only to a small part of his disposable income. In any case, he had not been around a great deal in the last six years to hand out a penny here, a sixpence there, to the unfortunates he chanced to meet.

We have the testimony of one parishioner. Some weeks after Woodforde died, Elizabeth Girling, the bright teen-aged youngest daughter of Mr. Custance's land agent, who was herself to die tragically young of the common scourge, tuberculosis, was writing to her brother, to keep him abreast of the local news. "We have lost Mr. Woodforde", she writes chirpily, bracketing him with two other people who had also died in the recent past. Then she goes on to discuss the new rector. "We are to have singing in Church", she

proceeds, pin-pointing one of the late Parson's more striking
deficiencies. Although he had come from Oxford, where there was
an abundance of good music, he had never troubled to provide any
for his parish, and the only times they ever heard singing were when
visiting choirs from other parishes took a hand in the services.

In her valediction Elizabeth plainly felt no more than any
young girl who has, so she thinks, a whole long, wonderful life
ahead of her could have felt for the passing of an elderly and
reclusive man whom she hardly knew. He had not taken a service in
church for over seven years, and his participation in the life of the
village, in these latter years, had been practically nil.

And it is likely, I think, that he was quickly forgotten in what
had been his parish. At the most, a few old people would think
kindly of him for his occasional charities, although he must have
always been looked upon as a "foreigner" in Norfolk, with his West
Country accent and past history spent in places far away from their
part of the world. The farmers may have been grateful to his
memory as the clergyman who had never, in all the years he had
been rector, increased the tithe burden, and contrasted that
forbearance with the conduct of the new man, whose first action on
being appointed was to double it all round.

The household of which the late Parson had been the head was
quickly wound up and its members dispersed. Nancy, who recounts
in her "Lady's Pocket Companion" style diary that on 20 February
she went to church with Bill "for the first Time since my poor Uncle
was buried", was "very low" and "Greatly affected at seeing my dear
Uncles Grave to-day". She had already paid off the servants (except
the new boy who was probably sent back home as soon as
Woodforde collapsed), since the receipts for their last year's wages,
for which they as usual signed or made a mark, are made out in her
hand. The servants were not left a penny in the Parson's Will; not
even faithful Ben Leggett, who had been with him for 26 years at
his unchanging wage of £10 a year. In June Sally Gunton was
married to her "Intended", Thomas Harrison the thatcher. Betty
Dade was a bridesmaid, and signed as one of the witnesses.[6] This
was for long our last sighting of her; but fresh information which
has only just come to light reveals that she did after all get married,
but not to Ben. She became the wife of a Mr Baldwin, lived at
Dereham and died in 1834, in her 70th year. Briton went to
Norwich, where in 1812 he was still a servant.

The sale of the late Parson's effects spread over three days:

19th, 20th and 21st of April. A total of £437 was raised, less than one might have thought, considering the heavy inflation of the war years. A comparison with the diary reveals that some of the items brought in no more than their former owner had paid for them, years before. Bill and Nancy were the only legatees, apart from the "poor" of the parish already mentioned; and the bequest scarcely amounted to a windfall, since the money accruing from the proceeds of the sale was offset by personal debts which amounted to £250. It was fortunate for them, and particularly for Nancy, who had no money of her own, that they had the much more valuable "Sussex Estate", left to them and their brother Samuel by their father, to fall back on.

It could not have taken long for practically every trace of James Woodforde's sojourn at Weston Longville to be obliterated, only his monument remaining to give posterity the bare statistics of his incumbency. The 73 small paperback and hardback volumes containing the priceless diary became William's property, and went back to Somerset with him. He may have vandalised a few entries in it that referred disparagingly to him (I do not think it was he who tore out the missing pages near to and at the end) but he must, I think, be forgiven, since he, and his son, and his grandson, and great-grandson all kept the record safe and preserved it for us.

And in the fulness of time the forgotten days of James Woodforde came gloriously back to life, to gladden the hearts of aftercomers who live in a different world from the one he knew and chronicled. The diary, after all, is his passport to immortality. It has become part of our historical inheritance.

CHAPTER 28

PORTRAIT
OF AN 18TH CENTURY CLERGYMAN

Woodforde's friend Anne Donne, Mrs. Bodham of South Green, Mattishall, had the immense life-span of 98 years. Born right in the middle of the 18th century, she survived until the high noon of the Victorian era, by which time the Industrial Revolution was steaming ahead towards a prosperity hitherto undreamed of, railway travel was commonplace, and the hugely inflated and overcrowded northern towns were grappling with their own social problems. And Woodforde's old familiar world had vanished for ever. He himself had died with that age, very early in the new century. There had, in truth, been many important and significant changes even by then, but by and large they had not taken place, or at least been seen to have happened in the parts of the country with which he was familiar. 28 years before the opening of the Liverpool and Manchester railway, 30 years before the passing of the great Reform Bill, 44 years before the repeal of the Corn Laws - he missed all these harbingers of the future by comfortable enough margins, and it is hard to believe that he would have enjoyed living in a world that contained them.

Woodforde is often called by commentators on his diary "a man of his time". And this is expressed slightingly, as though he were personally associated with such abusive features as the harsh penal laws, the corruption and venality of politics, the oppression of the working people. In fact, as anyone who has read the diary attentively enough will have discovered for him or herself, he avoided so far as he was able the discussion of "controversial" questions in his diary, and it is likely enough that he did the same in life. It is simply too easy to infer that he must have enjoyed watching the cock-fights, the bear baiting, and the other manifestations of cruelty to animals, because he does not go out of his way to attack them in the diary.[1] But such scenes occur only in the very earliest diary, and not very often even then. It seems likely that he quickly enough outgrew his taste for such displays, and quite soon came to ignore them. He once witnessed the hanging of a murderer, in Oxford, but seems after that never to have attended another public execution - not that there was any lack of such scenes, if he had wanted to view them.

It is true enough that he was, in nearly all things, a conformist, like most people in all epochs. Those who would have it that conformity to whatever idea or dogma or conviction that was currently dominant completely sums up his character and leaves nothing to be speculated about may adduce his picture, painted by his nephew Samuel Woodforde R.A. It certainly shows a bland, smooth, unlined face with very little expression in it. Yet one can place no more reliance on it as an accurate representation of Woodforde's features than the engraving by Droeshout or the bust by Cornelius Janssen can be accepted as likenesses of Shakespeare. It was painted in 1804, that is after the death of the subject, and based on a sketch which Samuel had made on a visit to his uncle at Weston more than 20 years before. [2]

Everyone knows that Woodforde had little liking for or even interest in books. One or two theological works while he was an undergraduate - and even here, he states only that he bought the books, not that he ever read any of them - a single volume recorded as a borrowing from New College Library; with a handful of popular novels borrowed from a circulating library, about make up the total for his early years. During his time at Weston, Fanny Burney's *Evelina*, "very clever and sensible" and *The Devil on Two Sticks in England*, both lent by Mrs. Custance, *Roderick Random* and "*Joan*, by Matilda FitzHugh", together with a few reference works and one or two volumes of sermons, practically make up his reading total for a quarter of a century. One night he sat up reading "The Life of Lewis 14. of France" until 2 in the morning, but that was only because the wind was very high and he was notoriously frightened of going to bed when it was stormy. The anecdote might stand as a symbol of his lifelong attitude to books.

He was no more attracted to politics than to literature. As a young man in the 1760s, he was on the side of (it is far too much to say that he supported) Wilkes, because everyone he knew was on that side too. Later, when the king had recovered from his first attack of illness, he became, and remained, quietly loyal. In 1784, at a time when he was on particularly cordial terms with the High Tory Mr. Custance, he went so far as to deck his servants out with cockades of the right colour for the Election. But in later years this fitful interest appears to have waned altogether.

When we come at last to look at him as a clergyman, we are on more difficult ground. There is no doubt that he would have considered any discussion of religious matters out of place in the diary. There is some evidence, too, which suggests that he would have been acutely embarrassed if the subject came up in ordinary conversation. So we cannot simply conclude that his silence in the diary reflects a lack of interest in his calling.

What we can say, I think, is this: Woodforde acquired at a very early age a set of simple beliefs, to him certainties, which were never questioned so long as he lived. There was no struggle against doubt and scepticism, and, I should say, very little sense of sin. Heaven was seen as an idealized version of Ansford, where no-one was ever sick, or poor, or hungry, and it was the reward of all the good.

At the same time, his real interests were those he could share with lay people, and the most perfunctory statements in the diary are those which describe his taking of the church services, where most times he has no more to say than "Read Prayers and Preached". Like most of his contemporaries, he was blind and deaf to the aesthetic appeal of medieval churches. To him, Weston Longville church was simply a building in which he worked, and it was cold, draughty and very uncomfortable. After he had suffered his fainting fit in the pulpit on Christmas Day 1794, he seems to have become afraid of it, and after he had ceased to serve it himself, in the following year, he never, so far as we know, entered the building again. Nor, in his long and distressing terminal illness, does he ever give the impression of deriving any benefit from the consolations of religion, but has his mind apprehensively centred in his own physical symptoms. Perhaps the only thing that can be said is that, in spite of his having spent all his working life in the service of the church, he was not a religious man.

So in the end, there is a double paradox about Woodforde. He was intellectually and spiritually limited, incurious about so much in the world that filled some others with delight and wonder. Perhaps he was not very intelligent. Perhaps, in the final outcome, all we can call him is a commonplace, ordinary man.

Ordinary, that is, except that he did one striking thing that is not ordinary at all. He wrote the diary. And the diary, although it may appear at first sight to be no more than the record of a life spent in the carrying out of routines, yet has the power to bring to life a whole, rich, miraculous world which he, writing every day of what he had done and seen, preserved from instant oblivion and has given to us to share.

APPENDIX

SEX AND THE CONSTANT BACHELOR

If James Woodforde and the diary had become known in the 19th century, and if some "wretched, rash, intruding fool" had been moved to write his life, this modest tailpiece is one part of the opus which the biographer would have been under no compulsion to write - rather indeed would the pressure on him have been not to write it. The reader of those times would quite naturally have assumed that, since the diarist never married, he found no difficulty in living a lifetime of celibacy. That, rightly or wrongly, is not enough for the modern reader, whose curiosity is likely to be awakened precisely because there is no discussion of the universal subject and who would at once suspect bowdlerisation and a "cover up". So let us see what we can discover about Woodforde's sexual nature, although the enquiry must be a "bricks without straw" sort of exercise, since the evidence, one way or the other, is so scanty as to afford little basis for speculation.

In the first place, there is in the human male very considerable variation in sexual potential, much greater, I should imagine, than in the males of any other species. Judged on a scale ranging from the sexually insatiable to the completely devoid of feeling, Woodforde must surely come quite low down on the list. Whatever his desires were, he had them firmly under control, without feeling any strain from living in the celibate society of New College.

When we first meet him he is in late adolescence, and he seems an agreeably normal young man. Clearly he likes and enjoys feminine company, and always knows which are the prettiest girls, and the best dancers in the ballroom. No doubt his encounters with girls of his own age and class led to nothing more than light flirtation. At the same time, although verbal indiscretions hardly ever seem to trouble the easy flow of his narrative, he never gives the impression of a young man without sexual experience. It is likely enough that some Jane Biggon or Jane Herod, one of those notorious lights o' love at Castle Cary whose illegitimate children and their reputed fathers are prominent in the registers - or even a "common strumpet" in Oxford - had taken care of his initiation. In his time as Pro Proctor, years later, he was to show kindness to at least one such woman. He was, surely, no male virgin, and quite unlike Kilvert born exactly a hundred years later, with his tormented sexual longings and frustrations. And it would be unthinkable to find a trace in Woodforde of the excited interest in flagellation betrayed by the later diarist. But then Woodforde was fortunate to have lived in a far less unhealthy moral climate.

In the later years of residence in his Norfolk parish Woodforde lived a contented celibate life. He had chosen as his companion a younger female relative of whom he was undoubtedly fond, although his affection for her seems to have worn rather thin towards the end. Nancy's presence in his household satisfied his taste for domesticity and his liking for a woman's company. No doubt when he was playing cribbage with her, a game at which he nearly always won, or when he read to her out of the *History of England,* he must often have felt that such a comfortable relationship brought with it all the social pleasures of married life without any of its disadvantages. It was not a way of living that would have satisfied most men; but then, he was not like most men, having sacrificed marital pleasures and family for the sake of his own special routines.

No doubt it had not always satisfied him. We know of two occasions in which, once certainly and once in all probability he sought for and obtained sexual gratification. We know of the first episode only because of his fear of the possible consequences, which shook him out of his usual discretion and made him reveal details in his diary of which, although later attempts were made to obliterate them, enough can still be deciphered to give the reader a clear enough impression of the event.

It all began with the fascinating Elizabeth Davie, to whom Woodforde was strongly attracted and, as I have remarked earlier (see Chapter 18) attracted in a directly physical way. In the summer of 1777 he had known her a little over a year, when he had an encounter with her in her Norwich lodgings that is described in a most cryptic way:

> Made a very late Evening of it being out after
> Supper & so engaged in Company that I could not
> leave them till near 2. in the Morning -

It was never Woodforde's habit to mention "Company" without giving the names of the people he was with; and this passage must surely contain a covert allusion to a return to, and long confidential session with Elizabeth Davie. But she was totally unattainable outside marriage. It was not until several years later that he even arrived at the fun and games which led to his being able to take off her garter, the high point of his relationship with her. But it is not at all surprising that it set up a sexual tension in him which there was only one way properly to relieve.

On 23 June Woodforde, accompanied by Nephew Bill and the servant Will Coleman, set out on the first of his holiday returns to the West Country since he had gone to reside in Norfolk. With his besetting tendency to hazard guesses which there was no need to make, Mr. Beresford says that the journey was "uneventful". I doubt if the diarist would have agreed. For a long way, indeed, it was a repetition in the opposite direction of the trip all three had made the year before. But at Thame, 15 miles from Oxford, instead of going on to look up some of his New College friends, he swerved off the road and went to spend the night at Abingdon.

Now Abingdon, like other little towns within easy reach of Oxford, may have had a bad reputation at this time, since it was outside the jurisdiction of the University Proctors and all the more attractive among the more rakish of the students. Four years earlier, while he was still a Fellow of New College, he had gone with some friends to the theatre at Abingdon, to see a performance of Addison's *Cato*, and observed a very raffish off-stage scene:

> There were two Gownsmen at the play in the Boxes
> with two noted Ladies of Pleasure, a Miss Alken
> & a Lady who goes by the Name of Miss Burford -
> A Mr Brown also of Queens Coll: was very much in
> Liquor at the Play & exposed himself much - 1

It is worth noting that he did not spend the night at the *Crown and Thistle*, where he had dinner on that earlier visit, and where it is conceivable that he could have been recognised. It was no doubt not until his nephew and the servant had gone to bed that he went out again. He recorded this in another of his sentences which reveal practically nothing:

> at a private House at Abingdon this Evening paid and gave - 7: 0 (2)

This took place on the night of 26 June.

And there he would have undoubtedly have left it, safe in the assurance that his cautious entry revealed nothing that he did not want to write about openly. But three weeks later, now in the middle of his holiday, he had a most nasty shock, which scared him so much that for once he threw caution to the winds:

> I breakfasted, and slept again at Mr Pounsetts -
> Very low indeed all Day long, being afraid that I am not
> right in Health having something (tho' at present trifling)
> not right with my Privities having a small Discharge
> from the same - owing to a private connection when
> at Abingdon with one Miss Clarke - which I am much fearful of -

Gonorrhoea was extremely common at this time, as we know from the experiences of such as Boswell, infected and reinfected over and over again, as well as from the many "cures" assiduously advertised in the newspapers. With the incidence of infection so high, even a casual, one-off encounter was dangerous. In Woodforde's case, the very long incubation period must cast some doubt on his having had gonorrhoea at all; but he undoubtedly thought he had contracted it, and he was too worried to retain his usual hearty appetite. "Tho' we had a very elegant Dinner was afraid to eat much", he wrote miserably.

Some two months later he was still having trouble, noting on 12 September:

> Ever since my return to Weston from the West I have
> had a very bad Pain in the inside of my Privities
> and this morning they were swollen and very sore -
> I apprehend by Friction in riding - to Day is
> something easier than I have been for many Days -
> It has made me very low on the above Account -
> I have made use of the Handkerchief bandage
> worn both up and a bed since Monday last -

"Low" he may have been, but the objective tone of this passage contrasts strongly with his panic in July, seemingly because he had hit on a much less embarrassing and shameful reason for the trouble that for a time was associated in his mind with Abingdon and Miss Clarke. At all events, he does not mention it again, and the condition he was complaining about must have cleared up.

In the following year (15/5/1778), after having been to see William Crotch, aged three, an infant prodigy in Norwich, "a very remarkable & surprising little Boy", who could play the organ, "and every Note in proper Tune", he adds:

This evening after Supper I took a Walk by myself and
called at a Friends House and paid -   0: 5: 0

This sounds like the Abingdon escapade all over again; but as no scare ensured, there is no further reference to whatever he was doing on that night. It is, of course, Woodforde's own fault if we look twice at these occasional cryptic passages. His diary is such an open document, it displays such a wealth of detail, that when we came across a passage in which the diarist seems to be writing evasively, we at once assume that he must have something to hide. It is rather like the situation in *Hamlet*, where the Prince in putting "an antic disposition on" and shamming madness to baffle his enemies merely makes them more suspicious of him.

Diaries are notorious for the presence of unexplained signs, initials and numbers, which by common consent are always taken rightly or wrongly to have a sexual significance, like the Greek letter "p", for "pleasure", used by Boswell. Most of Woodforde's marginal entries are clearly explained. For example, at one time he takes to measuring the level of the water in his "great Pond" and puts down the daily rise or fall. Applying the rule just mentioned, another set of figures with no explanation of what they may stand for naturally attracts attention.

The numbers were at first located on the blotting paper, opposite the weather notes; afterwards transferred to the margins of the diary proper. They begin in January 1776 and run in sequence for the whole of the year. There are 54 for 1776 and 41 for 1777; in other words whatever it was happened approximately once a week, and only on one single occasion did it take place on a Sunday. The occurrences are fewer as time goes on. There are 31 for 1778 and 28 for 1779. In 1780, instead of starting in January, they do not begin until 16 July. 1782 is the last year for the consecutive numbers. They go up to No. 17 on 25 July, then stop abruptly and are not again noted in subsequent years.

These unaccompanied numbers could of course mean anything, and could have safely been left to guard their own mystery; but we are trying to investigate here the sexual nature of a man who was normally and usually celibate. It is just possible, I suppose, that these could be records of masturbation. If so, the practice was more likely to have been resorted to as a health measure than a source of sensual enjoyment.

To understand this, it is necessary to recall the old doctrine of humours, which still commanded belief. Good health depended upon an exact balance of these within the body. Hence the great importance in this society of evacuation, which was held to get rid of peccant humours. Doctors prescribed, and patients enthusiastically accepted, the most murderous programmes of purging, emetics and bleeding, in the belief that they were all doing good. The same belief was held in regard to seminal fluid: it was inimical to health to let too much build up in the body. It is of course true that medical writers produced one lurid and terrifying account after another of the supposed dangers of "onanism", as it was called, which was held inevitably to cause blindness, curvature of the spine, insanity and premature death as well as any other morbid condition the authors could think of. At the same time, for the reasons just given, doctors did not think that absolute continence was healthy, although that view did not receive anything like so much publicity as the scaremongering aimed at boys and their parents, whose responsibility it was to suppress bad habits in the young.

There remains, then, the possibility that Woodforde practised masturbation as a form of therapy for a few years, carefully monitoring its incidence as he monitored the state of the weather and other natural phenomena, and then gave up the practice. Conversely, he may have continued the indulgence but ceased to record it. Or the theory may be entirely wrong and the numbers must refer to something quite different and, so far, unexplained. What is quite certain is that Woodforde lived a celibate life for the last 20 years or more of his existence.

A WORD ON SOURCES

The essential authority for the life of James Woodforde, from the age of 19 to a few weeks before his death at 62, is his manuscript diary, now in the Bodleian Library, Oxford (MS eng. misc. e. 645 and f. 101-73) which except for the first few months contains an entry for each day. The original 5 volume work edited by John B. Beresford and published by Oxford University Press (1924-31) reproduces only a third or less of the total number of entries, most of these are abridged and the diarist's early years in Somerset very much neglected. In 1968 Dr. W. N. Hargreaves-Mawdsley edited the full diary of the Oxford years, under the title of *Woodforde at Oxford 1759-1776*, as Vol. XXI, New Series of the Publications of the Oxford Historical Society (Clarendon Press, Oxford). More recently the Parson Woodforde Society has produced 9 volumes of the complete and extensively annotated diary covering the years 1759-81.

For the Woodforde family the basic source document is the unpublished *Family Book* compiled by Dr. R.E. H. Woodforde, great grandson of the diarist's nephew William. This incorporates other genealogical material, going back to the 17th century, and the first chapter of the present work is entirely based on it. Other unpublished material include the accounts book of the Rev. Samuel Woodforde, James' father, and a similar ledger kept by the diarist himself. There are important Woodforde archives in the Bodleian Library and in New College, Oxford, while those of Winchester College are also invaluable, particularly the Long Rolls, which chart James Woodforde's course as a pupil there from 1752 to 1758.

Concerning those aspects of the book which deal not so much with Woodforde himself as with his familiar background and environment, it is the product of a very long time spent living mentally in the 18th century and trying to understand its often baffling thought-processes and behaviour. I have tried to eschew speculation, in so far as this is ever possible, and base my statements on solid evidence, a counsel of perfection, no doubt, which I am quite certain I have failed to live up to; but my guides have been other diaries of the time, letters, contemporary newspapers and occasional literature, far too many to be listed here. The experience of editing the Quarterly Journal of the Parson Woodforde Society has given me insights into highways and byways of Georgian England which I would never otherwise have attained, through many valuable contributions to the Journal and equally stimulating and thought-provoking letters and conversation. I have received endless help from my friends in the Parson Woodforde Society. They are not to be held responsible for my errors.

Woodforde - Notes

CHAPTER 1 - ANCESTRY

1. For the Woodfords of Ashby Folville, see W. Burton: *Description of Leicestershire*, (1622), 22/3. Their blazon reads: Sable. Three leopards heads or jessant as many fleurs de lys gules. Crest on a wreath two lions or. It is practically identical to the arms of the see of Hereford. The Woodforde arms have substantially the same arrangement, and their crest is a "wood man". It has been suggested that this came from a "Supporter" of the armorial coat of Ashby Folville, which was mistaken for a crest.
2. Dr. R.E.H. Woodforde: *Family Book*, incorporating *Stemma Woodfordeiana* written in the 17th century: unpublished.
3. Northamptonshire and Rutland Wills 1st. series A148 - Northamptonshire Record office.
4. ibid. 1st. series 1204.
5. Parish Register, Old, Northants. - Northamptonshire R.O.
6. Northamptonshire and Rutland Wills 2nd. series C168 - Northamptonshire R.O.
7. *Records of the Borough of Northampton*, ed J.C. Cox. II (1898)
8. *Wadham College Register*, ed R.B. Gardiner, (1889), I, 456.
9. Samuel Woodforde, D.D., Diary, 17/10/1663 - Feb. 1664/5. Inscribed on cover: "Liber Dolorosus". - Bodleian library, Oxford, Eng. Misc. f.381. The autobiographical material cited earlier comes from this source.
10. John Aubrey: *Brief Lives*. "Edmund Spenser". Aubrey says Samuel told him that Spenser "lived sometime in these parts [Alton, Hants.] in this delicate sweet ayre; where he enjoyed his muse, and writt a good part of his verses". - Cresset Press ed. (1949), 51.
11. More information about Samuel Woodforde is to be found in the diary of his second wife, Mary Norton: *"Mary Woodfordes Booke"*, printed in modernized English in *Woodforde Papers and Diaries* ed. D.H. Woodforde (1932, 2nd ed. 1990). The original is in the Woodforde archive at New College, Oxford.

CHAPTER 2 - NEAR RELATIONS AND DIARY PEOPLE

1. T.F. Kirby: *Winchester Scholars - A List of the Wardens, Fellows and Scholars of Saint Mary College of Winchester, near Winchester, commonly called Winchester College* (1888), var. cit.
2. This could only have been the 2nd. earl, Charles Bennet, since by the time his son inherited the title, Samuel Woodforde was established both at Ansford and Castle Cary.
3. For the career of Robert Woodforde, see *Fasti Ecclesiae Anglicanae*, ed, J. Le Neve (1854), I, 183, 204. Robert lived for long enough to get. into James Woodforde's early diary, and died in 1761.

Woodforde - Notes

4. *Winchester Scholars*, op. cit. 228.

5. Wallace Notestein: *English Folk* (1938). One of the best short studies of Woodforde that has ever appeared.

6. Information about these members of the Woodforde family comes from James Woodforde's diary, the *Family Book* and the parish registers of Castle Cary, Ansford and Ditcheat, Somerset. The baptism of Clementina Sobieski is at Epsom, John Woodforde's marriage to Melleora Clarke is at Evercreech, Somerset. Heighes first wedding to Anne Dorville may be found at the Queen's Chapel of the Savoy, London.

CHAPTER 3
EDUCATION - FROM MARTHA MORRIS TO WINCHESTER

1. Sandford Orcas, now in Dorset but part of Somerset in JW's time. See Sir Mervyn Medlycott, Bt. and G. Suggs, *Anatomy of a Village* (1987), and review in Parson Woodforde Society Quarterly Journal. Vol. XXI, No. 4. Both show the tiny holdings owned by JW, as a detail from an Ordnance Survey map.

2. The depositions of witnesses in the trial of Reginald Tucker for the "wilful murder of Martha his wife", held at Wells on 25 August 1775, are all in a shilling pamphlet published by R. Cruttwell, proprietor of the *Bath Chronicle*. A copy is in the Local History Library at Taunton Castle. For the Somerset Tuckers, and their relations with the Woodforde family, see"Tucker's Affair - an Ansford Murder" in Journal VII, 1.

3. Reference to and quotations from the Rev. Samuel Woodforde's Accounts Book are given by kind permission of its owner, Oliver Heighes Woodforde Esq.

CHAPTER 4 - A CHILD OF THE FOUNDATION

1. General details about Winchester can be picked up from various books on the history of the school; of which the best is A.K. Cook: *About Winchester College* (1917). Also useful and worth consulting is T.F. Kirby: *Annals of Winchester College* (1892). But neither of these, nor any of the other books on the subject, is particularly informative about 18th century Winchester, no doubt owing to the paucity of records dating from that time; also perhaps because the writers did not consider it a very interesting period and are usually in haste to get to the reforms of the following century.

2. For the career of the Head Master, John Burton, see A.F. Kirby: *Winchester Scholars* (1888). JW mentioned his death in the diary which is more than he did for that of his successor, the much better-known Joseph Warton.

3. A "scob" or "scobb" was a double-lidded desk, of which the upper lid formed a ledge when opened. Four could be ranged together to form what has been called "a screen against the outer world" and provide a little much-desired privacy in the "Great Schoolroom", where they were kept. There is a picture of a Winchester Scob

Woodforde - Notes

in Jonathan Gathorne-Hardy: *The Public School Phenomenon* (1977). A "toys" (singular) was a box which each boy had by his bed in his dormitory or "Chamber".

4. Anthony Trollope: *An Autobiography*. Fontana Library ed. (1962) 33/4.

5. Cook. op. cit. The Head Master quoted was Dr. George Moberley. By 1862 the number of floggings had been reduced "to ten or twenty a year".

6. Anthony Trollope said that in his time at Winchester "we had no tea or coffee, but beer as much as you liked - beer at breakfast, beer at dinner, beer at supper, beer under your bed". - Cited in Cook, op. cit., 329.

7. T.A. Trollope: *What I Remember* (1887), I, 6.

8. *Norfolk Diary III*, entry for 15/11/1781.

9. Cook, op. cit., 349.

10. Cook, op. cit., 355.

11. Two stories which deal with bullying and the authorities' ambivalent attitude to it, dating from just after JW's time at Winchester are found in T.F Kirby, op. cit., and in *Good Times at Winchester*, Journal XXIV, 4.

12. Henry Bathurst: *The Life of Henry Bathurst, Lord Bishop of Norwich* (1837). However, since it appears that another Wykehamist, named Algernon Bathurst, admitted 1832, long after the future bishop, claimed to have memorized that exact number of lines, it is plain that some confusion of names has arisen. Cook, op. cit. 308.

13. *Oxford Diary*, 27/11/1761, see also 26/10/1759.

14. Cook, op. cit., 314.

15. *Long Rolls of Winchester College,* ed. C.W. Holgate and H. Chitty (1904).

CHAPTER 5 - ELECTIONS AND BRIBERY

1. T.A. Trollope, op. cit., I, 99.

2. *Ansford Diary V*, 1/9/1772. Three years earlier, the corresponding passage was rather more detailed: "... and then we held the Scrutiny that is, the Senr. Boy of every Chamber was sent for before us the New-Coll: Electors (the Winton Electors not being present) and examined with regard to their Victuals and Drink, and to the Schoolmaster &c. and all was well", - *Ansford Diary IV*, 5/9/1769.

3. The idea behind the institution of "Founder's Kin" is that as the benefactor had spent money on his charitable foundation which would otherwise have been left to his relations, it was only fair to let these be given privileged places on the foundation itself - G.B. Squibb: *Founder's Kin*.

4. This was a board, already of considerable antiquity in JW's time, hung in the Great Schoolroom, which set out the three options for the Winchester boys: he could learn what was being taught him, leave or be flogged for laziness. Pictures of a mitre and pastoral staff, emblematic of the bishopric that might eventually be the reward of a good scholar; an inkhorn and pen, representing law, and the soldier's sword, pointing to possible careers for those who left; and a rod alluded to the "third fate" that awaited the unsatisfactory pupil!

265

5. *Registrum Orielense*, ed. C.L. Shadwell (1902), II, 148.

6. Both in 1769 and 1772 "new Shillings" were handed out on behalf of the school by the former Usher Samuel Speed, a pronounced "Old Boy" type who appears to have spent most of his time at Winchester after giving up the post. The Wardens received two each, the others one. At the same time the Oxford electors presented those of Winchester each with four pairs of gloves. These last are not mentioned in 1772.

7. The explanation of the way these sums of money changed hands is given in the text as the most likely; but it was all very much a secret transaction, so it is impossible to look for confirmation in any official source.

8. The man whose Fellowship JW succeeded to is remembered for a violent action in which he participated, when he shot and killed a highwayman who had already robbed two other persons. - See *John Risley; or Death on the Highway*, in Journal XVII, 2.

CHAPTER 6 - NEW COLLEGE AND THE EARLIEST DIARY

1. William Gaunt: *Oxford* (1965), 51.

2. William Burland, of a noted Wells family, grandson of Dr. Claver Morris, physician and diarist, brother of Sir John Burland, the judge who tried Reginald Tucker for the murder of his wife in 1775.

3. "Norway Oak" was a trade name, usually standing for pine.

4. A trencher cap or mortar-board was the usual academic cap, so called because it was thought to be like a plate standing on a basin. The "tossle" survives as a decorative feature.

5. For E.C. Orthman, see *The Music Room* in Journal XXVI, 1. The "Catch Clubb" is mentioned in the diary entry for 5/5/1774. See *Oxford and Somerset Diary*, under date.

6. *Woodforde at Oxford 1759-1776*, ed. W.N. Hargreaves-Mawdsley, 38, f/n. One wonders, all the same, how the editor knew that all the fathers were tradesmen, or well-to-do, and it looks like a guess.

7. "Lambskinnet"; a corrupt form of Fr. "Lansquenet", itself derived from German "Landsknecht", a mercenary soldier. A card game dating from the 17th century.

8. This was the Benson Bennett mentioned earlier as having been admitted to Winchester in JW's year, 1752. He was now at Hertford College. J Foster: *Alumni Oxonienses Second Series*, I, 93.

9. Sir E. Godley: *Oxford in the Eighteenth Century*, (1908), 175.

10. Quoted in Godley, op. cit., 176/8.

11. The BCR was the Bachelors' Common Room, which JW and his friends were allowed to make use of a considerable time before graduation. Strangely enough he only once mentions the Junior Common Room.

12. For the Rooke family of Somerton, Somerset, see *Early Friends - the Rooks of Somerton* in Journal XXVI, 2.

Woodforde - Notes

13. JW's favourite coffee shop, originally in New College Lane, then on the corner of Holywell and Catte Street, Oxford; kept by Martha Kinnersley, who married John Baggs, "a breeches-maker". He objected to JW's habit of purchasing "on tick", or credit.

CHAPTER 7 - THE SOMERSET CURACIES

1. "It was a Place like a Stable you know ..." - James L. Clifford: *Hester Lynch Piozzi (Mrs. Thrale)* (1969), 408.
2. Berta Lawrence:*Notes on Thurloxton and District* in Journal VI, 3.
3. Parish Register, Thurloxton, Somerset Record Office, Taunton, Somerset.
4. Sir Thomas Acland, 3rd. baronet (1723-85), a member of a well known West Country family.
5. Berta Lawrence: *The Gappers and their Villages* in Journal XI, 1. Edmund Gapper was rector of Keinton Mandeville (d. 1775). He was one of JW's early friends, signing the "Testimonium" in support of his application for Priest's Orders in 1764.
6. For the successful career of Robert Penny, and the complicated transactions over the living of Evercreech, very characteristic of the time, see *Parson Penny and Young Master Rodbard* in Journal V, 1.
7. Ansford Parish Register records the burial of Mary Chrich in 1782, aged 75, so she was by no means old in the 1760s. But working women of the epoch no doubt tended to age early.

CHAPTER 8 - LIFE AT THE LOWER HOUSE

1. Ansford has greatly changed for the worse in recent years, notably through the building of an excessive number of houses which have filled in the entire space between the church and the Parsonage, destroying a scene which had remained unchanged since long before JW's time. From the master bedroom of the house, in which he was probably born, there used to be a clear view across what were known as the "Churchfields" to the tower of the church, the only part of the building he would have recognised, with no other structure in sight.
2. M.S. Diary, 15/9/1794.
3. This is made clear by entries in Samuel Woodforde's Account Book.
4. The apothecary, like the pharmacist of today, made up medicines to the prescription of the consultant, but was not supposed to examine patients or diagnose their complaints. However, as the diary shows in many places, the distinction between the two was blurred, and the same practitioner is often referred to as "doctor" and "apothecary" in turn.

Woodforde - Notes

CHAPTER 9 - "JUSTICE CREED" AND THE CARY SINGERS

1. Also reminiscent of *The Mayor of Casterbridge* was the custom, recorded by JW on two occasions, of singing a psalm in direct hostility to a person or persons against whom the singers held a grudge. See *Ansford Diary V*, entries for 26/2/ and 17/12/1769, and the corresponding notes.

2. Some very recent research has thrown more light on the earlier career of Cary Creed the younger. He was as a young man a clerk at the Excheque in London, along with his friend Frederick Alberton Hindley, who appears in the diary as a frequent visitor to Creed's house. The Cary Creed mentioned in numerous reference books of the late eighteenth and early nineteenth century who produced engravings of the sculpture at Wilton House in the 1730's was almost certainly not the same man but possibly a cousin. See *Cary Creed, Etcher?* in Journal XIV, I. and Robin Gibson: Mr Hindley - *Merry, Kind and Polite* in Journal XXVII, 2.

3. The connections of the Woodforde family with Stourhead are explored in *Samuel Woodforde R.A.*, Journal VI, 1.

4. William Melliar, the elder son of James and Fortune Melliar, was an attorney by profession, but also a man of wealth, Lord of the Manor of Puriton, near Bridgwater. His brother "Counsellor Melliar" of Galhampton, is like him frequently mentioned in JW's diary.

5. 'Shy in the sense of "cautiously reserved; wary in speech" (*O.E.D.*) was used by JW also to describe his own attitude at the last embarrassing meeting with Betsy White on the turnpike road - See below, Ch. 11, 100.

6. The George Inn, High Street, Castle Cary, still exists in the place where JW knew it.

7. As none of the actions came to trial, there are no references to them in the records of the Ecclesiastical Court beyond those noted in the text.

CHAPTER 10 - UNCLE TOM AND THE ANSFORD LIVING

1. *Ansford Diary IV*, 17/5/1771.
2. *The Farington Diary*, ed. Kathryn Cave (1982) Vol. 8, 2949.
3. *Ansford Diary V*, 25/5/1772.
4. *Ansford Diary III*, 4/9/1766.
5. William Phelps: *History and Antiquities of Somersetshire* (1836), Vol. I, Part 5, 382/3.
6. Mr. Beresford, who was no expert in 18th century idioms, thought that the living had been "promised" to JW himself, thus hopelessly confusing the issue for a reader. - *The Diary of a Country Parson*, commentary to Vol. 1, 107.

Woodforde - Notes

1. The baptismal records of the White family in this generation are all in the Ansford register.
2. Shepton Mallet register.
3. George Bridle, "Founder's Kin", of Leigh, Dorset, adm. Winchester 1732. He was Fellow of New College 1734, and retained the Fellowship until his death. - *Winchester Scholars*. op. cit. 237.
4. *Ansford Diary V*, 1//9/1773. The account gives a vivid description of the way such charity schools were run in the 18th century.
5. During the "Year of Grace", the Fellow could change his mind and turn down the preferment, his Fellowship remaining intact because he was not obliged to resign until after the expiry of the "Grace" period.
6. *Brother John - a Biographical Study of Woodforde's Brother*: Supplement No. 4 to P.W.S. Journal (1976).
7. *Oxford and Somerset Diary*, 28/5/1774.
8. Ibid., 16/5/1774.

1. Thomas Hayward, the immediate predecessor of JW's friend Oglander as Warden of New College, was appointed in 1764. Four years later he was killed in a riding accident while leading a "Progress", or survey of outlying college property, in Hampshire. *Winchester Scholars*, op. cit,
2. The staircase can be identified without difficulty, but the rooms in this part of the college have been much altered. The blocked up door at the top of the flight led to JW's rooms.
3. A "lease" or "leash" was a set of three: *Shorter O.E.D.*
4. The custom of standing up while the "Grace Cup" was drunk from is explained as "to prevent guests from following the charming old Danish custom of stabbing or cutting the throats of unwary drinkers, the Cup is not taken up until those on the drinker's left and right are also standing". Helen Howgego: 'Oxford Night Caps' in *Oxford To Day*, Michaelmas issue 1991.
5. Examples of academic Oxford slang. Asked if his friend was worthy to be awarded a degree, JW would have answered "scio" (I know). His other options were "credo" (I believe so) and "nescio" (I do not know).
6. Mr. Pounsett did not long remain the tenant of Ansford Parsonage, since Frank Woodforde, who married his cousin Jane Clarke on 23 November, ejected him as soon as he needed the house for himself. Pounsett then built himself a new home in his native hamlet, Cole Place, where in later years he was host to JW and Nancy when they revisited the West Country.
7. Washbourne Cooke, of Edmonton, near London, JW's colleague as Pro-Proctor

Woodforde - Notes

and soon to be his companion in the inspection visit to Weston Longville. He was baptized 2//5/1744, and a Fellow of New College 1765-93; later the rector of Hardwicke, a college living. *Winchester Scholars*, op, cit, 254.

8. 'Manciple' - "An officer or servant who buys provisions for a college, an inn of court, a monastery etc" - *Shorter O.E.D.* The name is still in use at New College today.

CHAPTER 13 - A COUNTRY PARISH

1. Francis Blomefield: *Essay towards a History of the County of Norfolk* (1805-11), 8, 285.
2. She was Rookwood's first wife. Her mother was a natural daughter of the first Duke of Norfolk - Blomefield, op. cit, 8, 291.

CHAPTER 14 - LIFE AT WESTON PARSONAGE

1. *The Diary of a Country Parson*, Vol. V, Appendix II, 417/18.
2. The letter corresponds to JW's diary entry for 22/8/1790, when the visit took place. He sounds less enchanted than his niece: "They came about 6. and went away about 8. o'clock. It was an awkward day for visiting, but it was Mr. Townshends appointment - ".
3. "Moreen" was a stout woollen or woollen and cotton material either plain or watered, used for curtains, etc. - *O.E.D.*
4. *Oxford and Somerset Diary*, 4/5/1775.
5. J. Boswell, *Life of Samuel Johnson* (Oxford ed.), 331.
6. *Woodforde at Oxford*, introduction, xii.
7. *Early Friends*, op. cit.

CHAPTER 15 - UNCLE AND NIECE

1. The Queen's Chapel of the Savoy in London had long been known as a place where runaway couples could be quietly married with no questions asked. About the middle of the century such marriages had been at a figure of no more than some 20 a year. The passing of Lord Hardwicke's Marriage Act in 1753, however, paradoxically gave a boost to the Savoy marriage, since the minister, John Wilkinson, decided to defy the law, other providers of clandestine marriages having been forced to withdraw their services. The number of marriages at the Savoy went up to nearly 400 in 1754, Heighes' year, and to nearly 1500 in 1755, before the law caught up with Wilkinson. He was arrested, tried and sentenced to be transported. Heighes and Anne were one of the seventeen couples married on 22 January 1754. - Registers of the Savoy Chapel, London: W.J. Loftie: *Memorials of the Savoy* (1883).*Brother Heighes* in Journal IV, 2. *Brother Heighes and Sister Woodforde* in Journal XXV, 4.

2. The very full parish records of Ditcheat are in the Somerset Record Office, Taunton.

3. Draft Will complete except for the signatures of witnesses, 25/6/1783 in Woodforde archive, New College. Cat. No. 9539.

4. Nancy Storace. A friend of Mozart and the original Susanna of *The Marriage of Figaro*.

5. For Nancy's letters see *Some Letters of Anna Maria Woodforde to Members of her Family*: Supplement No 1 to Journal, 1971.

CHAPTER 16 - FRIENDS AND ROTATIONS

1. For the University and clerical career of George Howes, see J. & J. Venn: Alumni Cantabrigienses, Part I, II, 418. For his life in general, see *Mr. Howes* in Journal, XXIV, 3.

2. For Thomas Roger du Quesne, see *Al. Cantab.* (Op. cit.) Part I, II, 77.
Articles on various aspects of his life have appeared from time to time in the P.W.S. Journal.

3. The Donnes and their connection with Cowper have been covered by Mary Bodham Johnson: *Donnes, Hewitts and Bodhams* in Journal V, 1 and *Mrs. Bodham*, Journal XIX, 2.

4. For the vicars of Mattishall at this time, see Mary Bodham Johnson:*Mattishall*, in Journal X, I, see note, 'Henry Goodall and John Smith'.

CHAPTER 17 - DISSENSION - THE FOURTH MRS. HOWES

1. It is not quite clear just what the diarist meant by "our" and whether it implies that there were more than one "hautboy", or oboe, in the house at the time. If he were the serenader, or one of them, this is the only reference in the diary to his playing a wood wind instrument.

2. *Norfolk Diary I*, 19/7/1776.

3. *Norfolk Diary II*, 26/1/1779.

4. On 12 January 1782 JW walked to Hockering through deep snow to attend Mrs. Howes' funeral. It was, as he said, "as decent, neat, handsome Funeral as I ever saw, and every thing conducted in the best manner", for which he gave the credit to Elizabeth Davie and her "good management". JW was a great connoisseur of funerals; not, I think, so much out of morbidity as from his feeling that a funeral could be taken as an index of the respect in which the person so commemorated had been held.

CHAPTER 18 - MRS. DAVIE AND MR. SMITH

1. This arrangement may have come about through the intermittent illness of Mrs. Howes, and Elizabeth Davie was perhaps at Hockering as a housekeeper rather than a guest.

271

2. JW had clearly been worried about possible scandal in 1778 when Sukey Buxley had become pregnant while living in a household made up of one other maidservant, a boy and four unmarried men, but appears to have taken no care about the damage which could be done to his reputation by such events.

3. M.S. Diary, 30/6/1781

4. For the Mattishall parson and his career, see *John Smith of Mattishall* in Journal, VIV, 1.

5. M.S. Diary 15/ 7/1784.

6. Ibid., 20/ 7/1784.

7. Ibid., 29/12/1785.

8. Ibid., 18/ 2/1786.

CHAPTER 19 - THE WALKER SCANDAL

1. JW may perhaps have had a special attraction to the name. There was even a third Betsy written of in the same unusually affectionate way: "I was very flat and dull on leaving my dear Miss Betsy Donne" - M.S. Diary, 3/7/1784.
This was Miss Donne from London, a cousin of his friends Castres Donne and Mrs. Bodham - *Donnes, Hewitts and Bodhams*, op. cit.

2. M.S. Diary, 3/3/1790.

3. M.S. Diary, 29/4/1790. According to this entry, Walker was 23 years old.

CHAPTER 20 - MR. AND MRS. JEANS - A CHEQUERED FRIENDSHIP

1. *Winchester Scholars*, 259. *Al. Ox.*(op. cit.) II 744. Jeans' career is discussed in some detail in *Another Parson: the Life of Thomas Jeans D.D.*, in Supplement no. 5 to Journal, (1978).

2. M.S. Diary, 14/4/1784

3. For Bathurst, see J.C. Hanekamp: *An Appeal for Justice - the Life of Henry Bathurst, Lord Bishop of Norwich* - doctorate thesis accepted by the University of Utrecht, 1992.

4. *Another Parson, Notes on the Life of Thomas Jeans, D.D.* op. cit.

5. M.S. Diary, 7/ 3/1795.

6. M.S. Diary, 4/11/1793.

7. *Jeans, Foster and the "College Land"*. Appendix to *Another Parson*, op. cit.

8. M.S. Diary, 15/10/1796. For Augustus Beevor and his quarrelsome life, see Jane Beevor, *The Beevor Story*.

9. *Another Parson*, op. cit.

CHAPTER 21 - SERVANTS AND SERVANT PROBLEMS

1. Much impressed, JW asked their names, which he later copied into his diary, having given them "what ever they could eat and drink" and a shilling each, besides

sending back a recommendation to the upholsterer "to pay them handsomely for their Days work". - M.S. Diary, 4/4/1793.

2. Sally Dunnell - "seems to be a mighty strapping Wench" and "a goodnatured Girl but very ignorant" - was dismissed and sent away with 3/- i.e. wages for 6 days at 6d. a day - Ibid., 10, 14 and 15/10/1784.

3. Ibid., 8/12/1788. All the boys, good, bad and indifferent, are to be found in *Skip Jacks*, Journal XIX, 1.

4. *Norfolk Diary III*, 5/1/1781.

5. M.S. Diary, 10/10/1796. 10 October was Old Michaelmas Day. The boy had been employed only since 11 June, having been taken "on trial".

6. Ibid., 10/10/1800.

7. Ibid., 17/ 3/1801.

8. Ibid., 21/ 5/1789.

9. Ibid., 3/11/1794. Mary was, however, in a much better position than many girls in her state. Her lover Sam Cudble or Cutbill, "a Carpenter of the Parish of Coulton", did not "make ... the least Objection to marrying her". The parish register of Colton reveals that they were married on 1 December and Mary's daughter was safely born in wedlock on Christmas Eve. She appears not to have had any more children, and died in 1802. - *Maidservants at the Parsonage* in Journal IV, 1.

10. Both in 1812 and 1819 the Poll Books give his name as "Briton Scurl".

11. In 1809 it was purchased for £122, far above the minimum value for an electoral qualification.

12. The archaic word "hath" appears in the diary only in the passages about Betty and Ben. See the entry for 8/9/1801, in which it is used three times. I believe the intention is ironic, as though JW had difficulty in taking seriously the love-lives of his servants.

CHAPTER 22 - TWO DESTINIES

1. Parish register, Taverham.

2. *Norfolk Diary I*, 4/6/1777.

3. *Norfolk Diary II*, 4/1/1778.

4. Ibid., 27/8/1778.

5. Ibid., 25/8/1778.

6. See Robert Bates: *Found, Woodforde's Missing Maid* in Journal xxvi, 3. Poor Law documents and a Will show that Humphrey Garrod and Sukey became quite prosperous citizens. His estate was declared as "under £300" (that is, just below that sum, a lot of money in 1824.) She died in 1831.

7. A petition for an increase in his salary as Parish Clerk shows that William Dade was a man of some literacy. The document is cited in *Mr. Dade asks for a Rise* in Journal X, 1.

8. M.S. Diary, 19/10/1784. All the diary references to Molly Dade are collected in *Molly Dade, the saddest Story*, Journal XXVI, 1.

9. There was an ancient, traditional belief that preparations of black currant were "good for" the common cold and, deceived by the catarrhal symptoms in some phases of tuberculosis, people of the time thought there was some relationship between them.

CHAPTER 23 - VILLAGE FOLK AND OTHERS

1. The Girling household was entered as having 15 persons, as against the Custances with 14. Mr. and Mrs. Custance had had eleven children, of whom four had died by this date. One son, George, was in India. Two of the youngest boys may have been away at school when the census return was made. This would allow for eight resident servants, a small number for the size of the house. The large number of people recorded as living in Mr. Girling's house is also inexplicable.
2. *Norfolk Diary I*, 13/1/1777.
3. This was apparently an East Anglian expression which JW had picked up since he had gone to reside in Norfolk. - Wright's *Dialect Dictionary*, 5, 191.

CHAPTER 24 - GOD BLESS THE SQUIRE AND HIS RELATIONS

1. Most of the factual information in this chapter and the cited passages come from L.H.M. Hill: *The Custances and their Family Circle*. Supplement No. 8 to Journal, 1989. Revised and corrected edition by Thomas Custance. Originally published in Journal III, 4.
2. Hill-Custance, op. cit.
3. Ibid. Sir E Bacon was 8th Baronet of Redgrave and 9th Baronet of Mildenhall.
4. Weston House was designed by Thomas Rawlins, an impressive but not particularly beautiful or graceful building. Completed and first inhabited in 1780, it was demolished in 1924, after the estate had been sold by Olive Custance, the squire's great-great-granddaughter.
5. Henry Walton, the painter of Mrs. Custance's miniature, was a pupil of Zoffany. JW, who calls him "A Mr. Walton who is a Portrait Painter from London", met him, together with the architect, for dinner at Weston House on 4/10/1781. The companion miniature of the squire is believed to be by Charles Grignion. Hill-Custance, op. cit.
6. The shipwreck of Nephew Bill's model vessel on the "Great Pond" is recounted in M.S. Diary, 10/6/1786.

CHAPTER 25 - CRIME AND CRIMINALITY

1. Tom Burge - *A Case to Answer* in Journal XX, 4.
2. For Reginald Tucker and his wife Martha (see above, Chapter 3 for her relations with the Woodforde family), the murder and details of the trial, see *"Tucker's Affair"* - *an Ansford Murder* in Journal V, 2 and *A Somersetshire Tragedy - the Tale of*

Woodforde - Notes

Reginald Tucker in Journal VIII, 2.
3. M.S. Diary, 20/11/1782.
4. *Norfolk Diary III*, 11/1/1781.
5. *Crime and Security in Woodforde's England*, Journal XVIII, 2.
6. M.S. Diary, 12/12/1785.
7. Ibid., 13/1/1788.
8. *Crime and Security*, op. cit.
9. Charles G. Harper: *The Smugglers* (1903). *Crime and Security*, op. cit.

CHAPTER 26 - AILMENTS AND DOCTORS

1. *Ansford Diary IV*, 12/12/1771.
2. Ibid., 18/12/1771.
3. *Ansford Diary V*, 10/3/1772.
4. M.S. Diary, 9/8/1783.
5. Roy Porter: *Health for Sale - Quackery in England 1660 - 1859* (1989). For health, doctors and the public in the "early modern" period, see Roy Porter and Dorothy Porter: *In Sickness and in Health - the British Experience 1650 - 1850* (1990).
6. *Health for Sale*, op. cit.
7. *Health for Sale*, op. cit.

CHAPTER 27 - "WE HAVE LOST MR. WOODFORDE"

1. *Oxford Diary*, 28/1/1762.
2. Ibid. 6/2/1762.
3. It is very clear that he did not have the "grand mal" type of epilepsy, as suffered by his servant maid Anne Golding, but I understand it cannot altogether be ruled out that the fainting attacks were epileptiform in character.
4. John Corbould or Carbould was the son of a wealthy hatter in Norwich, "from whom I have had many a Hat". JW had first met him on 10/2/1794 after Corbould, just married, had taken over Hungate Lodge, former home of Press Custance, the squire's brother. Corbould later had two livings in Norfolk, and was patron of a third, of which the incumbent was his father-in-law. He died in 1810, aged 42.
5. *The Diary of a Country Parson*. Vol. V, Appendix I, 414.
6. Weston Longville Register, 16/1803. This wedding was conducted by Thomas Dade, the last of Woodforde's official curates.

275

Woodforde - Notes

CHAPTER 28 - PORTRAIT OF AN 18TH CENTURY CLERGYMAN

1. JW did once buy a fowl to prevent its being "squailed"; i.e. used in a deplorable and repulsive pastime, in which the bird was fastened to a post and killed by stoning.
2. The picture now (1994) hangs in Weston Longville church.

APPENDIX

1. *Oxford and Somerset Diary.* 3/6/1774.
2. The M.S. booklets have survived the vicissitudes of time very well, but they were made of cheap paper to begin with, and the edges of some pages have tended to crumble. The line quoted here was written in very small letters at the foot of one page, which has now flaked away. It is, however, plainly visible and perfectly legible in the microfilm.